Parenting Dual Exceptional Children

of related interest

Being Twice Exceptional
Melanie Hayes
ISBN 978 1 78775 962 6
eISBN 978 1 78775 963 3

The Spectrum Girl's Survival Guide
Siena Castellon
Foreword by Temple Grandin
ISBN 978 1 78775 183 5
eISBN 978 1 78775 184 2

Dyslexia is My Superpower (Most of the Time)
Margaret Rooke
Forewords by Professor Catherine Drennan and Loyle Carner
ISBN 978 1 78592 299 2
eISBN 978 1 78450 606 3

The Parents' Guide to Specific Learning Differences
Information, Advice and Practical Tips
Veronica Bidwell
ISBN 978 1 78592 040 0
eISBN 978 1 78450 308 6

PARENTING DUAL EXCEPTIONAL CHILDREN

Supporting a Child who Has High Learning Potential and Special Educational Needs and Disabilities

Denise Yates

In partnership with Potential Plus UK and The Potential Trust

Illustrated by Paul Pickford

Forewords by Lydia Niomi Christie and Sal McKeown

Jessica Kingsley Publishers
London and Philadelphia

First published in Great Britain in 2022 by Jessica Kingsley Publishers
An imprint of Hodder & Stoughton Ltd
An Hachette Company

1

A CIP catalogue record for this title is available from the
British Library and the Library of Congress

ISBN 978 1 78775 810 0
eISBN 978 1 78775 811 7

Printed and bound in Great Britain by CPI Group

Jessica Kingsley Publishers' policy is to use papers that are natural, renewable and recyclable
products and made from wood grown in sustainable forests. The logging and manufacturing
processes are expected to conform to the environmental regulations of the country of origin.

Jessica Kingsley Publishers
Carmelite House
50 Victoria Embankment
London EC4Y 0DZ

www.jkp.com

For John, Jess and Seb.

I couldn't have written this book without you.

Contents

Foreword

Lydia Niomi Christie

This book focuses on improving the health and wellbeing of children who have something 'different about them', Dual or Multiple Exceptionality (DME) children with 'flashes of brilliance', who may need support in areas other children may take for granted.

As Denise Yates highlights in this book, identifying High Learning Potential (HLP) is only the fragile beginning, the first steps of a frequently difficult journey that may be a long way from the achievement of potential, in whatever form that may take.

And how about those DME children with special interests?

From primary school age, my personal reading regularly maxed out the library limit, with multiple books on loan at a time. I read somewhere that if you put 10,000 hours into learning a topic or interest, you can develop the skills to move into that sector in a professional capacity.

I suspect a lot of DME children acquire their volumes of hours on a topic of interest without realising, so would-be writers, musicians, engineers or sports people may have already gained a lot of background knowledge and practice in a particular subject or area before they reach adulthood.

My interest in reading developed into an interest in writing. When I was around ten, I started writing mini-magazines on a typewriter, grateful to mask my frequently unreadable left-handed scrawl. I later found out that I regularly write my 'Ps' and 'Rs' in reverse, as I likely have a mild form of dyslexia.

How does having one or more special interests impact those around a DME child? Is an interest inclusive or exclusive of others? Is the interest supported at school, or seen as a form of nuisance? How does a parent or carer know when the time is right to encourage an interest, or when to encourage other interests – without upsetting the child? These are the sorts of issues addressed by Denise, reflecting on her experiences working with DME children at Potential Plus UK.

Several years ago, I started learning the process of writing for screen, before writing my first script treatments. I later spent several months as a freelance agency scriptwriter, co-writing treatments, as well as writing or revising scripts for various crowdfunding videos, as part of campaigns that collectively raised over £1.5 million in 2021.

My career in writing has been an indirect path, and certainly not an easy one. I am a huge fan of the work Denise does, as she tirelessly supports the cause for improved assistance for DME children, to better equip those with special educational needs with the skills and support needed to navigate through the various pitfalls life loves to throw in the way, as they reach for their highest potential.

I hope this book further supports Denise's ambition of supporting both parents or carers and DME children to better understand each other, while improving understanding of those with something 'a bit different about them', as they find their way through the external world around them.

Lydia Niomi Christie's short story collection, *Magic, Tales & Other Stories* (2020), makes use of thousands of hours reading and studying the craft of how to tell ghost stories.

Foreword

Sal McKeown

If you are reading *Parenting Dual Exceptional Children* it is probably because you need answers. You are in safe hands. It is written for parents and carers by a parent who has gone through many of the experiences you are facing now.

Denise Yates has worked for many years in the field of helping and supporting children with High Learning Potential (HLP) and Dual or Multiple Exceptionality (DME) and their families. She has a wide-ranging knowledge of the education sector, from early years to post-16, and speaks knowledgeably about home schooling, alternative provision and the options for online learning, both in class and at home.

CHILDREN WITH DME

Some people are dismissive of high ability and the issues that can come in its train. 'We all think our little ducklings are swans', I've heard a headteacher say to parents who were anxious about their daughter's progress.

While it is true that families are not always objective (look at all those proud parent posts on Facebook), they are generally the ones who know most about their child, their passions and idiosyncrasies, obsessions and their violent aversions. They live alongside the child day in, day out, while teachers see them for just a few hours a day, or a week, and often as part of a crowd in a formal setting.

There is a lot of talk these days about 'getting the family perspective', particularly if a child is apparently under-achieving in relation to their ability, but sometimes this consultation appears tokenistic, particularly if the professionals don't seem to be listening.

But what if parents and carers are right in their assessments? It's hard to identify DME, but if your child shows an above-average ability or strength in one area but struggles to show that aptitude at school, you may be looking at DME.

ABLE, BUT NOT ACHIEVING

Many children do not fit the system: they struggle in mainstream education and have areas of great potential, but something holds them back. Perhaps they have exceptional understanding of science but can't manage the noise and smells of the lab, or they can formulate complicated arguments but can't get them down on paper in a way that others can follow.

Parents and carers sometimes worry that their child's progress is static or going backwards. Having been top of the class or in the top set, suddenly they are not doing homework and are withdrawing into themselves. It is not that they want to drop out or don't want to fit in; it's more that they don't want to stand out.

CHARACTERISTICS ASSOCIATED WITH DME

We used to talk about children being 'Gifted and Talented', but that painted a false picture because it suggested that they arrived with abilities that were fully formed and unchanging. A preferred term now is 'High Learning Potential', which is more accurate since it reflects the seeds of talent that will need to be nurtured.

However, children may not fulfil their potential because of:

- Excessive anxiety
- Strong fear of failure
- Sensitivity to criticism
- Experiences of intense frustration
- Low self-esteem
- Feelings of being different from others
- Poor social skills.

Some would immediately jump to a diagnosis of autism – and indeed, some young people with DME do have an Autism Spectrum Disorder (ASD) – but others have mental health issues, dyslexia, Tourette's Syndrome, dyspraxia or any number of neurodiverse conditions.

ALL ABOUT DME

It is difficult to know how many children or young people have DME in the UK. According to Denise's research, current estimates suggest anywhere between 40,000 and 80,000 children and young people, but these figures are for England alone, and do not include Scotland, Wales or Northern Ireland.

Figures may be further skewed because they are likely to miss out all those children with HLP who cannot be in school perhaps because of a medical condition, or anxiety, or who have been excluded because of their behaviour. If your child is not in the education system and not undertaking the same assessments as other children, it is hard to produce robust evidence of their capability.

Any parent or carer who has tried to get a diagnosis and access suitable provision for a child with Autism or Semantic Pragmatic Disorder will know that it's a Herculean task. Imagine, then, looking for support for DME, which is two separate conditions: a disability side by side with an apparent abundance of ability. This is a paradox that often baffles the education system.

WHY WE NEED THIS BOOK NOW

The current generation faces the greatest disruption to education since the evacuation of children in the Second World War. As a result of COVID-19, children have been out of school, away from classmates, and may have had limited contact with teachers for several months. Although some have suffered from a lack of stimuli and social interaction, others have thrived. For some children the return to school has been traumatic, especially those who set their own agenda and self-educated during lockdown.

Imagine the pleasure these young people have felt at having a school day that suits their diurnal rhythm, perhaps working all night and sleeping all day, being able to immerse themselves in subjects of their own choosing with the opportunity to spend days, and perhaps whole weeks, creating a piece of music, making an app, perfecting an animation. This has been a chance for them to spread their wings and develop their gifts, passions, talents, call them what you will.

Sometimes the system seems to be loaded against families who have a child with DME. Many of those featured in *Parenting Dual Exceptional Children* speak of their frustrations. This is why a book like this is such an important resource. Here, you will find contacts, details of organisations and advice that will carry you forward.

Family supporters – whether parents and carers or not – have so many roles. They need to be cheerleaders, monitor their child's physical health and wellbeing, and be advocates for children when they cannot speak for themselves. They need to be there to offer comfort when it all looks bleak, and to celebrate the many successes.

Books for parents and carers often prescribe unconditional love. Some of you may want to reflect on that when you are having a shouting match with your insomniac child at 3am. You are not on your own – this book will help you to help your child succeed.

Sal McKeown is a freelance journalist who writes about disability, education and technology, and is the author of *How to Help Your Dyslexic and Dyspraxic Child* (2012).

Acknowledgements

With thanks to the parent reviewers Tam, Charlotte and Nicolette, the peer reviewers Adam Boddison and Julie Taplin, and to staff at Potential Plus UK and The Potential Trust.

Also, my thanks to Lydia and Sal, who both wrote forewords that came from the heart.

Finally, thanks also to the many children and young people, parents and carers who have shared their passions and dilemmas with me over the years. I hope, in some small way, that I have helped you on your journeys.

What Is this Book About?

This book is for every parent and carer who has a feeling that their child is 'different' from the other children around them.

It might be 'easier' if your child were just 'bright' and could be put into the box that described them as 'More Able', which brings its own challenges, although there are plenty of other books on the market in the UK for you to be able to support them with their high ability.

If your child had a diagnosable Special Educational Need and Disability (SEND), they could be put into another box where there will be support – albeit maybe not all you need – and a number of organisations and resources to help both you and your child.

This book is about neither of these, and yet it is about both – it is for the parents and carers of those children who fall into both boxes. You look at them one way, and you are constantly amazed at the things they can do, which is why you cannot understand why they struggle with often the most basic things other children their age find easy. Or they communicate their feelings at not being able to do these things through their behaviour – stress, anger, meltdowns and more... Or they disappear altogether, seen as average and failing to receive any support at all.

If this sounds like the situation you find yourself in, then this book is most definitely for you. I hope that it will not only provide some answers about what your child is experiencing, but will also help signpost you to a range of resources and organisations that can help.

However, even if you are not a parent or carer of a child like this, but another family member or a teacher or other professional who is interested in finding out more about these children, who they are and how they learn,

I hope that you will read on to understand more about these wonderful quirky children and what they offer.

In the UK, these children have Dual or Multiple Exceptionalities (DME). In other countries, they may be referred to as 'Twice Exceptional' (2e), 'Gifted with Learning Difficulties or Differences' (GLD) or other similar names. Other phrases that are now growing in popularity include 'neuro-diverse', 'bright and quirky' and 'differently wired'.

This book takes a strengths-based approach towards supporting these children, building on their abilities and the things they *can* do first, and then using these to address the areas they find more difficult, for whatever reason. My 30 years plus experience of working with hundreds of children, young people and adults in different circumstances, including those who are More Able, make me absolutely convinced that this is the right starting point in getting the best from those we aim to nurture.

As a parent I make, and have made in the past, plenty of mistakes (like many of us!), and the road was sometimes bumpy. However, to misquote from the 1960 film *Pollyanna*, 'If you look for the potential in people, you will surely find it.'

HOW TO USE THE BOOK

You can use the book in a variety of different ways:

- Read the whole book, from start to finish.
- Dip into chapters that may help you with a specific question or challenge you are facing, such as working with your child's school.
- Go straight to the organisations in the UK and elsewhere listed in Chapter 8 that can help with any support needs you may have.

Go to www.jkp.com/catalogue/book/9781787758100 for subjects where you might want to know more. I have also suggested further reading and resources that relate to what was discussed, as well as some suggestions for a brief action plan of things to do – if you have time – related to that chapter. All pages marked with ⊕ can be photocopied and downloaded at www.jkp.com/catalogue/book/9781787758100. Other things to note, I have also:

- Included a list of abbreviations and terms in 'Glossary of Terms' at the end of the book
- Used the term 'parent and (or) carer' throughout. This is because I recognise the excellent work being done by carers as well as parents in bringing up these children, and I wanted to make this book as inclusive as possible
- Used quotes based on the views of real parents and carers and what they have said or written. Where these are attributed to 'parents', this also means some who may have adopted or who are carers. I have taken out the gender of any children (unless this is relevant to the point being made) because I don't want you to think a certain subject can only happen with a child of one gender. What parents and carers describe can be seen in every child, everywhere.

I hope that the book will provide some answers to the questions you have about your child, or at least signpost you in the right direction for more help.

CHAPTER 1

Why Is My Child So Different from Others Their Age?

Could They Have High Learning Potential?

INTRODUCTION

Many parents and carers are puzzled. They outline the amazing abilities they saw in their child in the early years. Maybe it wasn't even them that spotted what their talented child was doing; it was the health professional who saw them, the worker who looked after them when they went to nursery, grandparents or other family members or friends who could see what they were doing. Or maybe they saw their child playing alongside their friends or when they took them to playgroup.

> It was apparent from birth that our child was different… The doctor said my child had the reactions and demeanour of a much older baby, even though they were the correct size. (Parent)

Alternatively, they may recognise their child's ability and their need to learn. When these needs are nurtured, the parent or carer may have a different child.

> As a parent, certainly at the start of my child's journey, I was drawn to Googling about their difficulties and trying to work out what might be wrong and how I could support them. It wasn't about nurturing their gifts for their own sake; I never wanted to give my child *more*. I knew they could just do all those amazing things, why would I need to try and make

them do more? I found that providing toys, books and other things that interested my child helped to stop them screaming for 5 minutes from about their first week as a baby. If I provided stuff or gave them different experiences and they stopped crying or screaming, then I provided more of that thing. It was all about concern for my child's wellbeing. (Parent)

Does any of this sound like your own experiences? Maybe you wondered, 'What's going on?' You might have other children who didn't act in the same way as the child you now have. Or this might be your first child and you didn't know what they were supposed to be doing at what age. If any of this describes you, what was your first reaction?

Did you:

- Believe you were imagining any differences?
- Think it was just a phase your child was going through?
- Feel you had somehow caused this to happen?
- Wonder what was going on and were afraid to ask for fear of sounding silly, or being embarrassed?

Don't worry if you feel these kinds of emotions (or have felt any in the past). You are not alone.

It would be easy to blame parents or carers for an over-inflated view of their child's abilities, or for 'hothousing' their child (an ugly term). However, what if parents and carers themselves are right? What if their early perceptions of their child – their actions and behaviours – are accurate? This is where this book begins.

We want to start here because it's what happens next that matters – how your child's needs are recognised as they start to grow and develop, and the best ways in which their abilities can be nurtured. We want to explore why a child with so much potential could experience challenges as they grow older or find themselves in different settings. We also want to suggest what parents and carers can do, both on their own and in partnership with others, to help ensure that their child thrives.

This is a book to support all those of you who believe your child – whatever their age – is struggling with the challenges they are facing at home, at school or in society, while at the same time showing 'flashes of brilliance' that make you question what is going on with them. By helping you to find some answers to these dilemmas, or at least to point you in the right direction, we hope to help you improve the health, wellbeing and even happiness of your child along the way as well as your own health and wellbeing and that of your family. Improving what your child can achieve – both now and in the future – in education, in work and in life in general – would be an additional bonus, but is not the primary focus of this book.

Notwithstanding, many of the approaches suggested here will not only work for your child but for others too, and may help all of these things and more besides. This is not a book about children who are 'Gifted and Talented' or 'More Able'. Nor is it a book about children with Special Educational Needs and Disabilities (SEND). There are plenty of specialist books on the market that explore these subjects in detail (and which we have recommended). However, you do need to have at least an understanding of *both* High Learning Potential (HLP) and SEND – what they look like separately and also how they look in combination, to form something called 'Dual or Multiple Exceptionality' (or DME for short).

So, are you ready to start this journey with me and with all those people who have helped contribute to this book? We hope so.

A SHORT DESCRIPTION OF 'DUAL OR MULTIPLE EXCEPTIONALITY'

'Dual or Multiple Exceptionality' is not a term that is well known either among families or professionals, although it is recognised by the Westminster Government and other devolved Governments in the UK. It has different names in different countries, with common ones being 'Twice Exceptional' (2e) and 'Gifted with Learning Difficulties, Disabilities or Differences' (GLD), although phrases such as 'bright and quirky', 'differently wired' and 'neurodiverse' are also growing in popularity. We need to look at *both* high ability and SEND through the lens of the other, and how they combine to form DME. The first chapter does this with your child's high ability.

How many children with DME are there in the UK? Ryan and Waterman (2018) estimate that about 60,000 children at school may fit the definition of DME, although this figure may be an under-estimate. The truth is, we simply don't know. We may only start to learn the true numbers when more children and young people in different settings are correctly identified.

Finding out about DME can often be a relief for parents and carers who may have tried to find answers to explain their child's behaviour or work ethic, especially when that same child cannot keep quiet when they are passionate about a subject.

> It was such a relief to find out that something called DME existed and is recognised by others. It helped me to understand what was going on and to adapt our own behaviour as parents. We were fairly clear ourselves about our child's intelligence. The confusing bit, and what we didn't understand as parents, were their disabilities. (Parent)

DME is what those children and young people (and adults) are referred to as having when they have both a SEND and are also highly able. Figure 1.1 simply illustrates what we mean.

Figure 1.1. Dual or Multiple Exceptionality

Source: Based on information from Fact Sheet F01 (Potential Plus UK 2018–21) and Yates and Boddison (2020, p.6)

YOUR CHILD AT HOME: THE EARLY YEARS

After the initial shock or warm fuzzy glow of having your child enter your life, the hard work really begins. Your child will have their own quirks and traits, and armed with these, they will actively begin to shape their own lives. They will also learn from you and others and, as they grow, they (and you) will learn how to get along and what they like (and don't like); you will help them to shape themselves into the adult they will one day become.

Every child is amazing. However, you may soon notice that what they are doing is *really* amazing. They could be talking early, singing, putting plastic bricks together to make wonderful feats of engineering (or taking things apart to see how they work!), using a computer or tablet confidently. Anything.

> My child had a burning thirst for knowledge that was hard to keep up with. Computer programmes and iPad apps helped a lot until we had to get a tutor at age five. (Parent)

You may have little or no experience of others like your child, whose development exceeds what would usually be expected at their age. This might be why you picked up this book and started to read. If you are like lots of other parents and carers, you may have already gone down to the library or started reading or 'Googling' everything you could to explain what is going on and how you can help ensure your child's wellbeing. Or your child might have an obsessive interest in a particular subject or activity, and it can be hard work to keep coming up with new resources and things for them to do.

> My child has a new obsession and it is driving me spare! They have just got into *Star Wars*. One minute they are not interested and the next it is all they think about. Every conversation is about it, every game, every thought from the moment they wake up. It's always like this with a new obsession so I should be used to it, but it's only been a week and already my child knows far more about *Star Wars* than any of their friends who have been into it for ages. All previous obsessions are forgotten, for now at least. Mind you, my child's Yoda impressions are pretty cute! (Parent)

> When I was a child, the most important thing to me was to lose myself in fantasy or in my specific interests; and then doing fun things related to those interests any time. It made me feel that I belonged somewhere. (Adult who was a child with DME)

As well as trying to keep up with their interests and obsessions – which can be exhausting – the depth and breadth of your child's knowledge and their attention to detail as well as any behaviour linked to them (maybe their anger when being asked to do something else such as eat or sleep!) may begin to concern you.

■ Tips and hints: Listing positive and not so positive behaviours

Think about your child and what they were doing before they went to school. It doesn't matter when, although the odds are that you will still remember a range of things, like when they learned to walk and said their first word. Spend 5 minutes thinking about the positive (and the not so positive) things they did, and at roughly what age. If you have time, ask other people about these, those who saw your child frequently and those who only saw them only occasionally.

Here is our example, but remember, every child is different, and this list may be different from yours. That's fine – there are no rights or wrongs here.

Positive	Not so positive	Things that are just 'different'	Approximate age (years)
Started talking at a very young age	No idea of time and hated being interrupted from doing something	Interested in climbing	2
Wouldn't stop talking or asking questions	Used advanced language to argue about something didn't want to do	Loved limericks	2
Obsessed with pirates	Over-active imagination, prone to exaggerating or telling untruths	Enjoyed cooking	3
Liked dressing up and making up stories to act or tell	Bad temper if didn't get own way; argued back		3
Sarcastic/quirky sense of humour	Highly sensitive		4

Vocabulary beyond years	Perfectionist/hated to fail	2
Concentrated on something interested in for a long time	Prone to dramatic behaviour	4
Able to create 15-minute PowerPoint presentations	Difficulties in writing	4/5
Excellent visual maths skills	Poor basic maths skills	6+
Focused for long periods of time on things that interested them	Failure to pay attention in class	7/8
Excellent poet if could dictate work or type it	Severe problems getting them to do homework	7+
Compassionate, good buddy to other children	Extremely sensitive	7+
Excellent actor and musician	Labelled 'class clown'	9/10
Gravitated towards higher-level maths	Bottom set for maths	11

Now make your own list, using the blank template on the next page. Alternatively, copy down the headings onto a sheet of paper. Keep this list and update it as your child grows older and shows new strengths and challenges. It is a reminder of everything you see them doing at different ages. We will build on this list later in the book. It may also be useful to use it when talking to class teachers or if your child has any kind of professional support outside school.

Positive	Not so positive	Things that are just 'different'	Approximate age (years)

For me personally, I found myself searching for answers and in need of support from Day One. The places you look for help at that age are health professionals such as health visitors, midwives, doctors, etc. The ones I met appeared to have no understanding of babies with any of the things related to my child. At the time I was thinking Sensory Processing Disorder, Autism or Advanced Abilities. I really needed help early on. It didn't really make a difference in terms of my child's ability or needing any kind of assessment, but support from people with similar experiences would have helped when they were younger.

When you are parenting a baby who just screams and cries almost all the time and all you get from health professionals is the standard baby advice, it doesn't take long to decide firstly that you are a failure as a parent and secondly, later on, that you are in this alone and you might as well not attend health appointments. You work out anything you can by trial and error to survive. Part of that might be stimulation, linked with that need for support for their high potential. You notice you need to take a huge bag full of toys, books and activities to engage your tiny baby, while every other baby appears to sleep and feed for months before their parents even buy any toys. Those early years before nursery were in some ways the hardest for me. (Parent)

COULD YOUR CHILD HAVE GIFTS OR TALENTS?

These experiences are not unique and can make parents and carers question what they are seeing. However, according to Dr Linda Silverman, Donna Chitwood and Jana Waters:

> For many decades, parents' judgement of their children's ability has been disparaged. The most common cliché is that 'all parents think their children are gifted'. Research, however, has consistently shown that parents are much better able than teachers to identify giftedness in their children (Ciha, Harris, Hoffman & Potter, 1974; Jacobs, 1971; Martinson, 1974). Ciha *et al.* (1974) concluded that for kindergarten-aged children (about 5 or 6 years old), parents were more than three times as effective as teachers in assessing children's abilities. (Silverman *et al.* 1986, p.23)

If anything, parents and carers are more likely to under-estimate their child's abilities, especially in cultures such as in the UK. What this means for you is that if you are thinking it, you are most probably right. So what should you be looking for to see whether your child has high ability?

Dr Silverman has since assessed about 6400 children and young people from the US and elsewhere in the Gifted Development Center (GDC).[1] Based on her research and observations, with Chitwood and Waters, she identified a list of characteristics for parents and carers to look for.

Over the years, further research has been done to support this 'Characteristics of Giftedness Scale'. For example, research conducted by Karen Rogers at the University of St Thomas found that 90 per cent of parents and carers of gifted children endorsed the following characteristics:

Learns rapidly
Extensive vocabulary
Excellent memory
Reasons well
Curiosity
Mature for age
Sense of humour
Compassion for others
Vivid imagination
Long attention span
Ability with numbers
Concern with justice and fairness
Sensitivity
Wide range of interests.

In addition, 80 per cent of parents endorsed the following characteristics:

Ability with puzzles
High energy level
Perfectionism
Perseveres in interests
Questions authority
Avid reader

---

1   www.gifteddevelopment.org

Prefers older companions. (Silverman n.d., p.2)

Note: Those characteristics that are in italics were not in the original 'Characteristics of Giftedness Scale'.

It is not that these qualities are in *every* child or young person who has gifts or talents, or that other children cannot have these qualities, but the majority of highly able children will show at least some of them, and they will be seen at a younger age than on average and more intensively.

In *Gifted Children*, Kate Distin argues:

> If you feel different from a group of people with whom you spend most of your time then it can be a relief to hear that you are pretty normal by the standards of another group. Similarly, parents who may be struggling to comprehend or keep up with their children may be bolstered by an insight into what it is like to be a gifted child. (Distin 2006, p.22)

Gifted Children is an excellent book that can help others understand what having a highly able child means, and how what is normal for them might be seen differently by others.

Still unsure? Potential Plus UK is one of the few national charities that works with these children and their parents or carers in the UK, and it has a free questionnaire on its website where you can see if your child could be highly able.[2]

WHAT DOES 'HIGH LEARNING POTENTIAL' MEAN?

Before we move on, it may be useful to talk about the words that are used when we talk about these children. Children and young people (and adults later!) who have these characteristics are called different things in different countries, such as 'Gifted and Talented', 'Gifted', 'Highly Able' and 'More or Most Able'.

Between 2010 and 2012, informal research was done in the UK among children and young people, parents and carers and teachers to find out what they thought about these terms. Although British culture may play

---

2   www.potentialplusuk.org/index.php/online-questionnaire

a part in this, many felt that 'Gifted and Talented' was actually a negative term, which:

- Suggested that a child would always achieve success whatever their education. However, for many of these children this may not be the case, especially if they have other challenges in their lives as a result of their abilities
- Made people think they would be good at everything (while often they may not be)
- Doesn't make room for children and young people who under-achieve.

As a result, since 2013, many organisations that support children or young people, families or schools (as well as a growing number of schools themselves) have started to use the term 'High Learning Potential' (HLP). According to Potential Plus UK, a child with HLP will:

- Show flashes of brilliance from their earliest years
- Need opportunities, challenges, encouragement and different approaches to fulfil their unique potential
- Thrive on learning and new experiences and will flourish, succeed and achieve if they are nurtured. Conversely, if their potential is ignored, they will withdraw, under-achieve and lose their 'spark'
- Have distinct social and emotional needs that must be recognised and supported alongside providing the right challenge for their intellectual abilities and potential
- Need both their strengths and difficulties and any challenges they have to be supported effectively. This is essential to their wellbeing.

All of this must be done in an environment that understands that HLP is the very beginning and not the end destination – success, achievement and wellbeing are not determined by HLP alone. HLP is a good start, but requires constant support for the child to fully develop.

HLP is a term that is growing in popularity among children and young people, their parents or carers (and some schools and other professionals), and it is the phrase we use throughout this book. If you want to read more about it, see the Free Advice Sheets PA101, PA102, PA103 and PA104 produced by Potential Plus UK (2017–20), which are available to download on their website.[3]

Potential Plus UK[4] is an independent charity that has been work-ing with families and schools for the benefit of young people with HLP, including those with DME, since it was established in 1967.

It offers a range of support and training based on best practice so that parents, carers and teachers can understand, advocate for and improve provision for young people with HLP. The creation of a community is of huge importance to them, enabling young people to find their peer group and reduce social isolation. It empowers young people to better understand themselves so that they can make informed decisions and have a strong voice in society.

Potential Plus UK subscribes to Steven Pfeiffer's Tripartite Model of Giftedness[5] in identifying children with HLP, which chimes well with the inclusive practice that is generally favoured in the UK: it considers HLP through the lenses of high intelligence, outstanding accomplishments and the potential to excel.

Many of the things your child may do – both positive and more challenging – will have been seen by other parents or carers when their child was at an incredibly early age. In fact, according to a piece of research conducted in 2020 and funded by The Potential Trust, many parents and carers reported that they knew their child was 'different' from as early on as birth.

My child's gifts and talents were evident in babyhood. The fact that they were also sensitive, highly strung and anxious only emerged when they began school. (Parent)

When my child was about 19 months old I noticed they had quite an ear for music. When they were about two years old, I noticed my child didn't seem to be quite like other children in the toddler group. When they

3   www.potentialplusuk.org
4   www.potentialplusuk.org
5   https://potentialplusuk.org/wp-content/uploads/2019/05/Tripartite-Model.pdf

went to nursery it was more apparent there were some differences, though no one thought of them having Special Educational Needs or Disabilities...at nursery the teachers noticed my child was bright (with regards to numbers). (Parent)

Many parents and carers report that their child with the characteristics of HLP was running rings round the family by as early as two or three years old!

So what is the difference between a child who is 'bright' and one who has HLP (gifts and talents) in one or more areas? Some of the differences between a bright child and a child with HLP are shown below.

A bright child	A child with HLP
Knows the answers	Asks the questions
Is interested	Is highly curious
Has good ideas	Has wild, silly ideas
Works hard	Doesn't do any work if not interested, but may test well
Answers the questions	Goes beyond the answer to discuss in detail
Learns with ease	Already knows
Listens with interest	Voices strong feelings and opinions
Grasps what you mean	Draws conclusions from what you *don't* say
Is receptive to what you say	Is intense and stubborn in favour of their own ideas

Absorbs information	Manipulates information
Is a technician	Is an inventor
Tells jokes	Invents jokes or uses sarcasm

Do any of these characteristics describe your child? Some of these traits, such as the ability to put forward logical arguments, along with their advanced knowledge or abilities in one or more areas, are often seen as endearing by parents and carers at first, until they are worn down by their child's constant questioning or their seemingly limitless levels of energy. Other relatives or friends who see your child less frequently may have different views one way or the other. Many early responses from an adult can help to fuel some of a child's behaviours as they grow older, and what was cute at age three can be difficult to deal with at age seven or eight or even fifteen years old.

Despite these challenges and however tough the going gets for you, it is important to remember, both while your child is at home and as they go through life, that:

- You love your child
- Your child has lots of strengths
- Any challenging behaviour by your child is often a direct response to their needs, sometimes their innate personality (and how they communicate their needs) and the way their behaviour has been managed in the home or school environment, or both.

I think how school manages behaviours will often have a huge impact. Children often soak up stresses from school and explode at home where they feel safe. (Parent)

■ Tips and hints: What are your child's strengths?
Have you thought about your child's:

- – General strengths?
- – Strengths in specific areas?
- – Social interaction strengths?
- – Other strengths, such as sense of humour?

Build on these strengths instead of focusing on the challenges. For example:

- If your child enjoys building complex LEGO® structures, could you use this as a way of distracting them if they show any challenging behaviour?
- If your child finds a friend on the same wavelength, could you invite them over so that your child's attention is on them instead, rather than on all the questions they have for you?
- Could you introduce your child to a range of knowledge areas to broaden their areas of obsession, or even take it in new directions?
- What else could you do?

WHAT ARE SOME OF THE CHALLENGES YOUR CHILD WITH HLP MAY FACE?

The kinds of concerns that parents and carers often report about their child with HLP that are more challenging for them at home include:

- Asynchronous development
- Worry and anxiety
- Extreme sensitivity
- Anger and meltdowns
- Child being controlling
- Incessant questioning
- Obsessions
- Perfectionism
- Sleeplessness
- Poor organisational skills or short-term (or working) memory
- Writing difficulties
- Lack of friends
- Social, emotional and mental health difficulties.

There is also a danger that traits already present in the child with HLP can become more intense or challenging when seen through the lens of any SEND. In such situations, a child whose abilities and HLP have been recognised and nurtured may thrive, while a similar child whose abilities are ignored may have behavioural or emotional challenges leading to problems such as difficulties with their mental health, school anxiety, exclusion or worse. We explore some of these in greater depth in Chapters 3 and 4. For now, let's summarise the kinds of things that concern parents and carers at home because of their child's HLP.

Asynchronous development

For some, asynchronous development is at the heart of what it means to have HLP. Imagine a child who is five years old with the intelligence of an adult and the emotions of a child much younger than themselves. One minute they are talking to you about high-level concepts or reading books beyond their years. The next you have a child who bites someone at nursery or who cannot keep their emotions in check. And the greater their abilities, the more 'out of sync' a child might be – parents and carers do not know who their child is from one moment to the next. Worse still, they have to cater for both, and switch from one to the other with no notice at all.

Jen Merrill says in her excellent (and very funny) book *If This Is a Gift, Can I Send It Back?*:

> I never know exactly which age I am dealing with at any moment… In the span of a few minutes, I could have a child who looks his age, discusses cosmology and theoretical physics in great detail, whips out a few bars of his current favourite rock song, feels existential despair over the unanswered questions of life, then behaves with the emotional maturity of a child half his age. It's parent whiplash. I've toyed with the idea of returning the favor. Look like a mom, talk like an infant, dress like a teen and act like a toddler. (Merrill 2012, pp.62–63)

Where a child's cognitive (intellectual) development is higher than their emotional, social and physical development (sometimes by a lot more), they can find it difficult to cope in social and educational settings. While physically a child with HLP may appear to be like any other child, their intellectual development is speeding ahead. This can be a problem as it is difficult to know how to parent and educate a child with such different emotional, physical and intellectual needs.

Children with HLP developing asynchronously can often feel frustrated with their family and friends at home. Likewise, pupils with HLP at school can often feel frustrated with their friends and the professionals around them. The child or young person can also feel frustrated with themselves in both situations. This may lead to behavioural challenges and social, emotional and mental health problems. Sometimes the different characteristics of a child are so 'out of balance' that they become difficult to handle; it can be like having two separate children and you might not understand whether they are Jekyll or Hyde.

Your child's frustration at being misunderstood is sometimes made worse by another set of HLP characteristics – a strong sense of justice and fairness. Children with HLP can often feel that their parents or carers, teachers and the children at school are treating them unfairly, which makes it very difficult to reason and communicate with them. These children, overall, are eloquent and have fantastic memories, which also means that they will remember every detail and fact during a disagreement. They can also be extremely sensitive, deep thinkers and very emotional.

It is both difficult and important to be able to deal with this effectively, the worst years being when the child is between about four or five and nine or ten years old. After the age of thirteen the main challenges with asynchronous development have usually begun to calm down. But then there's puberty...

Worry and anxiety

While the ability to think deeply and 'beyond their years' can be a positive trait, for some of these children, particularly when they do not have the emotional maturity to reject some of these thoughts, this 'overthinking' may cause them worry and anxiety that they cannot control. Common questions when a child with HLP is at a very young age can include subjects such as thinking about death, worry about being separated from parents or carers, even for short periods (which can spill over into separation anxiety when they go to school), or even putting together two separate pieces of information to form a third, and then worrying about any conclusion they draw from this that may not necessarily be logical.

> In Year 4 our child really struggled with their mental health for several reasons. Our child's constant hypervigilance, huge knowledge of the world and exceptionally creative imagination led them down a path where they conjured up an elaborate scenario where everyone was trying to harm them... The professional working with us explained that he could not treat our child like a usual eight-year-old child because they had so much more knowledge and understanding of things in the world, but a certain part of our child's physical brain was not yet developed enough for them to apply reasoning to their knowledge. The professional also said our child was so creative that the scenarios they had conjured up were so elaborate and detailed that it had tricked our child's brain into believing them. (Parent)

Extreme sensitivity

Imagine any of your child's senses – how they touch, how they smell, how they see, or hear or taste, move or balance, or even know when they are tired or hungry. Now imagine being extremely sensitive about one or more of these senses, really sensitive, so much so that it causes problems for them.

> My very bright child who is four years old seems super-sensitive! They react to everything with high emotion and extreme intensity. They get upset by age-appropriate TV programmes; when they hear pieces of music my child cries, and when other kids are upset by things they get overwhelmed with emotion. My child seems to react more strongly to these things and I don't know how to help them. (Parent)

> From my own experience, if your child appears to have a lot of serious problems relating to sensory difficulties, it may be worth seeking an assessment from a sensory occupational therapist, as early intervention is key. I couldn't get this on the NHS early on, and in most cases this may not be done without a prior diagnosis of Autism Spectrum Disorder (ASD). Intervention at just turned two for my youngest was life-changing. (Parent)

Parents and carers up and down the country are cutting labels out of vests and jumpers, buying seamless socks and responding in a hundred other ways to their child's sensitivities. Did you think you were alone in this? I promise you are far from it! An excellent book to read about this is *Living with Intensity*, edited by Susan Daniels and Michael Piechowski.

We will discuss sensory processing difficulties (both avoiding sensory input and seeking it out) later on in the book.

Anger and meltdowns

Parents and carers report the extreme anger and meltdowns their child with HLP has at home, and often from a young age. There are many reasons for a child's anger. The child could be trying to communicate with you and others around them something they do not yet have the words to explain. They could be perfectionists who are dissatisfied with what they have drawn or written down and are angry that it isn't perfect (or as perfect as they think it should be). They could be letting out their frustration about something that has happened to them (or they are worried might happen). If you think of anger and other types of behaviour as forms of communication, what is your child trying to tell you through their anger? Could you play anger detective and find out (even if your child doesn't know or cannot put it into words)? We will return to this in Chapters 3 and 4.

> Our child was late for something they had to get to, something important to them. We couldn't find them anywhere. Finally, we found them in a wardrobe, hiding. When we got our child out, they exploded at us, they were really angry. Once our child came back from what they had to get to and had seen everything was okay, they confessed that they had been embarrassed as they had been late for the event and that was why they were angry. How were we supposed to work that out? (Parent)

Child being controlling

Parents and carers sometimes report problems with their child wanting to be in charge – of them, their family, their friends – and as a result they feel their child has become difficult to 'control'. It can start innocently enough, with everyone celebrating a child's early ability to speak well, tell people what they want and 'boss them around'. Soon, and often at a young age, the child looks as if they are in charge of the household and the parents or carers quickly lose control. This can spill over into other aspects of the child's life until a parent or carer suddenly finds they have a teenager causing real problems at home or at school, or both.

> When my child is playing with their siblings, they have to be in charge. They tell my other children what to do, how to play the game they want to play and will have a meltdown if the other children do something different. The same is true for us as parents too. It's my child's way or the highway. My child wants to decide their own bedtime and creates their own form of reasoning to justify the argument in favour of it. They say they don't want to go to school as they don't like English, but at home my child is writing their own novel at eight years old. (Parent)

Incessant questioning

Parents and carers often say they feel exhausted from the questions their child asks, from the moment they get up in the morning until the time they go to sleep: 'Why does a dog bark and a cat meow?', 'If penguins are birds, why don't they fly?', 'Why do we speak different languages?', 'Will there be a playground when I die?'

It's great when children ask questions; it's good to be inquisitive about life and what is happening. But often when parents and carers talk about this, they can be exhausted by all the questions, particularly those they do not have an answer for, or even where there is no answer.

Later on, this can be a problem in nursery or school where there are lots of other children in the class and the incessant questioning can be seen as a behaviour problem rather than a child's thirst for knowledge. Alternatively, if these questions are not handled effectively or are simply ignored, either at home or at school, their enthusiasm for learning or knowledge may eventually disappear.

> My child is in Year 1 at school [five or six years old]. They seem quite bright and have lots of energy. When they are at home, they ask questions constantly, love building things with LEGO® and read a lot. The feedback we get from their teacher is that they aren't paying attention. We are really surprised as at home our child can pay attention to their books or models for hours on end! (Parent)

■ Tips and hints: Supporting your child's questions

- Have a whiteboard or notebook for your child to write down all their questions or, if they can't yet write, they could either dictate them onto a phone or iPad (or buy them a Dictaphone or equivalent that is 'theirs'). Alternatively, find a way of using pictures so they can record their questions.
- Encourage them to research the answers, or spend a set time each day researching the answers to the questions together.
- Ask your child for their views on what they think.

All of this is great for learning and encourages something called 'critical thinking', which can help all children to learn at a higher level. We will explore critical thinking later.

The kinds of ways in which you support your child can also be shared with teachers to help them in class, if relevant. This supports the principle of behaviour as a communication of needs that requires support rather than consequences.

Obsessions

As we have already seen, a trait of some children with HLP can often be their obsessions about a subject – from pirates to dinosaurs to the solar system, animals and everything in between. A child will often have every collectible item in the range and know everything about the subject (and probably more than their parents or carers). However, many of these children will often flip from one obsession to another, or even abandon their obsessions altogether (usually when you have just bought them the whole range of whatever is their latest obsession as a present for them!).

My child was obsessed with pirates. We had pirate ships, pirate books, pirate flags. I even painted their room blue with waves in it and we put a ship's wheel on their bed. One day they wanted to make some ships biscuits with me to see what they were like, but I put a stop to them adding in worms and insects from the garden to make them 'real'! (Parent)

Perfectionism

Many children and young people with HLP are strong perfectionists. They have a vision in their mind's eye of what perfection looks like, and then, when they fail to reach this, they might have a meltdown or a tantrum (depending on their age!). It doesn't matter that the standards they were trying to reach were impossibly high in the first place – they felt they would only be happy when they reached them. Does your child spend a long time on something they draw or paint or write, only to tear up the piece of paper in tears and put it in the bin? Does your child handle any difficulties they have negatively or with extreme emotion? You might have a perfectionist on your hands!

> We play a lot of board games in our household, things like Scrabble™ and Monopoly®, and have done so since our child was young. I still remember them throwing the board and the dice across the room when they lost in Monopoly® or some other game. Even now they are an adult they still hate the thought of losing anything or being 'less than perfect'. (Parent of a child with DME who is now an adult)

While perfectionism is not necessarily a bad characteristic, it can lead to challenges for parents and carers such as behaviour problems resulting from making mistakes and fear of failure. To address such problems, many UK schools have been teaching about 'growth mindset' (Barry Hymer and Mike Gershon's *Growth Mindset Pocketbook* is worth a read). This may be something you have come across, and it is an approach that can be used among children with HLP who can often 'give up' whenever they find something too difficult.

■ Tips and hints: Helping a child with HLP to develop a growth mindset at home

Dr Carol Dweck developed the theory of the fixed and growth mindset (2017). To summarise, someone with a *fixed* mindset believes that their intelligence, character and creativity are all static concepts that cannot be changed. Children with HLP often have a very fixed mindset about their ability, which can give them a distorted view about themselves, believing things like:

- I am only intelligent because I know things. If I fail it means I don't know things, which means I am not intelligent
- I can never be as good as I think I should be, and so, if I make a mistake or get something wrong, it means I have failed, and I will give up as I will never be good at it.

This can cause problems for most children, but for a perfectionist who needs to be perfect in all they do, it can cause real difficulties, and may mean that they just give up as they fear failure.

By contrast, a *growth* mindset is based on intelligence being a flexible concept, which means that intelligence, creativity and character can all be changed by putting in hard work and learning from every experience. This leads to beliefs such as:

- If I take every opportunity to learn, my achievement levels will improve (or I will achieve more)
- Even negative experiences are opportunities to learn something
- Constructive criticism will help me learn and improve and is a positive thing
- If others succeed in something, learning how they did this can be positive for my own learning.

Parents and carers or other family members must be careful not to accidentally fuel negative beliefs. Positive ideas include rewarding or praising the effort put in rather than only the outcomes achieved. When a child makes a mistake or does something wrong, problem-solving with them what they would do different next time or what they had learned as a result and not putting pressure on them to always come top of the class or to be the best at everything can be more productive.

Being the best in the class or their area of strength can be great at first, but children with HLP need to see beyond that, or it can hold them back. Ideally, encourage them to take a challenge outside their comfort zone or to make mistakes, from a young age if possible, so they can learn that failure is a way to try new things and improve their performance, and is not something to be feared.

Sleeplessness

Many parents and carers speak about the challenges they face with their child's sleep (or lack of!) – that their child doesn't seem to need much sleep or cannot get to sleep easily or even at all. They have even said that they have had to do shifts with family members or friends, as their child is still awake in the early hours! It is important to explore all reasons for a child being unable to sleep, including challenges children and young people face such as overthinking, worry and anxiety.

> My child has never been able to sleep. When they were younger, I tried all the conventional approaches with them that were recommended by the health visitor: going to bed at the same time every night, having a bath and warm drink before bedtime, tough love. I was exhausted. Then I spoke to my child; they said that when they went to bed they started to think. They said it felt like a ping pong ball bouncing round the walls of a box. We worked together on coming up with solutions to this and it helped. They still didn't need any more sleep, but they said they felt happier. (Parent)

Poor organisational skills or short-term (or working) memory

Sometimes parents and carers outline problems at home with their child with HLP's organisational skills, processing speed or working memory, mentioning things such as:

- They are daydreamers, and don't seem to listen to what their parents or carers or others say
- When they are asked to do something, they forget what their parent or carer has said
- They seem to be disorganised and untidy
- They have difficulty moving from one task to another and can become angry when they are asked to do this quickly or without warning.

A perfect example of this is when children fail to get ready for school in time. More than one parent or carer has taken their child to school still dressed in their pyjamas or has threatened to do this as a warning!

Even in the early years, parents and carers often paint the picture of the 'absent-minded professor' whose brain is too busy thinking about problems and is learning at such a 'high level' that they forget about day-to-day matters such as eating their breakfast or getting dressed. While this may be frustrating at home, it can cause real problems at school, and can lead to different interventions being put in place, especially if linked to challenges such as poor writing skills or lack of attention in class.

Writing difficulties

Writing difficulties may not be obvious until a child enters formal education or as the work they are expected to do gets harder or the amount increases. Then, a variety of different problems may arise, including an inability to write for long periods of time, difficulty in forming letters and in starting or structuring what to write. This can make homework a particular nightmare for many families.

> Handwriting has been such a difficulty for my child and...created a web of problems at school. My child's self-esteem, school anxiety, relationships with teachers, ability to work in front of peers and, of course, my own relationship with their teachers have all been affected negatively. In Year 2, around about the time my child and their class were required to complete extended pieces of writing for assessment, things really started to go downhill for my child in the classroom. (Parent)

> My child is on the 99th percentile for verbal comprehension and had always read books beyond their years in terms of language, plots and ideas. But they just couldn't write more than a couple of sentences without becoming an exhausted, frustrated, emotional wreck. By Year 3, when they were being asked daily to 'c'mon, pick up your pencil and finish your work or you won't get playtime', my child responded by getting into their school locker, shutting the door and not coming out until home time. At home, I resorted to letting them use the dictate function on the computer. Through this, we discovered the witty, articulate and engaging stories hidden behind my child's inability to tolerate writing by hand. We hope we can persuade the school that my child isn't lazy or awkward; they are just frustrated and embarrassed by the difficulties handwriting poses for them. (Parent)

Some difficulties may be due to medical problems, such as double-joint-edness (also called hypermobility). Others may be due to an inability to structure the amount of knowledge that is in the child's head or to start a piece of work for the same reason. It could also be due to a range of other factors including inappropriateness of the topic and perfectionism, none of which may be connected to the obvious difficulty that is dyslexia, which we will return to later.

Lack of friends

Sometimes one of the biggest concerns of parents and carers is that their child has no friends. This can happen when the child is young and wants to do different things from others their age – making up complicated games that nobody else wants to play or simply wanting to read or do maths indoors rather than run about outside. When children are at a young age, they often have no sense of 'self' and don't get upset when they want to do different things from other children their age, but as they grow older (and certainly by the end of primary school), they may suddenly realise that they are 'different' and develop social, emotional and mental health problems as a result. Being unable to meet like-minded peers is a problem that can continue for these children, even progressing into adulthood. This is what makes finding people who accept them for who they are and who are on the same wavelength so important, and certainly by the time a child mentions it as a problem.

> I was bullied and the teacher said I was overreacting. One friend manipulated other friends into them all shunning me collectively. But they were very sneaky about hiding how much they were hurting me from anybody. The social pressure on people to fit in and conform and achieve certain social standards was very negative. (Adult who was a child with DME)

> I was incredibly lonely, always. No one understood me or wanted to. I had no one to talk to, no one to confide in. I had suicidal ideas from about eight years old. (Adult who has a child with DME)

Social, emotional and mental health difficulties

Some children with HLP can develop social, emotional and mental health issues as a result of one or more of the other challenges listed above, and this can happen for a variety of reasons. Sometimes the child has a high cognitive ability – they 'overthink' and start to worry about problems that might never happen in the future, or about things that have happened in the past and that they think about time and time again, exaggerating them out of all proportion.

> My sibling watched a science documentary on the television about the fact that eventually the Sun will die out so life on Earth would become impossible. The programme also talked about the fact that if the Sun exploded it would be around eight minutes before we knew about it on Earth. The combinations of these two revelations meant my sibling couldn't sleep at night for worrying about the end of the world. Even when it was explained to them that this was many thousands of years away, they struggled to move on from the anxiety of it all. They were seven years old at the time. (Sibling of an adult who was a child with DME)

> If I'm not careful, in the evenings I start to think about things that have happened that day, what somebody meant when they said something or how they looked, about why things have happened in the past and what I could have done differently. I found it too difficult to go to school as a result of this and developed Social Anxiety Disorder and began to self-harm. (Young person with DME)

As the child 'over worries' or becomes over-anxious and even extrapolates what will happen from a variety of pieces of information that may be unrelated, this can lead to difficulties sleeping at night or being unable to rest or relax or regulate their behaviour. Ultimately, this can also have an impact on their long-term social, emotional and mental state.

Sometimes the child's needs are not met. Growing social, emotional and mental health difficulties can be the *consequence* of a lack of identification or support of their needs and not the original cause, and may disappear or reduce once their needs are met.

> Finding a school which recognised HLP as a Special Educational Need was a massive help to our family. Once our child was in an environment and challenged, their need for emotional support diminished. (Parent)

> A range of professionals have tried to intervene to say that the right education needs to be provided for my child. Without this I have seen my child's mental health get worse and worse until they have needed specialist intervention in hospital. It breaks my heart. (Parent)

There are other reasons why social, emotional and mental health difficulties can arise, but in terms of HLP, the question that may need to be considered by parents and carers who are going through situations such as this is: Are their child's emotional or mental health difficulties a *result* of their HLP or the *consequence* of lack of identification or effective support they receive? We will leave this for you to think about, but remember this question as you read through this book.

Of course, you may not face any of these challenges, or these areas of concern may not be the only ones you worry about with your child with HLP. However, without the right understanding and support for any of your concerns at home, such problems can increase in other settings and as your child grows older. In particular, your child with HLP can be affected by what happens to them when they go to school, how others act towards them in a learning environment, because of the support they are given or their experiences. The impact of these can also be felt once again, in the home environment. This is covered later, in Chapter 6.

THINKING ABOUT HAVING YOUR CHILD WITH HLP ASSESSED?

Many parents and carers facing challenges like this with their child with HLP choose to have their child assessed by a specialist. Contrary to popular belief, this is not usually done because they want to discover 'how bright their child is'. Instead, it is far more likely that they are looking for an in-depth understanding of their child and how best to support them.

If you are thinking of getting an assessment for your child, it is important that you do this with someone who understands about HLP, what it looks like and how it can be nurtured. If it becomes relevant, such specialists should also have an understanding of SEND, or at least those most commonly diagnosed in children like this. These could include Autism Spectrum Disorder (ASD), specific learning difficulties (SpLD) such as dyslexia, dyscalculia and dysgraphia, and also Attention Deficit Hyperactivity Disorder (ADHD). Sensory processing difficulty (SPD) is usually recognised as part of another condition, such as ASD. As well as being able to identify HLP and SEND, it is also critical that the assessor has a deep understanding of what these two areas can look like in combination, as DME.

Finally, parents and carers need a practical action plan for how they – and others – can support their child effectively. In Chapter 6 we will explore the pros and cons of using different types of assessor as well as providing more information on the assessments used for such children. For now, here is what some parents have said about the benefits of going down the assessment route:

> I've made massive changes in how I support my child since having the assessment. I now know exactly what they need. I acted on the advice the assessor gave us and we have had a few sessions with another specialist to address their mood swings. Life is much smoother. (Parent)

> Following the assessment, we gave the report and action plan to the school. Since then, our child has been accelerated a year in maths. The school is now looking into changing the way they teach English and especially writing. They are allowing our child to do reports in the class related to topic work. The assessment validated our concerns, and the school is now taking us seriously. The staff also seem to understand our child more. At home we are trying to clearly communicate our expectations and give our child checklists to reduce their frustration. (Parent)

RECEIVING APPROPRIATE SUPPORT

Before we move out of the world of the child with HLP, there is one more important question that needs to be considered by all parents and carers of children with HLP, which is, from everything you have read so far about the child with HLP:

- Should HLP be identified as a Special Educational Need, especially where children with HLP face challenges as a result of their HLP?

Many parents and carers would argue that, just as with asynchronous development, such characteristics are part of being a child (and later, an adult) with HLP. Here is what Dr Silverman says:

> Giftedness is not what you do or how hard you work. It is who you are. You think differently. You experience life intensely. You care about injustice. You seek meaning. You appreciate and strive for the exquisite. You are painfully sensitive. You are extremely complex. You cherish integrity. Your truth-telling has gotten you into trouble. Should 98% of the population find you odd, seek out the company of those who love you just the way you are. You are not broken. You do not need to be fixed. You are utterly fascinating. Trust yourself! (Silverman 2012, quoted in Merrill 2012, pp.61–62)

However, in the UK allowances are not often made for these traits. There is no school (yet) for children with HLP. How, then, can a child with some of these traits receive appropriate support for their learning?

Within the education system, children with diagnosed SEND such as ASD and ADHD can also have some of the same characteristics as a child with HLP. This can make it even more challenging for them to be identified correctly, which has led to growing suspicion among parents and carers that some children with HLP are being misdiagnosed, either by accident or deliberately, as this is seen as the only way a child in school will receive the support they need. But what if the label of 'SEND' could also be applied to 'HLP'? What would be the result?

There are many situations where amending the how, the where or even the what and when a child is taught can enable that child or young person (or adult) with the characteristics of HLP to learn effectively. Sometimes, however, the child needs more than is provided through this differentiation within the inclusive classroom. Many should be identified as having an additional need for support, and just what to do about this need is certainly something that should be considered by the school or learning setting.

Before we move on, you may have already started the search for a greater understanding of your child and be trying to find answers to explain their actions, emotions and behaviour. You may even have begun to wonder whether your child could have a SEND. Alternatively, you may not have thought of SEND at all. That is until someone – perhaps your child's nursery worker, their teacher when they started school or one of your friends – may have mentioned these and you may have begun to wonder whether they could be right. This is the focus of the next chapter.

CONCLUSION

This chapter has been about introducing you to the term 'High Learning Potential', what you need to look for in your child, and some of the common challenges you may come across along the way. But remember – every child is unique. Just because we've highlighted some things you may be facing doesn't mean that there aren't others you may experience, or even that you have experienced none of them. If in doubt:

- Talk to others who know your child.
- Observe the kinds of things your child does and how they behave in certain situations.
- Talk to people who have experience of these challenges (a list of some of the key organisations is provided at the end of this book). Some of those that work with parents and carers provide online webinars for you to watch or regular blogs you can read.
- In all of this, don't forget the support *you* need as a parent or carer. This is vital. You will find information and ideas about this in Chapter 5.

Identifying your child's strengths and the challenges they face is important if they are to be supported effectively at school and in their learning. However, before we talk about DME, it is also important that you have a clear idea of the SEND framework in your own country. This will enable you to understand what *could* be provided for a child with diagnosable SEND. We turn to this in the next chapter, which focuses on SEND.

Want to know more? Further information can be found at www.jkp.com/catalogue/book/9781787758100

FURTHER READING
Growth mindset

Carol Dweck (2017) *Mindset: Changing the Way You Think to Fulfil Your Potential* (6th edition). Robinson.

Barry Hymer and Mike Gershon (2014) *Growth Mindset Pocketbook*. Teachers' Pocketbooks.

Barry Hymer and Will Hussey (2017) *Puffed Out: The Three Little Pigs' Guide to a Growth Mindset*. Crown House Publishing.

High Learning Potential (HLP)

Kate Distin (ed.) (2006) *Gifted Children: A Guide for Parents and Professionals*. Jessica Kingsley Publishers.

Valsa Koshy and Elizabeth Koshy (2017) *Find and Nurture Your Child's Gifts: Boost Your Child's Learning and Wellbeing (4 to 11 Years)*. enrichchildrenslives.

Valsa Koshy and Elizabeth Koshy (2020) *Help Your Children to Succeed in Life: A Guide for Parents, Grandparents and Carers with Children Aged 4–11 Years*. enrichchildrenslives.

Linda Kreger Silverman (2013) *Giftedness 101* (The Psych 101 Series). Springer Publishing Company.

James Webb, Janet Gore, Edward Amend and Arlene DeVries (2007) *A Parent's Guide to Gifted Children*. Great Potential Press, Inc.

Living with intensity

Elaine Aron (2015) *The Highly Sensitive Child: Helping Our Children Thrive When the World Overwhelms Them*. Harper Thorsons.

Susan Daniels and Michael Piechowski (eds) (2009) *Living with Intensity: Understanding the Sensitivity, Excitability, and the Emotional Development of Gifted Children, Adolescents, and Adults*. Great Potential Press, Inc.

Sal Mendaglio (ed.) (2008) *Dabrowski's Theory of Positive Disintegration*. Great Potential Press, Inc.

Lisa Rivero (2010) *A Parent's Guide to Gifted Teens: Living with Intense and Creative Adolescents*. Great Potential Press, Inc.

Lisa Rivero (2010) *The Smart Teens' Guide to Living with Intensity: How to Get More Out of Life and Learning*. Great Potential Press, Inc.

Angie Voss (2011) *Understanding Your Child's Sensory Signals: A Practical Daily Use Handbook for Parents and Teachers*. CreateSpace Independent Publishing Platform.

Angie Voss (2014) *Understanding Your Baby's Sensory Signals*. CreateSpace Independent Publishing Platform.

YOUR ACTION PLAN

1. Make a list of everything your child is doing or did when they were younger – both positive and more challenging. Pin them to the wall or somewhere you can see them. Remember what is on your list if things get more difficult.

2. If you think you would find it useful, do the free Potential Plus UK online questionnaire to see whether your child could have HLP.[6]

3. Observe what your child is doing when their actions or responses are challenging, and develop an action plan for each, involving your child where you can.

4. Be consistent in your approach with your child, and make sure the rest of the family do the same.

---

6 https://potentialplusuk.org/index.php/online-questionnaire

CHAPTER 2

I've Been Told My Child Has Special Educational Needs and/or a Disability

What Could Be Going On?

INTRODUCTION

Every child is unique, and their differences should be celebrated, and every parent and carer should remember that each child has amazing strengths as well as challenges to face along the way. While you may still feel that your child has High Learning Potential (HLP), something in your child's behaviour may also have led you to a growing suspicion that they might have a recognised SEND which, somehow, has been missed so far.

> When I was younger, people never realised that I knew as much as I did, nor that I struggled as much as I did. (Adult who was a child with DME)

You might already have family members who show characteristics of a SEND, so you may already be aware of them. Or someone might have pointed you in this direction as a possibility. This includes the specialist attached to your child's school, a teacher or other professional. Or you might have watched a TV programme or read a book or searched the internet about this very subject. You may even have read Chapter 1 of this book and felt that something more was going on with your child than 'just' HLP. In fact, there are many ways in which your suspicions might have been aroused:

- Are you right? How do you know if you are right?
- Is whoever has told you giving you their own views or those based on a thorough assessment of your child? How do you know if they are right?
- If you don't think they are right, what does this mean for your child?
- If you *do* think they are right, what does this mean for your child?

Before we explore these and other questions, it is important for you to understand what is meant by 'Special Educational Needs and Disabilities'.

THE LEGAL DEFINITION OF 'SPECIAL EDUCATIONAL NEEDS AND DISABILITIES'

It is important that parents and carers of children with HLP (especially those with challenges) and also children with Dual or Multiple Exceptionality (DME) understand the legal framework in place. In September 2014, the Government in England introduced the Children and Families Act.[1] This covered many different topics related to children and young people. Chapter 6, Part 3 was about improving support for children and young people with Special Educational Needs and Disabilities (often shortened to SEND) and their families. It defined the age this support might be provided as 0–25, to allow for early identification and also preparation for adulthood.

According to Chapter 6, Part 3, the legal definition of 'Special Educational Needs' is:

1. A child or young person has special educational needs if he or she has a learning difficulty or disability that calls for special educational provision to be made for him or her.

   A child of compulsory school age or a young person has a learning difficulty or disability if he or she –
   a. Has a significantly greater difficulty in learning than the majority of others of the same age, or
   b. Has a disability that prevents or hinders him or her from making use of facilities of a kind generally provided for others of the same age in mainstream schools or mainstream post-16 institutions.

---

1   www.legislation.gov.uk/ukpga/2014/6/part/3/enacted

The Special Educational Needs and Disability Code of Practice: 0–25 years (Department for Education and Department of Health 2015) is easier to read and provides statutory guidance on the duties, policies and procedures relating to Part 3 of the Children and Families Act 2014 (go to www.jkp/com/catalogue/book/9781787758100 for more information on this).

One of the key points to this legislation is that it is based on the comparison of one child with another of the same age. This is well represented in Figure 2.1.

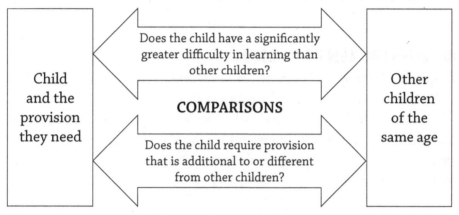

Figure 2.1. Comparisons to support the identification of SEND
Source: Boddison (2021, p.3)

However, what happens if that child is performing at a significantly higher level than others their age, and any difficulties they have are masked or counterbalanced by this? Does this make any SEND invalid? Or, hypothetically, what happens if every child in a class or year has HLP? How would the comparison work then? Or alternatively, where every child is performing well below average?

We will return to this topic again later. Notwithstanding, experience suggests that many children with HLP have developed significant behavioural, social, emotional and mental health problems as a result of inappropriate education before any SEND intervention is considered. Once it has been, parents and carers may need to convince schools to support their child's strengths rather than their areas of challenge.

Lack of identification or misidentification can lead to growing problems. By the time the child is identified with a recognisable SEND or DME it can be too late. Either the child has stopped going to school, is a school refuser or anxious or has even been excluded from school, or a lot of resources have been invested to sort out the child's social, emotional and mental health problems that are seen rather than getting to the root cause of why they are happening – DME.

Of course, not every school setting is so inflexible, and there are plenty of examples of good practice in this area around the country. But this is the point – it is often left to the leadership of one headteacher, one board of governors or one class teacher to provide the support needed.

Surely there must be another option?

IDENTIFYING SEND IN SCHOOL

Chapter 6 of *The Special Educational Needs and Disability Code of Practice* outlines how SEND should be identified and supported at different times within education (such as in the early years and in schools). Reading current guidance like this can be useful for parents and carers to evaluate what schools should be doing in such areas. Paragraphs 6.17 and 6.18 are particularly important:

> 6.17 Class and subject teachers, supported by the senior leadership team, should make regular assessment of progress for all pupils. These should seek to identify pupils making less than expected progress given their age and individual circumstances. This can be characterised by progress which:
>
> - is significantly slower than that of their peers starting from the same baseline
> - fails to match or better the child's previous rate of progress
> - fails to close the attainment gap between the child and their peers
> - widens the attainment gap.
>
> 6.18 It can include progress in areas other than attainment – for instance where a pupil needs to make additional progress with wider development or social needs in order to make a successful transition to adult life. (Department for Education and Department of Health 2015)

In other words, if a child's progress is deteriorating over time, or if they have other needs outside their attainment levels, their SEND should be recognised in school.

Four broad areas of need are identified that should be planned for in school (paras 6.28–6.35, pp.97–98): communication and interaction, cognition and learning, social, emotional and mental health difficulties and sensory and/or physical needs. It is important for parents and carers to remember that these should not be seen as all the needs that could be identified. Some children might have SEND that span all four areas; others may have needs that change over time. Section 6.27 clearly states:

> The purpose of identification is to work out what action the school needs to take, not to fit a pupil into a category. (Department for Education and Department of Health 2015, 6.27, p.97)

As we shall see later, reaching for 'off the peg' definitions of SEND without effective assessment can lead to inappropriate support and interventions being followed for some children with HLP.

Before we move on, let's look at the four broad areas of need in a little more detail.

Communication and interaction

This covers children and young people with speech, language and communication needs, which means that they find it difficult to communicate with others. For example, they might find it difficult to say what they want to, have difficulties in understanding what someone says to them or they might not understand the social rules of communication. An example of this would be a child with ASD. It could include someone with a speech and language problem.

> My child refuses to speak at school! They are incredibly quiet normally, but they really withdrew into themselves when they started the local primary school. It is quite large (about 500 pupils) and my child does admit to finding it a bit overwhelming with the noise and hustle and bustle of school life... I don't have a problem at home; they are happy at school and are happy to go in every day. It is a real problem for them in school, though. (Parent)

Cognition and learning

Support for learning difficulties may be needed when children and young people learn at a slower pace than their peers, even when changes are made to the way they are taught (called 'differentiation'). This covers several difficulties including moderate learning difficulties (MLD) and severe learning difficulties (SLD) through to profound and multiple learning difficulties (PMLD), where children are likely to have severe and complex learning difficulties as well as a physical disability or sensory issue. Specific learning difficulties (SpLD) affect one or more aspects of their learning, which includes conditions such as dyslexia, dyscalculia and dyspraxia.

> When I was younger, I had many people who tried to put limits on what I could achieve because they saw me as a dyslexic child and didn't look at what I'd already accomplished. I also encountered people who tried to tell me what they thought was best for me and who didn't trust my opinion when I could tell them why it wouldn't be beneficial to me. (Adult who was a child with DME)

Social, emotional and mental health difficulties

Children and young people can have lots of different kinds of social, emotional and mental health challenges (sometimes shortened to SEMH). For example, they could become withdrawn and depressed, or they could show challenging or disruptive behaviour. The way a young person acts could be because of underlying mental health difficulties such as anxiety or depression, self-harm, eating disorders or Body Dysmorphic Disorder (BDD). They could also have diagnosed conditions like Attention Deficit Hyperactivity Disorder (ADHD) or Attachment Disorder.

Sensory and/or physical needs

Some children or young people need special support in education because they have a disability that stops them or makes it difficult for them to join in with the learning or other things on offer. This could include children or young people who are visually impaired (VI) or hearing impaired (HI) or who have a multi-sensory impairment (MSI), where they have both hearing and sight difficulties. It could also include children and young people with a physical difficulty (PD) who need extra support or special equipment so they can learn with their classmates.

I remember being in the top set at primary school. I loved maths and writing, and I was good at languages. But all the teachers saw, especially at secondary school, was my hearing disability. That made me anxious. (Young person with DME)

We knew our child was bright, but they just were not achieving at school. So, we had them assessed. The assessment indicated that our child had visual perception problems and so had further tests. A pair of tinted glasses later and our child had progressed rapidly from being the worst reader in the class to the best, reading at about four years above their age. (Parent)

These areas of disability give the 'D' that makes up the 'SEND' approach parents and carers may see in schools, an approach that is so important for inclusion. However, this book is not about just SEND. There are many publications that give details about individual SEND as well as organisations that offer support in different aspects of SEND, but one that deserves a special mention here is nasen (National Association for Special Educational Needs).

NASEN (NATIONAL ASSOCIATION FOR SPECIAL EDUCATIONAL NEEDS)

This is a charitable membership organisation whose aim is to promote education, training, advancement, development and care of all infants, children, young people and others of whatever age with learning differences by providing relevant information, training and resources to enable the needs of all pupils to be met.

While nasen does have parents and carers as members, it is primarily for education professionals such as Special Educational Needs coordinators (SENCos). The information it provides about SEND and how schools approach this topic is always up to date and relevant. This is useful for parents and carers in understanding about different SEND; in looking at what schools could do to support children and young people with SEND; and in exploring new ideas for supporting children with SEND that could be useful for supporting a child at home.

Since January 2021, nasen membership has been free for every-one.[2] Membership includes access to the most up-to-date knowledge and support; exclusive online access to nasen's *Connect* magazine six times a year; easy-to-access information via email including a monthly member newsletter and discounts from a range of selected SEND organisations; and access to the SEND Gateway, a one-stop-shop for SEND.[3]

England, Scotland, Northern Ireland and Wales each operate within slightly different structures and within different definitions. Other countries around the world also have different approaches towards children and young people with SEND, depending on what they believe is important or most relevant to their cultures (go to www.jkp.com/catalogue/book/9781787758100 for more information).

Legislation and approaches to SEND are changing all the time, so it is best to see the latest Government framework in place in your area or country when you need it, as well as the latest approaches your child's school is planning to take. Don't forget – many fee-paying schools may not have chosen to follow some of the frameworks in place in state schools (although many have), so it is worth checking with the school about their approaches and policies if you are thinking of sending your child to one outside the state system.

---

2   To become a member, log on to www.nasen.org.uk. As information is provided online, contact nasen at 01827 311500 to discuss other ways of getting information.
3   https://sendgateway.org.uk

IDENTIFYING AND NURTURING YOUR CHILD'S AMAZING STRENGTHS

Regardless of your child's HLP and any SEND, every child is more than the sum of their parts. There is no such thing as the 'average child'; every child is a complex mix of strengths and struggles. Some people do not see SEND as a problem for the child, but rather, they see SEND as 'differences' that are a positive part of every individual – superpowers, if you like – which need to be recognised and nurtured. If anything, it is argued, the problem lies with the structures and attitudes of society and its establishments (such as schools) that fail to recognise and celebrate differences, and that are inflexible in their approach towards these differences.

This problem stems, in part at least, because the approach to SEND (in England and elsewhere) is based on a *medical model* of intervention. Although this is changing, this medical model is quite negative and implies that there is something 'wrong' with the child that needs to be 'put right':

> The medical model is premised on the concept that a person with SEND needs to be 'improved' or 'cured' through medical, social or educational interventions. The social model focuses more on the environmental barriers to participation and learning and how these can be removed or reduced, including through wider societal change. (Boddison 2021, p.5)

Our book supports the *social model* of SEND. In fact, we go further and say that many of the characteristics identified as SEND in the right environments should be seen as *strengths*. The failure is in the 'system' – in society – to recognise and make room for those differences so that these strengths can flourish.

> I was working in a busy store. There were lots of people around and it was hectic. My manager was right on the other side of the large shop floor and he asked someone to get something for him. Nobody else could hear him. He was absolutely amazed when I passed him what he wanted. He didn't know I could lipread so well. (Young person with DME)

There must be room in any model for medical and other interventions where needed, and this book does not seek to trivialise the very real challenges that those with SEND live with – and struggle with – on a day-to-day basis. However, there must also be room in any society to look at SEND through a strengths-based social model, which should also be a consideration for schools and parents and carers (as well as children and young people themselves).

Let's take a few examples of this to highlight what we mean.

DYSLEXIA

If you have a child who has (or may have) dyslexia, books such as *The Dyslexic Advantage* by Brock Eide and Fernette Eide are useful. Alternatively, *Dyslexia Is My Superpower (Most of the Time)* is a book about children and teens with dyslexia told by the young people themselves (coordinated by Margaret Rooke).

Some challenges seen with *dyslexia*	Some strengths seen with *dyslexia*
• Poor skills in seeing the detail	• Ability to see the 'big picture'
• Difficulties with reading and/or writing	• Highly creative
• Difficulties in learning	• Enjoys practical tasks
• Low self-esteem	• Appears bright, highly intelligent and articulate
• Poor processing skills (such as needing more time to answer questions)	• Good oral skills
• Poor working memory (e.g., manipulating two words to form another)	• Good social skills
• Difficulties in organisation skills	• Able to 'think outside the box'
• Problems with exams based on recall	• Able to think imaginatively
• Difficulties with time management	• Good at developing strategies for the future
• Lower achievement levels in exams	• Able to think in pictures
	• Confident talker or presenter
	• Able to find patterns in things
	• Good entrepreneur

Source: Various, including the British Dyslexia Society, Dyslexia Scotland (n.d.) as well as parent and carer feedback

ATTENTION DEFICIT HYPERACTIVITY DISORDER (ADHD)

Parents and carers who want to know more about what it is like to grow up with ADHD might find *Andrew and the Magic Giveash**ometer* by Whitehouse an interesting read.

Some challenges seen with *ADHD*	Some strengths seen with *ADHD*
• Makes careless mistakes • Appears forgetful • Loses things • Unable to stick to tasks that are tedious or time-consuming • Appears unable to listen or carry out instructions • Constantly changes activities or tasks to something else • Difficulty in organising tasks • Unable to concentrate in certain situations • Fidgets constantly • Physically moves excessively • Talks excessively • Interrupts others while they are speaking • Has poor listening skills • Unable to focus on one skill area (or job) at once • Unable to wait their turn • Acts impulsively (or without thinking) • Has little or no sense of danger	• Able to think creatively • Flexible • Enthusiastic and spontaneous • Highly energetic • Has a brain that never stops thinking • Able to think about lots of things at the same time • Brilliant multi-tasker • Able to focus for long periods on something that interests them • Strong innovator • Highly productive when focused • Outgoing (a 'people person') with lots of friends • Has lots of different talents • A risk-taker • Successful, if in the right job

Source: Various, including the NHS, The ADHD Centre, ADHD Foundation (n.d.) as well as parent and carer feedback

AUTISM SPECTRUM DISORDER (ASD)

Books worth reading on Autism Spectrum Disorder (ASD) include *Aspergirls* by Rudy Simone and *Ask Dr Tony* by Craig Evans and Tony Attwood.

Some challenges seen with *ASD*	Some strengths seen with *ASD*
• Needs strict daily routines and has difficulties coping with change • Has sensory difficulties with things such as bright or flickering lights and strong smells • Has sensory overload • Takes things literally that others say to them • Vulnerable to bullying, manipulation and social exclusion • Finds it difficult to understand other people • Unable to understand what others are thinking or feeling, and can be socially isolated and withdrawn because of this • Finds it hard to make friends or prefers to be on their own • Shows challenging behaviour in certain situations • Has poor processing speeds • Has a physical and/or emotional meltdown in stressful situations • Has social, emotional and mental health problems • Difficult to detect, e.g., girls with ASD may present differently and be harder to detect	• Has strong attention to detail • Has good visual perception • Has strong mathematical and programming abilities • Has interests or expertise in specialist or 'niche' areas • Able to think clearly 'without the clutter' • Able to focus on one activity, often for long periods • Able to systematically approach tasks • Highly focused in a crisis • Strong attention to detail • Logically able to analyse problems • Accurate and able to detect errors • Loyal • Able to work towards high quality in what they do • Honest and trustworthy • A unique thinker

Source: Various, including the NHS, Autistica (n.d.), Auticon (n.d.) as well as parent and carer feedback

When I was a child, people thought only boys with a learning disability had autism. I was a girl and hence went undiagnosed. My family thought I had a learning disability and ignored my intellectual needs. My sister was regarded as the smart one and all the attention was focused on her. So, I ambled along and fought my way into a school where I could do A-levels and then get into university. My family still thought I had a learning disability (even though I did a science degree at university and then a further degree in a specialist area). I always struggled with the social demands at nursery, school and then university. While at university, I started to realise that I wasn't intellectually disabled but the opposite! I was faster, brighter and much more interested in the subject than my peers. After my professors asked me to stop asking so many questions as they could not answer them, I looked up Mensa for support. It took me some years to finally have my IQ tested, and when I had the results, they were quite unbelievable. And a revelation. And a relief. Five years earlier I had finally received an autism diagnosis. That was even more of a relief. Now I could finally understand myself! (Adult who was a child with DME)

Remember that whoever your child is and whatever challenges they face, it is about identifying their strengths and nurturing these, so that the child can:

- Believe in themselves
- Recognise they have strengths and what they are
- Build on these for the future.

Building first on the strengths of a child or young person and using these as a way of supporting the difficulties they have (what we refer to as 'scaffolding') is important, we believe, for any child or young person (and adult). However, as we shall see in the following chapters, this approach is absolutely vital for a child or young person with DME if they are to become the best version of themselves they can be.

■ Tips and hints: Strengths and challenges

Make a list of all your child's strengths. Remember – these are the most important things about your child.

If you want, make a list of the challenges they face.

Now see if you can use their strengths to support their challenges by:

- Finding out what your child enjoys doing
- Relating these to your child's areas of strength
- Using these to support the challenges your child faces.

For example, if your child is obsessed with dinosaurs and has difficulties with understanding what others are thinking, saying or feeling, you could role-play using dinosaur cards with emotions on them and tell your child a story about dinosaurs where they have to identify their emotions. This may help them to slowly learn how to recognise and correctly identify emotional or other cues.

Many parents and carers may still not feel that the 'identification' or diagnosis of their child that they have been given (or that has been suggested to them) is right. What's the problem? Let's now spend some time looking at the kinds of questions parents and carers raise in these situations.

HAS MY CHILD BEEN MISDIAGNOSED?

You may have been thinking when you were reading the lists above that many of the characteristics identified seem to be like those identified in Chapter 1 for HLP.

You would not be wrong.

SEND OR HLP?

You may still be wondering whether your child has SEND or HLP. What would your answers be to the questions below?

- Should a child with HLP be identified as having a communication problem when they merely seem to operate 'on a different wavelength'?
- If an eight-year-old has the potential to work to the level of an eighteen-year-old but is only given the work of a nine-year-

old, are they working one year ahead or ten years behind their potential?

- Many children and young people have anxiety and other social, emotional and mental health difficulties for a range of reasons related to their HLP. Many of them may not have an underlying condition, but could this develop because of their learning experiences? What comes first, SEND or HLP?

- Does SEND arise only because the education framework is wrong in some way for the child, or because it is not adapted correctly?

- How often are children misdiagnosed at school? In other forms of learning? In home education?

This was the argument put forward by James Webb and colleagues in *Misdiagnosis and Dual Diagnoses of Gifted Children and Adults*, a book first published in the US in 2005. This book is an important piece of work for those of us involved in this field and it is certainly recommended reading. It explored possible misdiagnoses of Gifted children (children with HLP) who had been identified as having ADHD, Asperger's Syndrome (AS), depression and other disorders:

Assigning a diagnosis to behaviors that are normal for gifted and talented persons is, in our opinion, a significant and widespread problem. Classifying such behaviors as mental health problems occurs too often. As health care professionals, we are trained to evaluate and categorise behaviors and symptoms. Sometimes those symptoms resemble a clinical condition, and labels are applied. In gifted persons, sometimes there is a better explanation than pathology. (Webb *et al*. 2016 [2005], p.1)

Webb *et al*. talk about a variety of different conditions and highlight their similarities with giftedness. They ask whether a child who is Gifted could be misdiagnosed or have *both* HLP and SEND. They go on to clarify:

We are not implying, however, that gifted individuals are immune from emotional or behavioral disorders. They certainly can have attention deficit disorder (ADD), Asperger's Disorder, or any of the other disorders described in DSM-5. We are not attempting to excuse inappropriate or maladaptive behavior on the basis of giftedness, or to explain away any real psychological or medical disorders. However, we do believe that the characteristics of gifted children and adults can sometimes imply pathology when there is none. Our goal for parents, healthcare professionals, educators and others is to help them view certain behaviors as normal for gifted individuals and then 'reframe' the problem behaviors in ways that will allow them to more appropriately guide and shape those behaviors, rather than to label them with a diagnosis that results in treating the behaviors to extinguish them. (Webb *et al.* 2016 [2005], p.26)

Taking Webb *et al.*'s model and comparing HLP with some of the characteristics of SEND identified in the Children and Families Act 2014, you can see how it would be easy to confuse or even misdiagnose them instead of HLP. We are not concerned with the why at the moment, just what you, as a parent and carer (or a teacher or other professional), may see.

Characteristics associated with some children with *dyslexia*	Characteristics associated with some children with *HLP*
Poor reading and/or writing skills	Poor writing skills
Poor processing skills	Poor processing skills
Poor organisation skills	Poor organisation skills
Poor time management skills	Poor time management skills
Poor achievement in exams	Achievement below expected levels in exams
Vivid imagination	Vivid imagination
Ability to put disconnected pieces of information together to come to a conclusion	Ability to put disconnected pieces of information together to come to a conclusion
Characteristics associated with some children with *ADHD*	**Characteristics associated with some children with *HLP***
Poor concentration levels	Poor concentration levels
Easily bored	Bored in certain situations
Impulsive	Impulsive
Brain never stops thinking and thinks about lots of things at the same time	High activity level, often needs less sleep, brain always 'on the go'

Difficulty following rules/instructions	Questions rules and won't follow them unless they make sense
Characteristics associated with some children with *ASD*	**Characteristics associated with some children with *HLP***
Dislikes or resistant to change	High levels of concentration or dislikes being pulled away from what they are doing
'Obsessions' about one hobby, interest or issue	Passion or obsession about one or a limited number of things
Poor social interaction or lack of understanding of other children or young people	Not interested in other children or young people as 'not on their wavelength'. Gravitates towards interaction with adults
Challenging behaviour in certain situations	Can challenge others' opinions, especially when they believe they are right
Sensory issues	Hypersensitivity
Physical and emotional meltdown in stressful situations	Can be part of HLP or as a result of lack of appropriate understanding of or response to it
Social, emotional and mental health issues	Range of mental health issues as a result of HLP or lack of appropriate response to it

Source: Based on Webb et al. (2016 [2005], pp.76–94)

You may think of other characteristics that are similar between both SEND and HLP and the characteristics you see in your child.

In 1981, Dr Webb set up SENG (Supporting Emotional Needs of the Gifted)[4] in the US to provide support to both children and adults. This organisation is excellent, and well worth looking at for support.

Many parents and carers are left with three outstanding questions:

- Has my child been misdiagnosed, and do they have HLP or SEND?
- Whatever the answer, in school, how far will these labels take us?
- If it is not one or the other, could it be both? What is going on?

The wrong diagnosis was given of ASD when my child was eight or nine years old, and the correct diagnosis was given (of ADHD) when they

---

4   https://sengifted.org

were in their 20s. The information I had been given on ASD was therefore not entirely helpful and there was no mention of HLP. (Parent)

Understanding HLP helped when talking to the professional who assessed our child as they wanted to label them as having Autism Spectrum Disorder (ASD) without looking at the HLP aspect. When I told the professional about HLP they said they didn't know enough about it. (Parent)

Our child's school incorrectly suggested our child had Autism, even though this didn't fit with our experience. Our child was tested for Autism, even when we were flagging ADHD. We started asking for diagnostic help from when our child was about five years old. Our child is now seven years old, and we still have a 3+ years waiting list to see diagnostic services where we live. (Parent)

The school thought my child had Autism and that was the reason for their challenging behaviour. As parents, we Googled the traits and came up with 'Gifted'. The teacher said, 'I've taught many Gifted children, and this is not the profile of a Gifted child.' At that time, when school was pushing the Autism agenda, I spoke to specialists in HLP and they confirmed that what I was describing was exactly the profile of a Gifted child. (Parent)

While we are not saying that every child who has ASD actually has HLP instead, or that every child with ASD has the wrong diagnosis, the fact that misdiagnosis *could* happen should give both parents and carers and those professionals working with children and young people pause for thought.

DOES MY CHILD NEED A DIAGNOSIS AT ALL?

It is important to remember that, according to the *Special Educational Needs and Disability Code of Practice*:

The purpose of identification is to work out what action the school needs to take and not to fit a pupil into a category. (Department for Education and Department of Health 2015, para. 6.7, p.97)

In spite of this, schools may turn to the more commonly identified SEND as labels (almost shorthand) for describing a child or young person as they go through school, sometimes even before a rigorous diagnosis has taken place. There are many reasons why this could happen and why it may sometimes start to happen relatively early on in a pupil's school life.

It could be because:

- Of the correct identification of SEND
- Additional support is required, and identification and labelling provide the quickest way for the child to receive this support, or
- In England at least, increased funding may go towards supporting a child with a diagnosed SEND. Without a recognised diagnosis, that funding might not be forthcoming, which could mean that they might not get the support they need due to lack of resources.

However, isn't HLP a Special Educational Need? At present, in England at least, HLP is not identified as a SEND within the education system. However, legislation that does seem particularly inclusive comes from Scotland, where provision is made for additional support for 'highly able learners' (what we would call 'children with HLP') within the Education (Additional Support for Learning) (Scotland) Act 2004 (as amended in 2009).[5]

The *Code of Practice* (Third Edition, 2017) from the Scottish Government that supports this Act states:

> The definition of additional support provided by the Act is a wide, inclusive one... What is central to all these forms of support is that they have been identified as additional provision required to help individual children and young people benefit from school education, taking account of their needs and circumstances. The examples below refer to particular situations but should be understood more widely. They can be used to suggest how the law may apply in analogous situations. However, the examples are illustrative not comprehensive, and they do not constitute an authoritative or exhaustive interpretation of the legislation. (Scottish Government 2017, p.20)

It goes on to outline examples of the types of additional support that could

---

5   www.legislation.gov.uk/asp/2009/7/pdfs/asp_20090007_en.pdf

be provided, including for: 'A highly able child at the later stages of primary school receiving support to access the secondary mathematics curriculum' (Scottish Government 2017, p.20). The inclusive approach in Scotland of identifying the *additional needs* of every child and young person is a welcome approach and one that enables children with HLP to be supported. We mention this specifically as it shows that where there is a will, legal provision can be made to support children with HLP. Hopefully, it is as positive in practice as it is on paper.

But what about in other countries where their policies are not as inclusive? What happens to parents and carers whose children with HLP need support? This dilemma has been discussed among parents and carers for years, and there are often no right or wrong answers, just personal choice. Some, for example, prefer to stick with the identification of their child as having HLP. Others prefer their child to be identified as having a diagnosable condition such as ASD or ADHD or equivalent. This is often the case even when a child has been formally diagnosed with SEND.

Let's look at some of the pros and cons of identifying your child as either having SEND or HLP.

	Child identified as having SEND	Child identified as having HLP
Pros	*In school:*	*In school:*
	If you believe your child needs additional support, it may be the best way to obtain this (even though the process may take time)	In the right school, you believe your child's HLP will be supported anyway
	In the state sector in the UK, funding may be available to the school to provide professionals and equipment to support your child, which may not be available otherwise	You may feel that your child with HLP will be supported to succeed rather than 'put right'
		You believe that HLP is a more positive label than SEND
	There is usually a clear framework and track record of support for children and young people with SEND to draw on in school	It could provide the potential for vertical teaching structures where children could be taught in years or groups above them in age
	There is a framework in law to support your child, with a clear structure and process	*Outside school:*
		It could provide access to organisations or groups that recognise your child's cognitive abilities and needs
	Your child's needs should be recognised and supported	It could provide access to peers who are similar

Cons	You may believe the SEND label will be a stigma for your child going through school	You may believe that your child with HLP may not be supported appropriately
	You may believe that the school will not seek to identify or support your child's HLP	There may be no or little funding to support a child identified as HLP on its own
	There may also be problems with a diagnosis 'leading the interpretation and response' to a child's behaviour in school rather than looking for other reasons for the behaviour	You may believe that a child with HLP who is struggling could be labelled as 'lazy', a 'troublemaker' or worse, and could be excluded from school
	When there are problems such as with behaviour, you may believe that any reasons for this behaviour (such as lack of stretch and challenge) will not be investigated further	Social, emotional and mental health issues may not be investigated further if your child is seen as having HLP

When I was younger, they reinforced the stereotype that because you have a Special Educational Need, you have less hope of having academic ability. (Parent who was a child with DME)

MY CHILD IS AN INDIVIDUAL, NOT A DIAGNOSIS!

It is important to see your child as an individual who is more than the diagnoses – any diagnosis – that anyone gives them, whether that is SEND or even HLP. However, if your child has any *additional needs* that their school or teacher needs to be aware of or where you feel your child should receive extra support, make a list of these to discuss with the teacher. (We will talk about school and learning later, in Chapter 6.)

When my child argues with a teacher over the teacher's misidentification of a rock or having a disagreement with a child in the playground, it is interpreted as them having 'a need to control' the environment – with a response of 'Oh, they need social skills training because of Autism Spectrum Disorder' rather than the teacher themselves simply being incorrect or the other child being unpleasant to mine. (Parent)

The term *additional need* seems more neutral than SEND or even HLP, and it is a term we support. Some children with SEND or HLP can be supported effectively (or with appropriate differentiation) in an inclusive classroom.

They may therefore have no additional needs or require any specialist inter-vention. Where a child does have additional needs, the focus should be on meeting each characteristic or need individually and not on the overall diagnosis – in the first instance at least – that has been given, until the specialist has collected all evidence and is certain of their diagnosis or identification. This includes with the more informal identification of HLP. Then the parent or carer (and the child or young person) should be able to decide for themselves what to do next.

As we have seen, many of the individual characteristics and needs of different conditions overlap and can result in misdiagnosis. Saying these children have additional needs is a more inclusive way to identify their needs. Even this approach, however, may leave many parents and carers left thinking 'Isn't there a third way? Can't a child or young person be identified as having *both* HLP *and* SEND?'

The short answer is, yes, they can.

Having strengths (such as being clever) AND a Special Educational Need (such as social, emotional and mental health issues) means that many people will not judge you on two counts, but they will only look at one or the other. Hence your strengths may be overlooked by people contemplating your Special Educational Needs OR those managing your Special Educational Needs will not utilise your exceptionalities. It is very important to understand that people need help on a far greater scale when compared to just a single issue. (Adult who was a child with DME)

This is where we were with our eldest. They were in Reception class when their teacher called us in to say she had concerns and wanted to start an assessment by an educational psychologist [ed psych]. While going through the assessment we also spoke to my partner's parents and they told us about their experiences and the support available from organisations like Potential Plus UK.

When the ed psych wanted to take us through the assessment as she believed our child to have Autism, our first reaction was 'But what about their HLP?' The answer we received was that the ed psych didn't know enough about HLP to make an assessment. This is when we booked our HLP assessment with Potential Plus UK and were told, yes, our child has

HLP, but upon this assessment there was a note to say that there could potentially be ASD traits as well.

We went back to the ed psych with this information, and they went ahead with the ASD assessment, only to find that our child is borderline ASD. Our child has very few ASD characteristics; however, where our child does have them, they are so profound that they did get an ASD diagnosis as well as HLP. (Parent)

We'll explore this further in the next chapter.

CONCLUSION

In this chapter, we have seen an exploration of SEND and how it is relevant for HLP. The whole topic of SEND and HLP is extremely complicated, for yourself as parents and carers, for schools, for teachers and for the other professionals who work with children and young people such as yours. There is no doubt that it can be a minefield, and it's no wonder that it can become a struggle for everyone to find their way through. It can also be a contentious topic, with strength of feeling on both the SEND and HLP sides of the argument.

Despite this, a good place to start, we feel, remains in identifying the strengths of your child and using these to support any areas that may be more challenging for them. When looking at education, it is also useful to forget about the labels and to think of any *additional needs* your child has and how these could be best supported. This could include the things they struggle with *and* the things they love to do to stretch and challenge themselves.

Current structures seek to identify the characteristics and then, if needed, label the child. Given this, why not have dual labels, to identify both SEND and HLP? Hold on to that thought as we go to the next chapter.

Want to know more? Further information can be found at www.jkp. com/catalogue/book/9781787758100

MORE READING, IDEAS AND SUGGESTIONS
UK organisations offering support and advice for families with a child with SEND

These sites may not cover all the topics about which parents and carers may be concerned, but they will help signpost to other national and more local organisations.

AccessAble provides detailed information before going out, to see whether somewhere will be accessible: www.accessable.co.uk

Action for Children offers general advice and support for parents and carers: www.actionforchildren.org.uk

Autism Education Trust provides information, advice, support and resources relating to education to ensure every single child with Autism reaches their full potential: www.autismeducationtrust.org.uk/for-parents

Child Law Advice provides specialist advice and information on child, family and education law to parents or carers and young people via email and telephone (operated by Coram Children's Legal Centre): www.childlawadvice.org.uk

The Communication Trust and Consortium is a coalition of 50 not-for-profit organisations working to support children and young people in England to support their speech, language and communication: https://ican.org.uk/i-cans-talking-point/professionals/tct-resources

Contact (Contact a Family) exists to help families of children with disabilities feel valued, supported and involved. They support families with information, advice and guidance and bring families together both online and in local groups. They also help families to campaign, volunteer, fundraise and shape local services to improve life for themselves and others: https://contact.org.uk

Council for Disabled Children provides information and resources for parents and carers of disabled children (including legal advice): https://councilfordisabledchildren.org.uk/resources-and-help/im-parent

The Dyslexia-SpLD Trust aims to ensure that all those with dyslexia or specific learning difficulties succeed in school. The site has information and resources to support parents, carers and professionals: www.thedyslexia-spldtrust.org.uk

IPSEA (Independent Provider of Special Education Advice) offers free, independent, legally based information, advice and support to help parents and carers get the right education for their children with SEND: www.ipsea.org.uk

MindEd provides resources including online training about a range of issues affecting the mental health of children, young people and older adults (coordinated by NHS Health Education England): https://mindedforfamilies.org.uk

NNPCF (National Network of Parent Carer Forums) is the independent national voice of parent carer forums. Their mission is to deliver better outcomes for families living with SEND. This includes empowering members to ensure their voices are heard at a local, regional and national level and sharing good practice and knowledge: https://nnpcf.org.uk

NatSIP (National Sensory Impairment Partnership) is a partnership of organisations working together to improve outcomes for children and young people with sensory impairment. A list of members on specific topics can be searched and contacted: www.natsip.org.uk

SEND Gateway is an online portal offering easy to access resources and training for meeting the needs of children with SEND. Designed for education professionals, but useful for parents and carers (coordinated by nasen): www.sendgateway.org.uk

Sky Badger is an organisation where parents and carers can find help for children with physical disabilities, SEN, mental health problems and support for the whole family. It has resources on a range of issues, articles and a directory of information: https://skybadger.co.uk

Other useful organisations with resources to explore and purchase

The CEA Card is a national card scheme that enables a cinema guest to receive a complimentary ticket for someone to go with them to a participating cinema (terms apply): https://ceacard.co.uk

Connevans offers a range of solutions primarily to support those with a hearing impairment and other issues: www.connevans.co.uk

Harkla mainly provides products for children and adults with sensory difficulties. It also has a regular blog on topics related to sensory need, autism, etc. It is based outside the UK. One per cent of every sale goes to the University of Washington to fund research and therapy for local children: https://harkla.co

Incentive Plus offers a range of social, emotional, mental health and wellbeing resources to help fulfil the potential of children and young people of all ages: https://incentiveplus.co.uk

Multi-Sensory World is a sensory toy company committed to providing products, equipment and activities that encourage development through the stimulation of the senses. They also have a blog: www.multi-sensoryworld.co.uk

SEN Magazine is a leading UK magazine for SEN, with articles, products and more: https://senmagazine.co.uk

Tes SEN Show is a conference and exhibition for parents or carers and professionals where parents or carers can go to free sessions, attend training sessions (for which there may be a charge) and look at different products available to support children with SEND: www.tessenshow.co.uk

Again, these are just some sites that other parents and carers have found useful. We do not recommend these to meet your own child's specific needs nor say anything about the quality of what is offered. Parents and carers would need to decide that for themselves.

Some books you may find useful
The SEND framework in the UK

Beate Hellawell (2018) *Understanding and Challenging the SEND Code of Practice*. SAGE Publications Ltd.

Melinda Nettleton (2015) *Special Needs and Legal Entitlement: A Practical Guide to Getting Out of the Maze*. Jessica Kingsley Publishers.

Misdiagnosis

James Webb, Edward Amend, Nadia Webb, Jean Goerss, Paul Beljan and F. Richard Olenchak (2016) *Misdiagnosis and Dual Diagnoses of Gifted Children and Adults: ADHD, Bipolar, OCD, Asperger's, Depression, and Other Disorders*. Great Potential Press Inc.

The strengths-based approach in general

Anders Ericsson (2017) *Peak: How All of Us Can Achieve Extraordinary Things*. Vintage.

Jenifer Fox (2009) *Your Child's Strengths: A Guide for Parents and Teachers*. Penguin; illustrated edition.

Dewey Rosetti (2020) *Parenting Bright Kids Who Struggle in School: A Strength-Based Approach to Helping Your Child Thrive and Succeed*. Prufrock Press.

Books for children on their strengths
Younger children

Elaine Marie Larson (2006) *I Am Utterly Unique: Celebrating the Strengths of Children with Asperger Syndrome and High Functioning Autism*. EDS Publications Ltd.

Alana Moore (2020) *ADHD Is My Super Power and It Comes with Great Super Strengths*. Winn Publications LLC.

Nikki Saunders (2019) *My Awesome Autism: Helping Children Learn About Their Autism Diagnosis*. Independently published.

Older children

Siena Castellon (2020) *The Spectrum Girl's Survival Guide: How to Grow Up Awesome and Autistic*. Jessica Kingsley Publishers; illustrated edition.

Yenn Purkis and Tanya Masterman (2020) *The Awesome Autistic Go-To Guide: A Practical Handbook for Autistic Teens and Tweens*. Jessica Kingsley Publishers; illustrated edition.

Margaret Rooke (2018) *Dyslexia Is My Superpower (Most of the Time)*. Jessica Kingsley Publishers; illustrated edition.

Support for parents and carers with children with SEND

Sarah-Jane Critchley (2016) *A Different Joy: The Parents' Guide to Living Better with Autism, Dyslexia, ADHD and More...* Writingscorpink.

Ronald Davis (2010) *The Gift of Dyslexia: Why Some of the Brightest People Can't Read and How They Can Learn*. Souvenir Press; 3rd revised edition.

Brock Eide and Fernette Eide (2011) *The Dyslexic Advantage: Unlocking the Hidden Potential of the Dyslexic Brain*. Hudson Street Press.

Edward Hallowell and John Ratey (2006) *Delivered from Distraction: Getting the Most Out of Life with Attention Deficit Disorder*. Ballantine Books.

YOUR ACTION PLAN

1. Learn more about your child and their needs to gain a better understanding of their areas of strength and struggle.
2. Explore your child's understanding with them of how they see the strengths and challenges they face by listening to what they say.
3. Write down how you can turn any of your child's challenges into strengths.
4. Discuss with loved ones the pros and cons of getting a formal diagnosis or assessment of your child's needs.
5. Think about and discuss with loved ones what your view would be on going down the formal SEND route in school. Do you think your child could have SEND or HLP, or do neither of these fit exactly? It may not matter at the moment (or ever), but you should have some idea of where you stand on this subject should you need it.

CHAPTER 3

How Could My Child Have Special Educational Needs and Disabilities and High Learning Potential?

INTRODUCTION

This chapter examines how Special Educational Needs and Disabilities (SEND, in school jargon) can exist alongside High Learning Potential (HLP), what it looks like and what it is called (if you need another label!). It also explores how to support a child you think may have these characteristics and the kinds of decisions you may need to make as a result.

> Professionals were great at understanding our child's special educational needs and their learning difficulties. This helped in terms of supporting our child (and us!) so they could cope with some of the more negative aspects of what we were all going through. It also enabled us to access support which would not have been there without the diagnosis. However, there was little or no support or encouragement from any professional for the HLP side. This was never recognised on Individual Education Plans (IEPs) or other formal documents. (Parent)

This experience is far from unique. What we also explore in this chapter is what can happen when SEND and HLP exist together, particularly if one or even both of these areas is ignored or remains unidentified.

CAN SEND EXIST ALONGSIDE HLP?

The short answer is, yes it can. In fact, it most definitely does.

Some of these children may have been formally identified as having a SEND and have a lot of support, but parents and carers and others around them feel that they would have much more to offer if their gifts or talents were only recognised.

Some of them may be identified as 'More Able' or 'Highly Able' in school and may take part in classes and programmes for such children. However, they may then be criticised for things like failing to hand in work, not working hard enough or 'messing about' in class. This can lead to a range of sanctions for the child or young person and ongoing problems for professionals and parents and carers.

Some of these children and young people seem to find one or more areas of their learning harder than others, while at the same time (with understanding and sometimes with support) they learn or do other things in a way that astounds those around them. However, they may not have been identified as having SEND. Neither may they have been identified as having HLP. Instead, depending on the circumstances and the school, they may be given a range of labels, such as 'troublemaker' or 'challenging child'. Or they may have begun to actively hate school or be anxious about attending altogether.

However, in a small but growing number of schools and other education settings, these children may have been correctly identified. The results can then be amazing:

> We took the assessment we had had done into school to 'prove' our child's needs and strengths as well as the things that were a challenge for them and why. The primary school our child attends has responded brilliantly by organising an afternoon a week or fortnight doing practical chemistry, computing and biology at the secondary school and providing a 1:1 maths session in their school aimed at Year 7 [11 to 12 years old]. All of this was done because, as the headteacher said to us, 'We notice that your child's behaviour is better when they are stretched.' At last! (Parent)

These children could have Dual or Multiple Exceptionality (or DME for short). This is the phrase used in the UK, although in other countries it is known by other names such as 'Twice Exceptional' (or 2e), 'Gifted with Learning Difficulties or Disabilities' (or GLD) or neurodiverse. There are also some new phrases being used by parents and carers that are also growing in popularity: 'differently wired' and 'bright and quirky', to name just two. Whatever name you decide to use, they all mean the same or similar things.

Children and young people with DME have always existed, having gifts and talents as well as their SEND. The box below highlights just a few examples of the people who we feel may have DME.

SOME EXAMPLES OF FAMOUS PEOPLE WITH A SEND WHO MAY ALSO BE DME

Ade Adepitan (1973–), a talented television presenter, wheelchair basketball player and Paralympian – who is also a wheelchair user because of childhood polio.

Maggie Aderin-Pocock (1968–), a British space scientist and science educator who, from 2014 onwards, co-presented the television programme *The Sky at Night* – she also has dyslexia.

David Beckham (1975–), a talented ex-professional footballer, model and celebrity, president and co-owner of Inter Miami CF and Salford City and UNICEF Ambassador – who also has Obsessive-Compulsive Disorder (OCD).

Evelyn Glennie (1965–), a talented, award-winning percussionist – who is also hearing impaired.

Will Smith (1968–), a talented, award-winning actor, producer and rapper – who also has dyslexia.

Emma Stone (1988–), a talented award-winning actress – who also had mental health difficulties as a child.

Satoshi Tajiri (1965–), a gifted video game designer and director, best known as the creator of Pokémon – who also has Autism

Spectrum Disorder (ASD) (what some people still refer to as Asperger's Syndrome).

Justin Timberlake (1981–), a talented singer, songwriter, actor and record producer – who also has OCD and Attention Deficit Disorder (now seen as part of Attention Deficit Hyperactivity Disorder, ADHD).

Stevie Wonder (1950–), a talented musician, songwriter and record producer – who is also visually impaired.

While these people may be described as DME, this doesn't mean that they don't have a SEND or even a gift or talent. DME highlights that they have both and that they are part of all three communities – the SEND community, the HLP community and, of course, the community of those with DME.

> When my child was about 19 months old, I noticed they had quite an ear for music. When they were about two years old, I noticed they didn't seem to be quite like other children in toddler groups (for reasons which we now know were to do with autism). When they went to nursery it was more apparent there were some differences, though still no one thought of autism. At three or four years old they also joined a dance class with which we had a lot of problems, and it became very apparent this was because of a special educational need and/or disability. (Parent)

At different times, children and young people who have DME have been recognised by governments or educationalists, and supported effectively, particularly in school. In the UK, the closure of the Westminster Government's 'Gifted and Talented Programme' meant that by the end of 2011 there was no statutory provision or structure in place in England to support Gifted and Talented (or HLP) children (including those with DME) in schools, so schools then became responsible for any approach they took towards – and the funding of – the identification and support of these children and young people. With no national framework in place, no structures and no accountability, these children (both HLP and DME) were quietly brushed under the carpet. And where these children's needs are not recognised or supported, they can frequently struggle in school.

> My child is eight years old and really bright. You would think that they loved school, but they don't. They hate it and don't want to go in almost every day. They complain of stomach aches and headaches and say they feel sick. I have had them checked with the doctor who says there is nothing wrong with them physically. It seems to be due to anxiety. But how can a naturally academic pupil dislike school so much? It is getting more and more difficult, and mornings are becoming stressful for all the family. (Parent)

In these situations, parents and carers, often with the involvement of, or even sometimes led by, their child, look for reasons to explain their concerns, which may mean exploring alternative approaches to learning such as online learning and home education (more on this later).

WHAT DOES 'DUAL OR MULTIPLE EXCEPTIONALITY' MEAN?

> Our child was talking in whole paragraphs by the time they were two years old and used to come to us with facts and ideas about a wide

variety of things. Our child was fine in nursery. In fact, the nursery suggested that they should move to pre-school as soon as possible. They felt our child needed to learn as their behaviour was getting worse and believed our child was bored (their words, not mine).

At school, as the work got harder though, our child began to struggle, and we didn't know what to do. They struggled with their writing (and even shortened their name because of it).

After a lot of worry and searching for answers to explain our child's behaviour, in the end we had our child assessed when they were nine years old. Then we discovered that, despite having a verbal IQ of 133 and a reading age of 15, our nine-year-old child had dyslexia and possibly dyscalculia and dysgraphia. We asked the school to support our child, but the Special Educational Needs coordinator (SENCo) said that they didn't have a support programme for our child as they were 'too bright' (their words). (Parent)

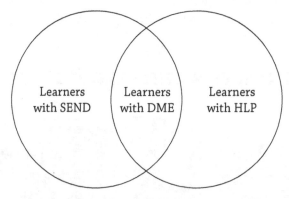

Figure 3.1. Diagrammatical representation of DME, SEND and HLP
Source: Yates and Boddison (2020, p.6)

As shown in Figure 3.1, think of one group of children with one or more SEND. Then think of another group with HLP, with strengths and abilities in one or more areas. Where they cross over in the middle represents those children and young people who have *both* SEND and HELP. They have Dual or Multiple Exceptionality, or DME for short.

How many children and young people with DME are there? Could your child be one of them? According to Ryan and Waterman in *Dual and Multiple Exceptionality*, around 60,000 pupils fit within their definition of DME. However, Yates and Boddison suggest in *The School Handbook for Dual and*

Multiple Exceptionality that the number of children and young people with DME in the UK could be closer to 80,000, if not more. The simple fact is that we cannot be accurate about how many children there are with DME, as we do not count the numbers across the UK either within schools or in other settings (such as in home education).

Much more useful for parents and carers, children or young people or others may be exploring how to recognise your *own* child with DME and what this means at home and in other settings.

HOW DO YOU RECOGNISE IF YOUR CHILD HAS DME?

It is not easy to spot a child or young person with DME, as their abilities may mean they can hide (or mask) their SEND and their SEND can mask their abilities, making them appear 'average, with flashes of brilliance'. This means that their teachers or others in school and elsewhere – and even parents or carers and their family – often get very few clues about the extent of their child's true abilities or SEND.

Sometimes, this can cause arguments or tensions between family members and even between parents or carers and professionals, as different people see different characteristics of a child.

In our case, we had a four-year-old, 'Rising Five', with a fabulous feel for numbers and writing. The teacher and teaching assistant [TA] of a new school my daughter would be attending came for a home visit. They were sitting in our living room, chatting, when suddenly our child started to reel off sums, very enthusiastically and spontaneously. Our child had been attending a local nursery attached to a primary school and the teacher there had picked up on our child's talents and let them go to their lessons in Year R [Reception] and Year 1 for maths and English. Sadly, we couldn't stay in this school for their primary education, so we had to move our child to the more local school.

The teacher and TA in Year R who were about to take our child into the school (hence my meeting with them at home) were amazed that they were saying sums like this, but then it later transpired that professionals thought we had put my child up to saying these sums in front of them and that we had been drilling sums into them. After all, how else could our child know their sums when they were only four years old?

This assumption from these two professionals really skewed the relationship between us and both of them, because they had made up their mind and they would not believe anything we said.

This was not helped as they saw a 'perfect' student, even though our child was struggling in some areas. The school definitely did not see our child as a 'Gifted' student in their eyes, just 'average'. Even when it turned out that our child struggled with their reading, there was no reason to look at why they struggled. After all, our child was still seven months ahead of their peers.

Meanwhile, we had a child who would have massive meltdowns at home, who hated going to school and who now, aged 12 years old, is still struggling with mental health issues and processing all the bullying she has had to endure from professionals as well as our child's peers. (Parent)

Sometimes I get frustrated as I know the answer to the question, but something goes wrong between what I think and what I write on the page. I feel so stupid and I wish I knew what to do about it. (Child with DME)

Potential Plus UK has compiled a list of characteristics of children identified as DME after over more than 50 years of working with these children (see below). While not all of these characteristics will relate to all children with DME (and will depend on the SEND of the child), they can help to show the kinds of things parents and carers should look out for. However, as they explain:

While it is difficult to generalise about such a diverse group of children and much will depend on the type of issues alongside their high learning potential, dual or multiple exceptional children share some characteristics. The characteristics relate to their intellectual strengths, academic difficulties, emotional and behavioural characteristics.[1]

In other words, you need to look out for both your child's intellectual strengths or abilities as well as their difficulties. Your child could be talented

---

1   www.potentialplusuk.org

in lots of different areas – art, music, theatre, making things – or be good at numbers or science or words or languages. However, they may struggle in other areas such as writing or reading or listening or understanding what is being said to them.

> My child would thrive with a high-paced education where they can race through the content as they just absorb the material. Otherwise, they can get easily bored while they have to wait for the rest of the class to catch up. However, my child has eyesight and eyesight tracking problems. They also have mental health difficulties, and their Autism challenges them in many ways within school.
>
> If my child were sent to a school for children with Special Educational Needs, they would probably be bored stiff and fail academically. While I recognise that my child might be supported for their Autism and other Special Educational Needs and Disabilities, I don't feel that a specialist school for Special Educational Needs could provide the speed of learning that my child needs. So, even though my child would be well placed on a Special Educational Needs level, I would be doing a disservice to their intellect, their academic and artistic abilities and my child wouldn't reach their potential.
>
> In a mainstream school, on the other hand, my child may excel in academic work, but they may not be best placed to support the Special Educational Needs arising from their Autism to the extent needed. My child's Autism is causing such issues that they are now not in the right mental place to learn and would then fail in both types of school.
>
> This is a concern because my child falls between the two types of education. I believe there are so many children that end up being educated at home or otherwise because of this discrepancy in the education system in the UK. (Parent)

When you read the list below, it is also worth thinking about which comes first. Or, to put it another way, do children with certain strengths and also challenges in the classroom find other outlets where these challenges become a strength? For example, in the last chapter, we explored the potential strengths of dyslexia, where children with dyslexia are good at things like seeing the 'big picture', thinking imaginatively, being creative, telling stories, finding patterns and being confident talkers.

> With hindsight, the best thing I could have done was support my child at five years old when they begged me to take them to the local drama group in our town. Not only did it enable them to develop something they found they were good at, but it also gave them something positive to hold on to when school seemed so negative. Something else I did not expect was that their passion then turned into their future career. (Parent with an adult who was a child with DME)

Just as an example, think of the number of extremely talented actors who have said they have dyslexia – Whoopi Goldberg, Goldie Hawn, Keira Knightley, Tom Cruise, Will Smith, Orlando Bloom, Keanu Reeves, Jennifer Aniston... The list could go on. These people have talents and have also chosen professions where their talents have become their strengths. Is this by accident or because their SEND – used effectively – has become the strength on which they have based their career? This is just for dyslexia. What is your child's superpower, and could it be used in a different way, like this? The list below, therefore, only gives examples of the kinds of ways to spot a child or young person with DME. If you need to check whether you are right about the things you see with your own child, talk to someone at Potential Plus UK or one of the other agencies that are skilled in this area (see the list provided at the end of this book), and they will be able to help.

Things to look for in a child with DME
Intellectual strengths

- Ability or expertise in one or more specific areas
- An active imagination
- An extensive vocabulary
- Exceptional comprehension
- High performance in tasks requiring abstract thinking and prob-lem-solving
- Excellent visual or auditory memory
- Creativity outside school
- The ability to take part in broad-ranging discussions.

Academic difficulties

- Poor handwriting
- Poor spelling
- Difficulty with phonics
- Inability to do seemingly simple tasks, although they often have the ability to do tasks that for others are seemingly more complex
- Success in *either* mathematics or language subjects, but often challenges in the other
- Poor performance under pressure
- Difficulties in completing tasks with a sequence of steps
- Inattentive at times.

Emotional issues

Managing a range of academic issues, especially at school, can mean that children and young people with DME can often develop the following emotional characteristics:

- Minor failures that create feelings of major inadequacy
- Unrealistically high or low self-expectations
- Feelings of being worthless academically
- Confusion about their abilities
- Strong fear of failure
- Sensitivity to criticism
- Experiences of intense frustration
- Low self-esteem
- Feelings of being different from others
- Poor social skills.

Behaviour

Emotional issues or responses may result in behavioural characteristics, such as:

- Disruptive in class
- Sometimes overcompensates or tries to hide difficulties (e.g., saying an issue is boring or becoming the 'class clown')
- Often off-task

- Disorganised
- Unmotivated
- Impulsive
- Creative when making excuses to avoid tasks they find difficult
- Can be intensely frustrated at times; sometimes this can spill over into anger or aggression
- Withdrawn at times.

> People blame you for being lazy or rude and yet don't also look for what you know. It makes me feel bad that I can't do anything right. (Child with DME)

WHAT CAN HAPPEN IF A CHILD WITH DME ISN'T IDENTIFIED OR SUPPORTED EFFECTIVELY?

As you may have already experienced, your child's response to their needs is not clear-cut. In *Raising the Achievement of All Pupils in an Inclusive Setting*, Professor Diane Montgomery argued that the way a child responds to anything is based on a combination of three separate issues:

- Their culture or upbringing – the child's background and how it supports the child with DME. This could include things like working hard to overcome difficulties, not complaining and just 'getting on with it' or being in a more relaxed environment where the child 'does their best' and doesn't worry about anything else.
- Personal issues – a child's personality can also support or hold back a child with DME. This could include things like taking risks, their motivation and their ability to bounce back when things go wrong (their resilience, or 'bouncebackability').
- How they are taught both at school and at home. This could include things like whether they are supported 'effectively' (for them) and whether someone understands and inspires them.

Professor Montgomery's argument was based on whether a child with DME achieves their best in school. However, we would also argue that these kinds of things are just as important for the child's health and wellbeing at home, in family life and for the way both parents and carers and the child cope with any challenges they face as the child gets older. For example, the child might be very motivated and resilient and may push themselves through any setbacks they experience. Or they might have been taught to get on with their work without complaining, and at school may be a 'teacher pleaser'. They might be the child whose work seems to be 'average' and who raises no 'warning bells' for the teacher that they are anything more than that 'average' pupil. Everybody then fails to discover what they are capable of achieving. Yet, what they do at home, or when left to follow their own passions, is amazing.

These children can 'turn off' to education, sometimes without realising it. They then either coast along, achieving the average that is expected of them, or they want to do more, but are not able to. This makes them increasingly withdrawn, or upset, or at risk of developing a range of social, emotional and mental health difficulties. They can often 'go in on themselves' as a response to their situation.

> My child is five years old and has always developed ahead of other children the same age. They could count to 10 and knew their alphabet at 18 months old. They started to read at the age of two-and-a-half years old and could add and take away when they started school. When we had our child assessed some of their scores came out really high. However, after going to a parents' evening recently, I feel like their teacher and I are talking about a different child. When I raised the results of the assessment, the teacher said they are not sure why my child would score so highly as they are not showing this at school. I feel like maybe I have it wrong. (Parent)

Alternatively, the child might be dissatisfied with their struggles and 'hit out' in the classroom or at home. This may get them noticed by those around them, but it may also get them identified as a child with 'behavioural problems'. While this can often lead to their identification as having SEND, it can also lead to responses that take no account of their ability. At its extreme, it can lead to a child being excluded from the classroom or even the school, on a temporary or permanent basis.

> My child is six years old. At the last parent–teacher meeting, their teacher told me that their behaviour in class is terrible. I was told my

child often talks back and argues with their teacher during lessons, they are disruptive and generally have no respect for authority. At home, my child rarely loses their temper and seems to be happy with many varied interests. However, they do complain that they are bored at school and cannot understand why they must go as they do not learn anything. The school also tells me that my child's negative behaviour is affecting the rest of the class. (Parent)

If faced with a situation such as this, more may need to be done to identify exactly why the child might have had behavioural problems in the first place. If it was because they have HLP that has not been supported, the child with DME needs to be educated appropriately for both their SEND and their HLP.

Parents and carers often report differences in behaviour between boys and girls. They report situations where boys 'hitting out' will lead to a range of sanctions. Thus, training courses run in the past for parents and carers on topics such as 'Challenging behaviour' may often have an audience almost exclusively composed of parents and carers with boys. But this is not always the case, and it is important that any identification and interventions that take place are neutral of characteristics such as race, ethnicity or gender.

There is also a case in school where the 'good girls' are identified as high achievers and placed on programmes for Highly Able pupils. Consideration of both these sets of characteristics should be free of 'bias'. The fact remains, however, that those children who seem to give the teacher the fewest problems may be treated one way, while those who hit out may be treated another way entirely (and often for negative reasons). Both groups could have within them children or young people with DME.

If parents and carers feel that their child could be in either of these groups (for whatever reason), they could explore this further by keeping a log of the kinds of things their child does at home. Once they have more evidence, they should talk to the teacher about their experiences. Doing this following a formal assessment of the child will often strengthen the evidence they can show to them.

Our child seemed academically only just above average, with reading just seven months ahead of their peers. Their teacher in Year 1 did notice that our child struggled a little, but because they were still seven months ahead of their peers, she didn't think it was enough of a struggle to investigate dyslexia. They put some one-to-one support from a teaching assistant in place, but that was about it. We had an assessment for HLP by Potential Plus UK and they indicated that our child could have what they termed 'stealth dyslexia' where their dyslexia was masked. They were also recognised as having High Learning Potential. After several requests going nowhere with school, we were recommended to see a behavioural optometrist. It turned out that it was not dyslexia but ocular motor dysfunction that they had. (Parent)

For many children, DME can be difficult to spot when they are younger. However, by the time they are in secondary school, identifying their DME can become almost impossible. By then, they have often become skilled at hiding their strengths (or the things they struggle with) and have found ways to avoid or cope with either the strengths or challenges related to their DME, or both. Alternatively, if DME has not yet been correctly identified by then, there is a very real danger that their frustration, behaviour or difficulties relating to their social, emotional and mental health may have become quite extreme.

While these difficulties can often be a response to the problems or frustrations they face, they can sometimes be misunderstood or misinterpreted, leading to problems at home or at school. In some cases, specialist agencies may eventually become involved to support the family, the child or young person, including mental health specialists or even social services.

To prevent things like this from happening, it's a good idea to seek information or advice from organisations that are specialists in DME. Consideration of a formal assessment of a child may also help parents and carers to identify both their child's strengths and areas of difficulty, and to develop an action plan and a programme of support that will be effective for the child. Even where a child's behaviour or emotional issues are not a problem, a skilled professional would be able to look for a range of characteristics associated with HLP and also those associated with SEND. However, this cannot be done in isolation because of the complex interaction between the two. For example, as we have seen in Chapter 2, many of the characteristics of high ability are similar for children with ASD. Indeed, the two are often confused, and there is a high level of misdiagnosis of one (often ASD) for the other.

Let's take a step back, and ask the question, what can happen to a child or young person with DME? A clear way of showing this is given in Figure 3.2. This comes from *Dual and Multiple Exceptionality (DME)* (Ryan and Waterman 2018, p.6), which is sourced from the free fact sheet (F01) from Potential Plus UK on DME.[2]

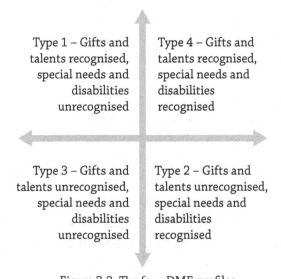

Figure 3.2. The four DME profiles

Source: Ryan and Waterman (2018), based on information from Potential Plus UK

This suggests one of the following four things can happen to a child or young person with DME:

Type 1 – The child's gifts and talents are recognised, but their special educational needs and disabilities are not. Sometimes, a child's gifts and talents are recognised. This usually happens at home and when the child is younger at school. However, as the workload or the skills required increase, depending on the child's response and the level of their HLP, they can become increasingly stressed or depressed. Alternatively, they may hit out at school (or whatever learning setting they are in), at home, or in both settings. In the end, everybody wonders whether the child has the gifts or talents that were first identified.

---

2   https://potentialplusuk.org/wp-content/uploads/2019/11/F01-Dual-or-Multiple-Exceptionality-191121.pdf

> It's hard to get recognition and support for the difficulties faced by children with High Learning Potential and their Special Educational Needs or Disabilities can be overlooked. This is detrimental to their self-esteem but also their academic performance. It can also have a negative impact on their social, emotional and mental health. (Young person who has DME)

Type 2 – The child's gifts and talents are not recognised, but their special educational needs and disabilities are. Sometimes, a child's SEND is recognised but not their HLP. These SEND are often easy to spot (however, how many children have managed to hide a hearing impairment or dyslexia from their parents or carers and even the professionals for a long time, sometimes even into adulthood?). Sometimes, however, they are harder to identify and will depend on the child and such things as their level of ability or their response to what is going on with them, especially at school. Eventually, for one reason or another (sometimes because of emerging behavioural, social, emotional and mental health problems), their SEND may be seen and supported.

However, even where a child's SEND may be identified, there is a danger that traditional approaches, learning programmes and other interventions put in place will not work or will not be as effective as they should be in supporting the child's SEND.

> Because of my disability I was encouraged to take a BTEC when I chose my exam options. I suppose they thought I wasn't capable of anything more. I worked out after a couple of weeks that there was nothing the teacher could teach me that I couldn't teach myself; and better. I went to ask the teacher and they agreed that I could learn what they taught in other ways. Later, I educated myself at home and also worked in a dog kennels to get experience. When I did the exam, I came top of my course. The school didn't say a word. That still annoys me. (Adult who was a child with DME)

In addition, when a child's SEND is identified, there is the danger that everyone – parents and carers, teachers and others – focuses on the child's SEND to the exclusion of everything else. While this is entirely understandable for some families (and professionals), unlocking untapped potential, if it were part and parcel of the SEND structure, may still be worth considering. In other words, identifying a child's SEND is only one half of the child with DME.

Unless a child's SEND can be supported within the context of their HLP, the child may be frustrated and angry, or hit out. Alternatively, they are at risk of developing a range of social, emotional and mental health problems. This means that the child is in danger of turning away from the support they have been offered. In addition, in the long term, none of these responses is healthy and may ultimately cause damage, both to the child and to their relationships with their parents or carers or the professionals who are there to help them.

Adapting the approaches many schools already use with children with SEND and giving a child with DME the tools they need to help them can be an excellent approach for many children. Rather than removing any difficulties they may experience, reframing what they need in terms of their HLP will have more chance of success. For example, rather than removing more complicated words (that they do understand the meaning of), giving the child the tools to be able to read them may help. This could include giving the context of a piece of text and working with them on meaning. Likewise, explaining the theories behind *how* they write and analysing any problems they face with writing things down can make a real difference to a child or young person with DME who faces these difficulties.

Alongside this, providing topics to write about that enthuse them, rather than easier subjects in which they have no interest, will help to spark their HLP. Then, parents and carers and the child's teachers can use the approach that works for the child as a springboard on which to support their SEND.

For many children, such greater flexibility in the approaches used, and on occasion, even thinking outside the box, can make very real differences to discovering the untapped potential of a child or young person with SEND. This includes using digital and other tools or even adaptations to how work will be done. Simple examples of what we mean (and which are already used in many schools with children with SEND) include writing PowerPoint presentations or dictating work via 'speech to text' software instead of writing something by hand. This means professionals may need to consider, in this particular example, whether it is what a child *knows* or their *handwriting* that is the focus of an exercise.

This increased flexibility and the success the child achieves (and recognises for themselves) will all help to improve the child's further achievement, while at the same time boosting their health and wellbeing. Unlocking their untapped potential in this way, for some children and young people, also clearly indicates that they are a child with DME. Once the barriers to learning are removed, they are able to fly.

Many schools are already used to these kinds of approaches for children with SEND. The missing ingredient is the pace and level of the work required for those with DME.

Type 3 – The child's gifts and talents and their special educational needs and disabilities are not recognised. This is, debatably, the worst-case situation, where the child's HLP is not recognised, but neither is their SEND. At best, they can appear 'average', achieving what is expected of them in school or in their learning. At worst, they can go through life never believing that they are 'good enough', and never understanding why. Sometimes, they can experience these feelings well into adulthood. That is, unless something changes. Then, what has happened to them in life up to that point is suddenly given a new explanation and re-evaluated with new eyes.

> I feel bright and intelligent (at least more than average) but I have been unable to apply myself when it matters. I suffer from depression and anxiety and other mental illnesses that I'm not sure I've been correctly diagnosed. I would like to study again with the Open University but I'm in the midst of mental fatigue. (Young person with DME)

This is one of the reasons why many parents and carers who come to have their child assessed suddenly realise that they also have the same traits – dyslexia, ADD, ASD – that they see in their child. For some, this is a positive outcome – a final piece of the jigsaw – after many years of feeling there was something wrong or something missing.

We hope that in the future fewer children and young people will be missed, and that parents and carers and professionals will be able to identify their gifts and talents *and* their SEND. However, as we have said repeatedly, DME is not easy to spot, and where a child is 'average' with no challenges, academically, behaviourally and emotionally, there is no reason to question anything is wrong. It is extremely important for parents and carers to constantly monitor the kinds of things their child is doing and to build up a complete picture of them, ideally starting this before they go to school. Some parents and carers film clips on their phone or iPad of their child engaged in activities. Collecting information in this way will provide evidence of what they can do (if needed), to show to professionals in the future (or at least provide a diary for parents and carers to remember the child when they were younger!).

Type 4 – The child's gifts and talents *and* their special educational needs and disabilities are recognised. On the surface, this can be the best outcome of them all, where the child's HLP is recognised by everyone – at home, at school, by friends and family members – as well as their SEND. However, it still comes with several provisos. For us, these include that:

- The child's SEND must be supported in a way that takes effective account of their HLP
- The child's HLP must be supported in a way that takes effective account of their SEND
- Ideally, the child's learning should be delivered by people who understand how to support both of these areas in their teaching
- There should be no myths around supporting those children with HLP and also with SEND, and vice versa (see below), either at home, in their education setting or elsewhere.

Music quite literally saved my life when I was a child. I went on a scholarship programme at an ordinary high school. It allowed me to be weird, different and non-conformist! It gave me a social group that was also made up of 'outliers' like me. (Adult who was a child with DME)

When I was younger, I had teachers around me who would listen and work with me to allow me to find the best method for me to achieve, as they trusted that I knew what would work best for me. (Adult who was a child with DME)

Ten myths (and the reality) about children with DME

Myth	Reality
Addressing any challenges (SEND) experienced by a child with DME must be the top priority	Not true. Actually, using the child's strengths to support any SEND should be the top priority (once any provision to meet medical needs has happened, e.g., glasses, hearing aids, etc.)
Children with DME are more mature than other children their own age	Not true. Sometimes a child with DME can appear a lot older than their years. However, sometimes, particularly emotionally, the same child can appear much younger than their age. Their behaviour can change instantly, and with little or no warning
HLP and SEND cannot be addressed at the same time	Not true. Using the child's HLP to address their SEND can help with both sides in a way that the child understands
A child with DME cannot lack basic skills; it just means they are lazy or aren't trying	Not true. Sometimes a child with DME is trying very hard to appear 'average' (e.g., to follow instructions or to do their schoolwork). They could be trying extremely hard, but cannot do what is asked of them
A child with DME struggling with their working memory or processing speed is simply not listening	Not true. Sometimes they are listening but forget what you have asked them, and sometimes they are slower at thinking through what you have just said. You might need to find out what is going on and how to support them effectively (such as writing things down you want them to remember, or giving them more time to think when they have been asked a question)
A child cannot have both HLP and SEND	Not true. Many children have SEND at the same time as HLP. This is called DME
Having HLP compensates for the SEND	Not true. It depends how the HLP and SEND interact with each other. Both should be considered to enable parents and carers or a professional to support the child effectively

cont.

Myth	Reality
Pupils with DME cannot have an Individual Education Plan (IEP), an Education, Health and Care Plan (EHCP) or equivalent to support and monitor their learning in school	Not true. Frameworks to monitor a child's education and the support they receive are ideal structures to evaluate both the child's SEND *and* their HLP or equivalent, provided both are reported on and monitored regularly
A pupil with DME is too clever to receive support from a school's SEND programme (or equivalent)	Not true. Based on their SEND and building on their HLP, there *are* programmes that can be developed to support them
Pupils with DME cannot go on to a school's HLP (or equivalent) programme; they would slow down the other pupils	Not true. If supported appropriately, a pupil with DME has a lot to offer to a school's HLP programme

SUPPORTING A CHILD WITH DME AT HOME

Having a child is an enormous responsibility for anyone. However, a parent's or carer's experience of a child with DME gives them a unique insight into DME and how to support the child's HLP and their SEND. What they identify in their child will, first, depend on their own experiences to a large extent as well as the experience and knowledge of other family members and friends about HLP, SEND or DME. This will send parents and carers (or may have sent them already) down a particular route shaped by this knowledge and experience:

- Does the parent or carer have other children with HLP? Could they therefore find it difficult to understand why their child is not similar? This may send them down the SEND route.
- Does the parent or carer have other children with SEND? Could they therefore find it difficult to spot some or all of these traits in their child? This may send them down the HLP route.
- Does the parent or carer have no experience of either SEND or HLP? This lack of relevant knowledge may make it difficult to know how to identify what is 'going on' with their child.

Parents and carers should look for some of the things their child does; not their strengths or weaknesses, but their actions and the activities they have noticed.

■ Tips and hints: Observing your child

If you have not done this already, make a list of things you have noticed your child doing. This could range from repetitive behaviour and obsessions with things to food preferences, things they like and don't like, or how they act when they are stressed or angry or tired.

This list can be updated and shown to your child's teacher or other professionals if it becomes relevant.

Try not to worry too much at this stage about the labels of 'Special Educational Need and Disability' and even 'High Learning Potential' that you or others may give to your child (unless there are medical reasons for you to get the matter treated, or because of any safety concerns about your child or others).

In talking to parents and carers both from the UK and around the world, when asked to name the most important thing that a parent or carer can give to their child, they say it is, without exception, unconditional love. Offering your child with DME unconditional love is extremely important for many reasons, one important one being that these children can develop low self-esteem and self-confidence. Unconditional love and support can help boost their self-esteem and self-confidence, and feeling positive about themselves can be vital for your child's wellbeing and even happiness. When it comes to it, isn't that important to you, too?

Beyond this, you may have some concerns that you want to address now to help lay foundations for your child's future. As your child develops, you will add other concerns to the list and develop strategies that work to support you and your child.

It is difficult to provide a list that identifies every challenge that may arise in every family. It is therefore almost impossible to provide all of the many solutions that parents and carers have discovered over the years – this would require a book of its own! Despite this difficulty, in Chapter 4 we outline some of the more common concerns raised by parents and carers and give some practical suggestions about how to address them. Many of the concerns mentioned by parents and carers about their child at home – often when their child is young – seem to focus on one or more aspects of their behaviour. Difficulties in areas such as reading, writing and learning do not often appear until a child has started school.

SUPPORTING A CHILD WITH DME AT SCHOOL

You are the best supporter of your child with DME they have. By the time they go to school, you will understand their characteristics, their behaviour and what to do to support them. You care about them and what happens to them, and can also understand what happens when things start to go wrong. That is enormously powerful, and you should not be afraid to use *your* superpower!

It is also important for your child to have an advocate in the education system, someone who believes in your child and who will make the case to others about their needs. This becomes even more important if your child experiences challenges as the complexity of their work increases.

> The teachers who trusted me allowed me to feel confident in my own abilities, as they didn't doubt that I could achieve the end goal. (Child with DME)

> One teacher in particular acted as my mentor. Basically, he gave me the confidence to do things which I found difficult. He was also there when I failed or had to make really difficult decisions. I owe him a lot. (Young person with DME)

The biggest challenge facing many children with DME is probably around poor self-esteem and lack of confidence about what they can do. Their own questioning about whether they have any abilities at all can be made worse – often by accident – by both parents and carers and professionals who do not see or understand the effort that these children are putting in to appearing 'average'. This can cause tension at both home and school, with such children often labelled as 'lazy' for failing to meet the standards expected or for seeking to avoid challenges at school or with their homework.

In a school that does not identify what is going on, the 'average' achievement or performance of a child does not merit special adjustments being made, such as extra time in exams or 'time out' from the classroom. However, where a child with DME is seen as functioning as 'average' (or even above average) within the classroom, they often do this at great personal expense to their own emotional wellbeing, which may cause severe behavioural problems at home, at school, or in both settings.

If you are Gifted and have Autism you are invisible at school. Everyone says 'Oh they're doing really well in lessons', but nobody cares that you are always bored. The other kids didn't like it when I could do things well and they bullied me for four years. School can be a foul place for children like me and I am really angry and upset that I can't go to any secondary school even if I wanted to because I don't have the right sort of brain for them. (Child with DME)

My child is well-behaved at school, for which I am grateful, but they are like a different child when they come home. As soon as my child leaves school, they often have a meltdown; they have punched me in the stomach more than once and kicked their sister. It's just like a pressure cooker has been building up during the day and it's the only way my child can let off steam. They find it so difficult. (Parent)

While this can be a minefield, it is important that you collect as much evidence about your child and what you see at home as well as any solutions to things you observe. This could be both positive (such as your child needing sufficient challenge in their reading) and not so positive (such as your child having problems with their behaviour at certain times of the day). In Chapter 6, we will look at what to do with this evidence and how to work in partnership with your child's teacher.

DECISIONS FOR YOU, AS A PARENT OR CARER

Just as every child is different, so, too, is every family, not only in terms of location, income levels and the size of the family, but also in terms of their preferences in education and teaching options and their views on how to support their family – including their child with DME – for the best.

Therefore, it is difficult for anyone to tell you the right way to bring up your children, and that includes your child with DME. Nonetheless, whatever the answers, there are some decisions that you may have to consider both before your child starts school and at key steps along the way, such as where or how they are educated, or whether they move school or leave school altogether. We discuss some of the main ones in Chapter 5.

Obviously, at different stages (and for some children with DME, from right at the beginning, before they start school), your child may want to play a strong part in any decisions made about them. One of your decisions will therefore be about how to help your child's voice to be heard.

CONCLUSION

This chapter has given you an overview of DME, what it looks like, how it can be recognised and some of the things that can happen both to the child whose DME remains hidden and the child whose DME is supported effectively. Now that, hopefully, you have a better understanding of DME, the next chapter is about the challenges your child can face because of their DME, and some of the decisions you may need to make – ideally with your child and others supporting them – as they grow older.

FURTHER READING

Susan Baum, Robin Schader and Steven Owen (2017) *To Be Gifted and Learning Disabled: Strength-Based Strategies for Helping Twice-Exceptional Students with LD, ADHD, ASD, and More*. Prufrock Press; 3rd edition.

John Inman (2020) *Twice-Exceptional Children Are Gifts: Developing the Talents of 2e Children*. Learning Exceptionalities Press.

Scott Barry Kaufman (ed.) (2018) *Twice Exceptional: Supporting and Educating Bright and Creative Students with Learning Difficulties*. Oxford University Press.

Deirdre Lovecky (2003) *Different Minds: Gifted Children with AD/HD, Asperger Syndrome and Other Learning Deficits*. Jessica Kingsley Publishers.

Jen Merrill (2012) *If This Is a Gift, Can I Send It Back? Surviving in the Land of the Gifted and Twice Exceptional*. GHF Press.

Diane Montgomery (2003) *Gifted and Talented Children with Special Educational Needs: Double Exceptionality*. Routledge.

Deborah Reber (2018) *Differently Wired: Raising an Exceptional Child in a Conventional World*. Workman Publishing.

Alison Ryan and Chris Waterman (2018) *Dual and Multiple Exceptionality (DME): The Current State of Play*. nasen.

YOUR ACTION PLAN

1. Explore the characteristics of DME with your loved ones. Do these seem to describe your own child?
2. What is your child doing at home that gives you cause for concern? Make a list.

3. What are you doing to address the things your child is doing at home that concern you? Write down your solutions.
4. Collect evidence of what your child is doing and how you can support them with the different challenges you face. These may be useful to discuss with teachers and other professionals in the future.
5. How are you going to bring up your child with DME? Talk with your loved ones about the approach you will take.
6. What do you do to praise the effort and progress made by your child at home?

CHAPTER 4

What Kind of Challenges Can My Child with DME Face?

INTRODUCTION

Children and young people with Dual or Multiple Exceptionality (DME) are neurodiverse. This isn't 'abnormal' or something to be 'cured'; it just means that they have a different way of thinking and looking at the world from other, 'neurotypical', children and young people (and adults), and we believe that these differences are to be celebrated.

> The behaviour change that made the biggest difference at home was mine. I accepted my child for who they are and that they are different and that makes us part of 'that family' and always will. Once I had accepted that, somehow it all seemed to make sense. (Parent)

However, many parents and carers can have concerns about the challenges faced by their child with DME and how they behave or what happens to them at home, at school or in different settings. These concerns can be particularly valid when that DME hasn't been recognised or supported effectively. What parents and carers can do to support their child with DME who faces such challenges is the focus of this chapter. This includes the decisions that you may need to make – often in partnership with your child – along the way.

We believe that failure to recognise a child's DME and to address any challenges effectively can lead to increased behavioural, social, emotional and mental health difficulties, at home and in other settings. For a child with DME who already overthinks or worries about things, having even more stress or anxiety piled onto them in this way may lead to a range of negative responses, such as incidents of extreme behaviour at home or school, leading to sanctions in the school setting (including temporary or permanent exclusion from school) or by the child or young person (such as self-exclusion or school anxiety), or a range of mental health difficulties including self-harm, depression, social anxiety, and worse.

We do not say any of this as 'proof' that your child with DME will go through any of this, but simply to highlight that the stakes have never been higher – especially within the UK education system – to get this right. The alternative, part of a generation lost, does not bear thinking about.

You may find it useful to remember that the attributes or behaviours of a child are often grouped together to provide a short cut – a label – to diagnose the support that an individual needs, including any medical intervention. However, the natural ability (intelligence, gifts and talents, High Learning Potential, HLP) of a child is often not considered as an explanation for their behaviour, which can be a mistake. Instead, we should look at the whole child, their strengths and abilities, rather than just their behaviours and any Special Educational Need and Disability (SEND) they have. These two areas should lead to their identification as having DME, and should then remain until it is either dismissed or confirmed that the child has both HLP and SEND.

> We were at our wits' end, knowing we had a bright child who was not properly served by the school and we could see their love of learning start to wane, as well as the vast well of potential not being realised and their resilience at a worrying low. There is no question that our child's mental health would have suffered and their potential left untapped. They just coasted along unchallenged at school. I am a firm believer that ensuring each child's potential is fulfilled is not just rewarding for themselves and their family but for society as a whole. (Parent)

ISN'T THERE A RISK THAT WE WILL OVER-IDENTIFY THE NUMBER OF CHILDREN AND YOUNG PEOPLE WITH DME?

Doesn't identifying children like this mean that we will over-estimate how many children and young people with DME there are in the UK?

Possibly. However, we suggest two responses to this question:

- Does it matter? There is an expression, 'a rising tide lifts all boats', which means that the approaches used to support the learning potential of every individual in the class, school or society raises everyone's achievement levels as a result, including those with DME.
- Until more professionals (such as qualified psychologists and other specialists and teachers) build in appropriate identification of and support for DME into their provision, this approach is the best we have.

Until you know more, identifying a child's strengths and ensuring effective provision to stretch and challenge their abilities and then using these to support any SEND must be the way forward. Remembering that a child or young person with DME needs to be 'in balance' in this way will help them to become the best version of themselves. Applied more generally, this approach is also a positive one for all children and young people (and adults!).

■ Tips and hints: Looking for a qualified specialist to assess your child?

What kinds of questions should you ask?

- What are your views on children and young people with HLP and SEND?
- What experience do you have in working with children and young people with HLP (More Able/Gifted and Talented/High Ability children)? Children and young people with DME?
- What kind of behaviours have you seen with both groups?
- How do you make sure you correctly identify children and young people with SEND such as Autism Spectrum Disorder (ASD), Attention Deficit Hyperactivity Disorder (ADHD), dyslexia, social, emotional and mental health conditions, HLP and DME?
- What other types of conditions have you seen with children and young people with DME?
- Do you provide a practical action plan to support the children and young people and their parents or carers after the assessment? Is this for support at home? Is this for support at school?

– What successes have you seen with these groups because of your
assessment?

COMMON CHALLENGES FACING A CHILD
OR YOUNG PERSON WITH DME

Here is a summary of the most common challenges that can be faced by
children and young people with DME, and that are of most concern to parents and carers at home. (Topics that are more school-focused are discussed
later, in Chapter 6.)

We have not reproduced the information, advice or other support that is
provided by the organisations listed in Chapter 8. They all support children
and young people with DME and you can look at the services they provide
and contact them. In fact, we recommend you do so as soon as possible.

If you are concerned about a topic, we have also provided examples of
the sort of practical suggestions from other parents and carers about what
worked for them, but remember, what works for one child with DME may
not work for others.

Many families may not have any questions or concerns about their
child with DME and could find that looking at this list and going to the
links for further information (as well as tapping into the services of the
specialist organisations) if a problem should arise is enough. This section
is for you. However, some parents and carers may need more than this.
Their child with DME may be experiencing a range of challenges that, if
left unchecked, can become more serious in nature.

This book does not seek to replace the specialist support available from
qualified professionals and other parents and carers to help you if your
child with DME (and you yourself) is facing more extreme challenges.
However, some suggestions are outlined as to why a child or young person
with DME might face these challenges and the kinds of things to try. (Go
to www.jkp.com/catalogue/book/9781787758100 for a little more detail
on two topics of concern to many parents and carers of children with DME:
sensory challenges and executive functioning skills.)

If you are at all concerned about the medical – physical or mental –
implications of something your child is facing, it is recommended that
you seek medical or specialist help. While many doctors and healthcare
specialists may not have explicit knowledge or understanding of the

characteristics or support needs of children and young people with DME, it can sometimes be useful to eliminate other causes of a problem before you go down the wrong route. If in doubt, talk to one of the organisations that supports families of children and young people with DME. We can almost guarantee that, even if they have no experience of your concerns, they will know someone who has!

While there will be more subjects or different topics on your list than given here, and you may struggle at first to find solutions that work for you and your child with DME, remember that your child with DME is bright; they may be able to help you solve the problem or find solutions to the challenges you all face.

Common questions and concerns parents and carers raise about their child with DME
My child asks so many questions. I'm exhausted!

- Write all the questions on a piece of paper or a board on the wall and give an amount of time to answering them during the day.
- When your child is old enough, ask them to research answers to the questions so you can discuss them all at once, at an agreed time.
- Give your child their own way of recording their questions (e.g., smartphone, Dictaphone, drawing pictures) and work together at a set time to answer them.
- Work with your child to come up with a fair system of answering their questions. This may also help them lay the foundations for asking questions at school.
- Use the 'speaking spoon' approach to encourage debate and discussion (our words!), around the meal table, for example. If you haven't got the 'speaking spoon' it is not your turn to speak, and you have to wait. This is great for encouraging turn-taking.
- Value and encourage your child's questions. Use open-ended questions and word puzzles to build on their skills.

A few websites and resources:

- '71 Thunks to make your child think!' (free Slideshare): www.slideshare.net/year5thepines/thunks-9947392

- Ian Gilbert (2019) 'A Tin of Thunks' [cards]
- '10 essential resources for building your learners' questioning skills': https://wabisabilearning.com/blogs/inquiry/building-questioning-skills
- Sara Distin (2016) 'Why it's a good thing kids ask so many questions': https://tinybop.com/blog/why-its-a-good-thing-kids-ask-so-many-questions
- Erinne Magee (2020) '63 fun questions to get your kids talking': www.parents.com/parenting/better-parenting/advice/questions-every-parent-should-ask-their-kid

Everyone focuses on my child's SEND, yet without creative challenge to stretch their mind, any other problems are much worse. I can't keep up!

- Join online learning groups and organisations offering online peer group support for your child. They will provide effective challenge!
- When your child goes to school, there is a risk that any SEND will be picked up by others, but their cognitive and other strengths will be missed. Make a list of all the things your child *can* do and the age they do it. Collect as much evidence on this as possible (including video clips on your phone, if you can). This may be needed when your child starts school.
- You don't need to be the one providing the challenge. At home just keep asking them questions or ask them to explain things to you. Let them do the hard thinking!
- Teaching skills such as critical and creative thinking is great for them at home. For example, once they have read a fairy tale like *Goldilocks and the Three Bears*, could they tell you the tale again from Daddy Bear's point of view? What about from the viewpoint of the bowl of porridge?
- Set them challenges at home that are real. Give them a small budget and challenge them to provide a meal for the whole family, for example. Then take them shopping to achieve this, even if they don't do the cooking on their own.

A few websites and resources:

- Book Creator: https://bookcreator.com
- Seesaw Learning Inc., Shadow Puppet Edu app: https://web.seesaw. me/shadow-puppet-edu
- Duck Duck Moose: www.duckduckmoose.com
- Twinkl: www.twinkl.co.uk
- Raising Creative Thinkers: www.raisingcreativethinkers.com
- Mantra Lingua: https://uk.mantralingua.com
- James Lehman (no date) 'Motivating the unmotivated child': www. empoweringparents.com/article/motivating-the-unmotivated-child

My child wants to be in charge

- Explain the boundaries clearly (with more 'do' words than 'do not!').
- Explain your reasons if something must happen in a different way.
- If they still want to be in charge, explain that you are sorry, but you need this to happen.
- Be positive when they do something they should, and try to ignore any negative behaviour.
- Give them a choice of two options so they can make a choice from a limited number (e.g., 'Do you want this or that for breakfast?') and stick to this. You may need to repeat it several times.
- Try and support a child with clear guidelines when they need to be in control when they are as young as possible, otherwise, the teenage years can be a nightmare.
- What is this controlling behaviour telling you? That they don't have control in other parts of their life? That they are cleverer than you and believe they are right (or that you can't keep up with them)? Or something else? Look at when it happens (and doesn't). Then come up with an action plan and stick to it. Reward effort and progress towards it.

A few websites and resources:

- YouTube sessions from The MEHRIT Centre about self-regulation and related challenges: www.youtube.com/c/TheMEHRITCentre

- Very Well Family: https://www.verywellfamily.com/social-and-emotional-problems-affecting-gifted-children-1449336
- The Australian Parenting Website: https://raisingchildren.net.au/preschoolers/play-learning/gifted-talented-children/behaviour-social-development
- Our Gifted Kids: https://ourgiftedkids.com/podcast

My child wants to know what we are doing that day/week, etc.

- Draw a timetable on a board or poster for the day/week, etc. If they can't read yet, do this with colours or pictures.
- Give them as much notice as possible and a daily or weekly schedule, and as much notice as possible if things change.
- Put events into two categories: things that are definite and things that may change.
- Clearly explain why things have had to change and the reasoning behind this.
- Always encourage your child with DME to have a 'Plan B' and what they think it should be. Sometimes doing this for both the little things and the bigger ones can reduce meltdowns as they have another action plan.

A few websites and resources:

- Widgit Online: https://widgitonline.com
- The Dyslexia Shop visual timetable boards: https://www.thedyslexiashop.co.uk/visual-timetable-board.html
- Visual supports from the National Autistic Society: https://www.autism.org.uk/advice-and-guidance/topics/communication/communication-tools/visual-supports
- Craftly Ltd, bespoke reward charts, calendars, educational boards and routine charts: www.notonthehighstreet.com/craftly

My child hates change

- Tell them what is changing and why.
- Give them as much notice as possible.

- Reward the effort put into coping with change and progress toward coping with it.
- Be positive when they cope well (and praise the effort they put in). If you can, try and ignore it when things go wrong until they have calmed down. Try to problem-solve what could have happened (but remember, behaviour is communication).

My child gets angry easily and has meltdowns

- When your child is calm, try to discover why they get angry.
- Remember, anger is a form of communication – think about what your child is telling you.
- You know your child best. Are they hungry or tired, or is there something else? Try and find out (and always have something your child can eat with you, for example).
- If your child becomes absorbed in what they are doing and is angry when you disturb them, give them 15 minutes' notice and then 5 minutes' notice to stop. Make sure you call their name each time; they might not have heard you or realised you were talking to them.
- Think about putting a reward system in place to identify effort or progress towards achievements.

A few websites and resources:

- Yellow Door, early years resources: www.yellow-door.net
- Ollie and his Superpowers: www.ollieandhissuperpowers.com
- Empowering Parents: www.empoweringparents.com

My child is so sensitive

- Make a list of all the ways in which they are sensitive.
- Turn into a sensory detective – what happens and when, and how do they react?
- If you can, remove the area of sensitivity or support it.
- Talk to a specialist organisation for sensory support if you are concerned.

A few websites and resources:

- Sensory Spectacle, advice and training about Sensory Processing Disorder: www.sensoryspectacle.co.uk/what-is-spd
- The OT Company: https://www.theotcompany.com
- Griffin Occupational Therapy: www.griffinot.com
- GoNoodle, YouTube channel for children who can't stop moving: www.youtube.com/channel/UC2YBT7HYqCbbvzu3kKZ3wnw
- GoNoodle website channel: www.gonoodle.com
- Beyond Autism: www.beyondautism.org.uk
- Sensory Planet – Twitter feed @SensoryPlanet

My child can't sleep

- Try and identify why they can't sleep.
- Make sure they have:
  - A consistent time for bed
  - A regular bedtime routine
  - A time to relax before going to bed, ideally with no technology being used, such as computers or television
  - A set time to read or wind down before sleeping.
- Stick with your routine and don't be thrown off it.
- If helping them sleep doesn't work after a few weeks, talk to them and listen to what they say.
- Problem-solve with them some solutions to why they can't sleep. Could it be:
  - They are overthinking things or worrying?
  - They don't like lying there in the dark?
  - They don't like the colour of the wallpaper or the feel of the duvet cover? Is it overwhelming them in some way, e.g., too bright or too itchy?
  - They have some other Sensory Processing Difficulty?
  - They love reading and want to get to the end of their book?
- Some parents and carers find products like weighted blankets and sensory sheets or other kinds of support in bed can help their child to sleep. Make sure you work with specialists who can find the right product (e.g., the right weight) that will be effective for your child.

A few websites and resources:

- HKD Solutions: www.hkdsolutions.com/index.asp
- Harkla: https://harkla.co
- Tink'n'stink: www.tinknstink.co.uk

My child has problems with food

- This can be an extremely difficult problem to unpick and could cover a range of mental, physical and other difficulties that you need to understand and support correctly. In the first instance, become a food (or eating) detective. Observe what your child does and what they say and the kinds of foods they want, and make a note of these to see patterns and any differences at times of day or in different situations.
- You could put different foods out in front of your child (e.g., colourful, bland, hard, soft, etc.) and see what they choose and what they say about each of them.
- If your child is young, play a game with them to explore their food preferences. Take it in turns to talk about different situations and what you would eat. For example, 'I am going to a picnic and I would eat XXX.'
- If they are a little older, ask them why they like (or don't like) a certain type of food. They still might not know, but you can ask questions like 'Do you like the taste?' and 'Do you like how it feels in your mouth?' Use this evidence to build up a picture of what they like and why.
- The challenge your child has with food can sometimes be a sensory one. Then you have a choice:
  - Accept this and give your child food that meets their sensory needs and avoid others.
  - Give a range of foods in small portions and hope that your child will eventually expand the kind of food they eat.
  - Seek support from specialists.
- Sometimes with a child with DME, the problem with food can be one of control. Then you have a choice:
  - Put your child in control of a limited number of choices (which

you have already chosen). For example, choose two things you are prepared to cook and ask your child 'Do you want X or Y?' Then they choose but are in control.

- If they still refuse to choose (and say something different), keep repeating the choice until they choose. If you have repeated this about five times or more (depending on the age of your child) and they have still not made a choice, tell them that you are going to choose for them. Then choose X. Sometimes your child may then say 'I don't want X, I want Y'. They have made their choice.
- Be consistent in your approach. If this doesn't work, this is where you may need specialist help.
- You may need more extreme solutions, e.g., if your child is older, could they cook for themselves?

• Something else may be going on in their lives. This could include bullying at school, lack of challenge in their learning or other problems which could lead to social, emotional, mental health or behavioural problems at school or at home.

- Talk to your child if you suspect something else might be going on in their life.
- If they don't feel able to tell you what it is (or they don't know what it could be), reassure them that you are there for them. Tell them that you love them and that you will listen and will love them whatever challenges they face.

• If none of these options seem to work, get specialist help to talk through what is happening and options for helping your child (and you) to address the challenges they face. The kinds of challenges that may need to be investigated include sensory processing problems, problems with swallowing and chewing and a range of other difficulties for your child with DME.

A few websites and resources:

- Annabel Karmel: www.annabelkarmel.com
- Vincent Iannelli (2020) 'A food diary for tracking your child's nutrition.' *Verywell Family*, 25 March. Includes things like calorie intake when your child is at different ages and an example food diary for

you to look at (please note that *Verywell Family* is based in the US): www.verywellfamily.com/printable-food-diary-2633949
- NHS England (2018) 'How many calories does a child of 7–10 need?': www.nhs.uk/common-health-questions/childrens-health/how-many-calories-does-a-child-of-7-10-need

My child overthinks everything and gets anxious

Depending on their age:

- Get a 'worry box' so they can write down or draw their worries (on individual pieces of paper) and put them away in the box (to get rid of them). This has the advantage that they have put what is worrying them into words and have put them away. It may help if you start this approach when they are young.
- Buy or make them a five-year diary. Encourage them to write in it every day so they can see what happened to them in the past and their progress (and ideally, that the world did not end!).
- Teach them how to problem-solve. For example:
  - Tell them 'You seem concerned/worried, what is the matter?' Then wait for them to tell you. Do not say anything, even if they remain quiet for a while.
  - If they can tell you, move to problem-solving. If not, ask if they feel able to tell you. If they can't, ask them if it is because they don't know or because they don't want to talk about it. If it is because they don't know, explore this with them. If it is that they can't (for whatever reason) talk to you about it, tell them that you are there for them.
  - If they know, listen to them. Then ask them what they think the solutions are. Get them to write it down, if it helps. Ask questions like 'What do you think the solutions are to your concern?' 'What is your action plan for solving it?'
  - If they don't know what the problem is (and are happy to talk about it), make a list with them of the things it could be. Do not give your child the answer – let them do the work. Hopefully, they will discover their concern and problem-solve the solution.
- Never say things like 'Don't be silly'. Listen to them and treat their concerns seriously.

- Do not problem-solve for them or give them a solution to their concerns. Solving the problem themselves will make your child with DME more resilient and more able to solve similar problems in the future.
- Tell your child that you love them and that you really believe that what they are saying is important.
- Listen more than talk to your child. Listening is sometimes all your child needs.
- There are many good books available on subjects like 'worry' and 'listening to your child'. Specialist organisations can also help you to support your child, and there are some good training courses out there.

A few websites and resources:

- Consortium calming cat worry toy and coaching cards: www.consortiumworldwide.com/calming-cat-worry-toy-and-coaching-cards-46563
- Eve Wilson (2013) *Little Tin of Big Worries* [cards] and the *Little Tin of Teenage Worries* [cards]: www.loggerheadpublishing.co.uk or https://incentiveplus.co.uk
- Joanna Faber and Julie King (2017) *How to Talk So Little Kids Will Listen: A Survival Guide to Life with Children Ages 2-7* (Audiobook). London: Simon & Schuster. Available at: https://www.audible.co.uk/pd/How-to-Talk-So-Little-Kids-Will-Listen-Audiobook/B01N1LV1TH?-source_code=M2M30DFT1BkSH11221601A7&&ipRedirectOverride=true&gclid=EAIaIQobChMI6Muc7Zzj8wIVB7rtCh1Tdw-waEAAYASAAEgIuJvD_BwE&gclsrc=aw.ds

My child gets angry in certain situations

- Investigate when they become angry. Writing these situations down (in a diary or somewhere to help you investigate the problem) can help you to see if there is a pattern to when your child is angry.
- Behaviour like this is a form of communication. What is your child telling you?
  - Are they tired and want to sleep?

- Are they hungry and want to eat?
- Do they need exercise or to get rid of excess energy?
- Are they being disturbed by you from an activity (such as reading) that they want to do?
- Is someone else disturbing them (or refusing to do something, e.g., join in with a game they've invented)?
- Look at what they do when they are angry.
- If anger is communication, try not to shout at them. Take your anger out of the equation, going out of the room if you need to calm down.
- If your child raises their voice in anger, lower yours to a whisper. This can help your child to calm down.
- Do not judge your child's anger. Make sure they know that you love them and will help them however you can.
- Practise anger management techniques with them until they can control their anger. This could include:
  - Counting backwards, from 10 to 1
  - Taking 'time out' where they take themselves off somewhere quiet to calm down.
- Show your child the behaviour you want them to have.
- Praise the effort your child puts into dealing with their anger positively and (as far as possible) ignore your child's negative behaviour or deal with it positively.

A few websites and resources:

- There are lots of good online training courses provided by organisations such as Bright and Quirky that can help with this: https://brightandquirky.com
- Cosmic Kids: https://cosmickids.com
- There are also some Positive Parenting leaflets available from the NSPCC: https://learning.nspcc.org.uk/research-resources/leaflets/positive-parenting

My child gets angry if they do not get their own way

- What is your child telling you? Look at the situations when this happens.

- If this anger is about your child controlling a situation, move onto how you deal with their controlling behaviour.
- Sometimes control could be about manipulation. Is your child able to control the whole situation because they know that you will 'give in' to their request so that they get their own way? If it is about control and manipulation, say what you mean and mean what you say clearly and positively, and then stick to it (easier said than done!).
- Remember, your child is clever. They may be able to twist your words and give you reasons why they should be able to do something (and then get their own way). They are communicating – whether they know it or not – the message that they are in control and can get whatever they want. Be aware of this problem before it escalates over the years, and seek specialist help and advice if needed.
- Learn assertiveness skills.
- Put rules in place with your whole family. Then stick to them. If that means no treats until homework is done, there is no deviation from this. This will help your child to understand that no means no.
- Phrase requests in the positive (say 'do this' rather than 'don't do that').
- Have a 'no blame' culture (e.g., 'the water spilled' rather than 'you spilled the water').
- Introduce 'time out' so your child can calm down.
- Encourage them to problem-solve with you what should happen in these situations (only do this when the situation is over, and they are ready to talk).
- If they become uncontrollable, remove them from the scene, but give them notice that you will do this.

My child is a daydreamer and forgets to do things

- Observe your child in situations where they daydream. If possible, see if there is a pattern to their daydreaming. For example, is it only in the morning, when they are getting ready? Do they forget things you asked them to do?
- Explore with your child where the problems lie. For example, how do they feel when they daydream? What are they thinking about? When do they do it?

- When your child is calm, ask them to help you to problem-solve what to do (e.g., could they help you plan the timetable for getting ready in the morning?).
- Give them notice for what they will do next on their timetable.
- Check if they hear you. If they do not have hearing problems (if you are concerned, get them checked), say their name. If that doesn't work, lightly tap them on the shoulder while saying their name. Many children with DME (and HLP) become so absorbed in what they are thinking or doing that everything else is blocked out.
- Talk to a specialist or consider having your child assessed with an organisation that understands about DME. This will give you an individualised action plan for supporting your child.

A few websites and resources:

- Comsmart sandtimers in six colours and times, available at: www.thewinfordcentre.com/product/comsmart-sand-timer or www.amazon.co.uk
- Watches to remind children to keep on track (ADDitude Editors 2013), or look for other technical solutions, such as a clock or alarm on a mobile phone or iPad

My child has no friends

- Listen to what your child says about friends:
  - Do they have friends that you don't know about?
  - Does having no friends bother them? It may not be seen as a problem until they become more 'self-aware' (often in late primary school/early secondary school).
  - Does them having no friends bother you?
  - Is it a question of numbers of friends? Is your child happy with one close friend while you think they should have lots of friends?
  - Is the problem having few or no friends or them not being invited to birthday parties or other events?
- If you discover that your child wants more friends, listen to what they think the problem is and any ideas for solving the problem. This could include:

- – Seeking out organisations that support like-minded children through face-to-face and online communities
- – Exploring extracurricular clubs in your child's area of interest (e.g., chess clubs).
- If your child goes to school, they could (depending on their age) invite all their classmates to their own birthday party (but be warned, this can backfire as these children may only talk to each other) or to a play date.

My child is a perfectionist

- Lay the foundations now to help address your child's competitive streak. Examples include:
  - – Praising your child for the effort they put into something, and not the results
  - – Being honest with them (e.g., not just saying, 'You were much better than the child who came first in the art competition, I don't know what happened')
  - – Praising something specific (e.g., saying things like 'I love the language (or colour) used to describe (or paint) this scene' rather than 'That's perfect' or 'It was a wonderful scene').
- Give your child a growth mindset (see Chapter 1).
- Challenge their learning, especially learning outside their 'comfort zone'. If done effectively, this will encourage them to work towards new challenges.
- Explain to them how the brain grows and makes connections (use the suggestion for this in Chapter 6 if you find it useful).

My child is obsessed with...

- Investigate your child's obsession. Is it something they have always had, or do they jump from one obsession to another?
- Could you use your child's obsession as a platform for exploring new things? For example, use it as a base for exploring things relating to it. If your child is obsessed with dinosaurs, could you use this as a base for exploring palaeontology? Could this take your child to archaeology? Could this take them on to history, and so on?

- If your child jumps from one obsession to another, see if there is a pattern. If there is no pattern, they may just have a mind that is obsessed with knowledge. Make sure that learning is fun for them and take them where they want to go. It could be deeper into a subject or broader into a range of subjects.
- If their obsession is not a topic or subject area that is followed at school, their passion may instead be something they can explore at home or in a specialist club. However, it is always worth talking to the teacher about their area of knowledge to see if it could be incorporated into a subject with which they struggle. For example, could they write their English essay on 'Fossils and what I've seen' instead of 'What I did over my summer holidays?' This may enthuse their learning and encourage them to get over any difficulties they may be experiencing with their writing.
- Don't write off their obsession because it is not seen as 'important'. After all, they could make a career out of it in the future!
- If you are concerned about their obsession (or feel that it could be related to a SEND such as ASD), consider having your child assessed with a specialist who can recognise HLP, DME and SEND and the complex interaction between them.

My child has a problem with handwriting

- Observe what is going on with your child when they write (or why they refuse to do so). Listen to what they say and ask questions such as 'How does it feel when you write?' 'What do you think would help you to write?'
- It may be worth considering an assessment with a specialist who understands the interaction between things like HLP and SEND (especially dyslexia, dysgraphia and eye problems), and how these can combine in a child or young person with DME. Common areas for further investigation that may arise out of an overall assessment include things like:
  - Joint Hypermobility Syndrome (double-jointedness), which, among other things, can cause pain and tiredness when a child writes

- Oscillopsia, where objects appear to jump or jiggle, or other eye problems that can make reading (and writing) difficult
- Dyslexia (including stealth dyslexia, which describes students with above-average or gifted reading abilities who use coping strategies to hide their dyslexia)
- Dysgraphia (which may involve looking at things such as how your child holds their pen or sits at their desk or even the weight of their pen)
- Working memory and processing problems.

There are also other reasons why a child with DME (and HLP) might have difficulties with writing. These include:

- Not being able to start a piece of writing because they cannot find the perfect sentence or paragraph to begin (giving an opening sentence or paragraph to your child can sometimes help with this)
- Having lots of different ideas, theories or concepts in their brain and being unable to structure them into any form of order (helping them with topics like mind mapping can sometimes help with this problem)
- Reading a question and thinking the answer should be more difficult than it actually is. Then answering the question incorrectly or being unable to provide any answer at all
- Failing to be inspired about the subject matter. Is there a difference, for example, between the subject material and your child's enthusiasm for writing? Could their teacher be persuaded to investigate this?

These are just a few of the reasons parents and carers have investigated to solve problems with handwriting. There are many others. As you can see, problems with handwriting can be extremely difficult to solve. If it is a physical problem, this can take you to specialist opticians, doctors, occupational therapists or a range of other organisations. However, if it is something more psychological and related to DME (or HLP), this will require further investigation by a specialist. For a child with DME, any specialist will also need to understand both SEND and HLP and how they combine in a child to form DME.

A few websites and resources:

- Learning Works for Kids, Dragon dictation, speech to text software: https://learningworksforkids.com/apps/dragon-dictation
- There are also lots of speech to text apps available as well as technology on phones and iPads, etc.
- Eide, B. and Eide, F. (2005) 'Stealth dyslexia': www.davidsongifted.org/search-database/entry/a10435

My child is so disorganised

- Investigate what is happening and how this affects your child. Where are the problem areas? How does this make your child feel? Once you have a clearer picture of the situation, contact a specialist organisation for help and advice.
- If your child's disorganisation is a problem for your child (and for you and others), identify the areas that need support and devise a plan.
- If needed (and welcomed by your child), give your child the 'scaffolding' they need to underpin their organisation skills. Depending on what you have found, some suggestions include:
  - Having a board to write on somewhere (which can be used again) where everyone writes down what they need to do that week, so they don't forget. Give responsibility to every individual to keep their own list up-to-date
  - Having a similar system, but using your smartphone or iPad
  - Putting a system in place to empty a schoolbag every evening. At first, you would be responsible for doing this. Once your child is used to the system, responsibility transfers to them
  - Having boxes of different colours somewhere in the house (ideally by the door) for each member of the family. This is where anything goes that has been left out and may otherwise be lost. If it works, your child will be able to find anything they 'lose' by going to their box
  - Teach your child how to tidy up; don't assume they know how to do it themselves. If possible, follow the 'nursery system' – all toys in one colour box, all LEGO® in another, etc. This will make it easier for them.

- Work with your child to devise a way of organising. For an older child, for example, having a three-tier letter tray on their desk can help with homework. On the top would go homework that is due now. On the second tray would be homework that is due this week. On the bottom tray would be homework that is due in the future. Then your child can be taught to transfer the work from one shelf to another depending on their deadlines.
- Praise your child for the effort they put in along the way.
- Tidy up to music. Put on a piece of music that is lively. Then tidy up as a whole family in short, sharp bursts. You will know how long it takes for your child to become bored of this activity.

Many ideas have been shared by parents and carers over the years, and you will have some of your own solutions. What you are trying to do is to transfer any systems you use into your child's long-term memory. To do this, you need to be consistent. However, some children will also have working memory difficulties or problems with processing skills. The first may mean that they will not remember what you or others have said (especially if they have to put two pieces of information together to form a third). The latter may mean that they need time to think about what you have asked them to do.

You may not be worried about this. After all, it may just be a part of who they are. However, if you (or, more importantly, they) or others have a problem with this, you may want to consider getting your child assessed.

A few websites and resources:

- Mindomo, mind-mapping software for children and young people: www.mindomo.com/mind-maps-for-education
- How to draw mind maps for kids: https://www.youtube.com/watch?v=nFYkj9fmlxE
- Parentkind – free resources to support learning https://www.parent-kind.org.uk/Parents/Free-learning-resources-for-children
- The ADHD Center: https://www.addcenters.com/articles/the-disorganized-child-strategies-for-helping-children-with-adhd-stay-focused
- The Brainy Child: www.brainy-child.com/experts/gifted-and-disorganized.shtml

- Your Modern Family: https://www.yourmodernfamily.com/disorganized-child

My child won't do their homework/schoolwork

- Investigate what is happening with your child at school (with their teacher), at home or elsewhere. Then you can problem-solve some solutions on your own or with others.
- This is a complicated area to unpick and can get to the heart of DME. For example:
  - Could your child have difficulties with handwriting? If so, why?
  - Do they have a SEND (dysgraphia, dyslexia, vision problems, etc.) at the same time as having HLP? Their DME needs to be clearly understood and supported by you and their teacher (or other professional).
  - What happens when your child dictates their piece of homework to you or types it or uses technology to support their writing? Is there a difference in what they write and how they feel?
- Experiment with different approaches that work at home (e.g., with homework) and, if successful, discuss these ideas with their teacher as solutions to any difficulties with schoolwork. Ideas include:
  - Using age-appropriate stepping-stones towards completion of homework
  - 'Chunking' the homework into sections and asking your child to complete a chunk and then to take a break
  - Using diamond ranking as a way of structuring an essay. Draw out a diamond shape and divide it into nine boxes, one at the top (the most important), two underneath, then three, followed by two and then one (the least important). Then encourage your child to think about which is most important...down to the point that is least important.
- Ask your child what would encourage their enthusiasm for schoolwork. Listen to what they say and advocate for this on their behalf with their teacher.
- Give your child 'the big picture' about why schoolwork (and exams) is needed. Some children with DME (and HLP) cannot understand why it is important, when their passions and enthusiasm are for subjects

either outside the curriculum or so far advanced that it makes the school exam structure almost irrelevant. However:

- Could these passions be nurtured in a different way?
- Could they be nurtured within school as part of the school week but outside the core curriculum? For example, some schools give pupils the opportunity to follow their own passion one afternoon a week.

• Consistency is sometimes important, especially for a child who is not engaged with homework. Consider having a set time for homework each day (even if there isn't any to do) and filling a toolbox with what they need to do it (pens, pencils, etc.) so they don't waste time looking for the tools they need. Also, if possible, have a permanent space to do their homework. Does this help?

• Could you negotiate with their teacher about homework (or even schoolwork)? For example:

- If you know what the point is of a piece of homework (including the skills your child will be learning), could you substitute it for something that took the skills to be learned or shown but did something different with them, or did additional bits? Take spelling, for example. A child with advanced reading ability may already know how to spell the words for a spelling test. Could they instead use those words in a sentence (or use them all in a story)? Working with them, you could help ensure your child is enthused by the homework set. Then, for a child with DME, this enthusiasm and their strengths could be used as a building block to underwrite the areas in which they struggle.
- If the homework is about finding out what they know, could they record this in different ways rather than through their writing? Perhaps a PowerPoint presentation (or equivalent)? Or even notes or diagrams? Once your child's mind loses its constraints, you – and others – may be amazed at what they can achieve!

A few websites and resources:

- Twinkl: www.twinkl.co.uk
- SparkleBox: www.sparklebox.co.uk/misc/homework
- TTS set of resources from the US: www.tts-group.co.uk/a5-homework-diary-20pk/1006306.html

DEVELOPING AN ACTION PLAN FOR YOUR PRE-SCHOOL/EARLY YEARS CHILD WITH DME

The pre-school and early years are a precious time for you and your child. Whether you work full-time, part-time or as a homemaker, letting your child take the lead in the activities that interest them and having fun is important and will often feel to you like the only time in their lives that you and they are able to follow their passions without the pressure of home-work and everything else that their future selves (and you!) will encounter. Many parents and carers say that their child's pre-school years are, for them looking back, a valuable time of learning and discovery.

From research that has been conducted in the UK (such as a survey carried out by The Potential Trust in 2020) and anecdotal evidence about children and young people with DME, we believe that parents and carers, even if they have no knowledge that their child could have DME, start to see the signs usually before their child goes to school (if they are not home educating), and certainly by the time they are in the first few years of primary education. This makes it important to be aware of the kinds of behaviours and actions that can be associated with DME, especially in the early years.

Many parents and carers worry during this time that their child's obsessions for such subjects as maths or reading or writing will look to the outside world as if they are 'hothousing' their child, or somehow forcing them to learn skills they will need in their future schooling. They think that this makes them look like 'pushy parents', trying to turn their children into geniuses, whatever their child might want.

> My child started to teach themselves to read by using the subtitles on the television. I don't even know how they turned them on. I'm worried that other people will think that I pushed my child into reading before they started school. I was an early reader, and my experiences at school were fairly negative because of this. I don't want the same to happen to my child. (Parent)

Try not to worry about this. Even at this age, many children with HLP and DME do not want to play in the sandpit but would prefer to read a book or to play with older children who can understand the games they have invented, rather than with children of their own age. Your role with your child at this age remains to:

- Help your child follow their passions
- Introduce them to a range of new ones, to see which of these interest them
- Be aware of what activities they enjoy doing the most, so that you can build on these in future
- Lay the foundations for the behaviours they need.

In the case of the latter, it can be useful to develop household rules for how your family will act and its core values. These can be built on in the future and possibly even reviewed once a year. The items on this list can range from the small to the huge. The important thing is that the rules outline how you are going to act and what you expect from others. They will also help to give you the building blocks for your child and your family as your child grows up.

Here is an example of rules and values. You may not agree with everything on the list, and yours may look totally different. That's fine – every family believes in different things. What is important is that you discuss and agree a set of rules that you can apply consistently. That way your child knows what is expected of them and others in the family.

What we believe in	The things we will do
Being positive towards each other every day	Praising the effort people put in
Treating our house and others with respect	Saying 'please' and 'thank you' Taking off our shoes when we come into the house Tidying up at least once a week
Everyone has a voice	Giving everyone a voice on family decisions Talking to each other round the table at mealtimes
Everyone has a choice	Having the right to speak our mind Understanding that we, the parents (or carers), must sometimes make the final decision
Everyone has their own space	Having space where each individual can relax Having bedtime routines that are discussed and agreed and followed
Helping other people	Helping with chores Allocating chores fairly between family members Doing a good turn every day for someone else
We believe in education	Supporting our child's learning Speaking up for every member of the family with others

As you can guess, these 'rules of the family' were written by an adult. As your child grows up and they become more involved, expect a few things coming from their rich mind. As this particular family believes that everyone has a voice, you might add them in!

Speaking up for your child's needs may start to happen at this age, in the early years, especially if they go to a nursery or other organised childcare, and you might want to prepare yourself for this next stage.

In England, the 'early years' are defined as when a child is aged three to five. In school terms, this is their first stage of education and might cover their time in nursery to Reception class. The key focus in these environments is about getting children used to routine and formality in a more structured environment than the one they might be used to at home.

According to the UK Government website on school admissions in England, most children start school full-time in the September after their fourth birthday. This means they'll turn five during their first school year. If you do not think your child is ready to start school at the usual time, they can start later. They can start part-time or part-way through the year in the school year after they turn five as long as they are in full-time education by the time they reach 'compulsory school age'. This is on 31 December, 31 March or 31 August following their fifth birthday.[1]

Countries vary in the age they expect children to start school, and it is very much a cultural issue. In countries like Finland, for example (which arguably has one of the best education systems in the world), children are not expected to start their compulsory education until the year in which they turn seven.[2]

How you are going to support your child with DME in their early years is probably one of the first formal decisions in your action plan that you will need to make:

- Is your child with DME getting restless to meet other children or to learn with others?
- Do you think your child is not yet ready and needs to be at home with you?
- Do you know what kind of early year setting you want them to go to?

---

1   www.gov.uk/schools-admissions/school-starting-age
2   www.infofinland.fi/en/living-in-finland/education/the-finnish-education-system

There are no right or wrong answers; it is down to every individual child and their parents and carers. For a child with DME, the areas where they need support may not be a problem (or even appear) before any formal teaching begins. Other children may not yet have the maturity to cope with some of the things expected of them in a more formal setting. Others may already be teaching themselves and can't wait to go to school to learn more formally.

Deciding to send your child with DME to nursery or to a childminder may be the first time you need to get someone else on board to meet their needs.

> We found it hard to explain to our child's nursery that they were a 'bit different'. We were initially met with disbelief (of course your child can't do sums, they are only two years old!) but then acceptance and interest. We found it a positive experience in the end. (Parent)

However, common problems that can arise for a child with DME at this stage include things like the child:

- Making up complicated games that no other child understands or wants to play
- Having a strong sense of justice and fairness and being unable to express these properly
- Not yet having the language skills to say what they are feeling and so resorting to, for example, biting or kicking instead
- Still being obsessed with something and wanting to spend all their time on this, to the exclusion of everything else
- Being distraught about leaving you.

While many of these may be experienced by children who do not have DME, a child with DME's behaviour may be much more intense and more complicated to unravel or support appropriately. If nursery or other staff raise these kinds of challenges, it is a good idea to work with them on a joint action plan to support your child.

IS YOUR CHILD UPSET BY THE THOUGHT OF BEING SEPARATED FROM YOU, EVEN FOR SHORT PERIODS?

This can be quite common, especially for children with DME (or HLP) who are already anxious about things, who overthink everything, who hate new environments or change or who are hypersensitive... So, while lots of children may be anxious when starting something new, a child with DME's behaviour and reasoning can sometimes be intense, extreme and complicated to unravel.

You could try:

- Talking to your child when they are calm and finding out why they are concerned. They may not know (or be able to come up with the words to explain), so you might have to suggest a few reasons, but give them time to think and talk about their fears. You can then respond appropriately and in ways that they can understand, given their age
- Taking your own fears, concerns and behaviour out of the equation. It is understandable that you might also feel anxious (whatever your child's age) when they are left in a new setting for the first time, but a child who is sensitive will pick up on this and it can make it even harder for them (and therefore you!) to cope.
- Putting in place a coping strategy, such as:
  - Giving your child something of yours to keep with them. It could be anything – a photograph, a scarf of yours or something else
  - Teaching them the time and telling them exactly when you will come back (just try not to be late!)
  - Talking to the person in charge to find out how your child was after you left. This may set your mind at rest the next time. However, their understanding is essential, as, without it, some professionals might believe that it is you who were concerned and not your child. If feasible, tell them the kinds of things they could do to distract your child
  - Practising before the event with shorter time periods apart from each other. You could gradually extend the time your

> child is left with someone else so that they can see that you
> will return to them each time
> - Seeking permission – in more extreme circumstances – to
>   accompany your child, until they are settled. This may not
>   be approved of in a more formal setting such as a school,
>   as it might disrupt routines, but it may be an option in
>   other settings.

Your decision about whether to send your child to school is a very personal one and there are no right or wrong answers. However, you might find it useful before you make your decision to think about the kinds of things your pre-schooler will be expected to learn. Again, this is very much a cultural decision, and what may be relevant in one country may be less so in another.

It is important to look at similar structures for your own country about what children are expected to be doing – at least in part – by the age of five (or when they start school), but be warned – laws change all the time. So it is worth looking out for the latest frameworks. The one below is from the *Early Years Foundation Stage Profile: 2021 Handbook*.

Don't worry if your child doesn't have all of the skills listed below at the moment. Children's development is rarely consistent in all areas, and this is quite normal. However, others may be able to do more in some or even all the learning areas. According to the Early Years Foundation Stage Framework:

The Early Years Foundation Stage (EYFS) framework in England sets the statutory standards for the development, learning and care of children from birth to age 5. The EYFS statutory framework sets the standards that all early years providers must keep to ensure that children learn and develop well and are kept healthy and safe. It promotes teaching and learning to ensure children's 'school readiness' and gives children the broad range of knowledge and skills that provide the right foundation for good future progress through school and life. (Department for Education 2021, p.8)

Although the language is official, we thought it would be useful to understand what kinds of things your child would be expected to do by the time they start school in England so that teachers (and parents and carers) can be aware of the characteristics of each child's learning, and so they can plan their Year 1 curriculum (drawn from Department for Education 2021, pp.27–31, 51–54).

	By the age of five, children should be able to:	What would they be doing if exceeding the targets? Then, children by the age of five would be able to:
1. Listening and attention	• Listen attentively in a range of situations. • Listen to stories, accurately anticipating key events and responding with relevant comments, questions or actions. • Give their attention to what others say and respond appropriately, while engaged in another activity.	• Listen to instructions and follow them accurately, asking for an explanation if necessary. • Listen attentively with sustained concentration to follow a story without pictures or props. • Listen in a larger group, e.g., in an assembly.
2. Understanding	• Follow instructions involving several ideas or actions. • Answer 'how' and 'why' questions about their experiences and in response to stories or events.	• After listening to stories, express views about events or characters in the story and answer questions about why things happened. • Carry out instructions, which contain several parts in a sequence.
3. Speaking	• Express themselves effectively, showing awareness of listeners' needs. • Use past, present and future forms accurately. • Have developed their own narratives and explanations by commenting on ideas or events.	• Show some awareness of the listener by making changes to language and non-verbal features. • Recount experiences and imagine possibilities, often connecting ideas. • Use a range of vocabulary in imaginative ways to add information, express ideas or to explain or justify actions of events.
4. Moving and handling	• Show good control and coordination in large and small movements. • Move confidently in a range of ways, safely negotiating space. • Handle equipment and tools effectively, including pencils for writing.	• Hop confidently and skip in time to music. • Hold paper in position and use their preferred hand for writing, using a correct pencil grip. • Begin to be able to write on lines and control letter size.

cont.

	By the age of five, children should be able to:	What would they be doing if exceeding the targets? Then, children by the age of five would be able to:
5. Health and self-care	• Know the importance for good health of physical exercise and a healthy diet, and talk about ways to keep healthy and safe. • Manage their own basic hygiene and personal needs successfully, including dressing and going to the toilet independently.	• Know about, and make healthy choices in relation to, healthy eating and exercise. • Dress and undress independently, successfully managing fastening buttons or laces.
6. Self-confidence and self-awareness	• Be confident about trying new activities and say why they like some activities more than others. • Be confident about speaking in a familiar group, will talk about their ideas and will choose the resources they need for their chosen activities. • Say when they do or do not need help.	• Confidently speak to a class group. • Talk about the things they enjoy, are good at and about the things they do not find easy. • Resourceful in finding support when they need help or information. • Talk about plans they have made to carry out activities and what they might change if they were to repeat them.
7. Managing feelings and behaviour	• Talk about how they and others show feelings, talk about their own and others' behaviour and its consequences and know that some behaviour is unacceptable. • Work as part of a group or class and understand and follow rules. • Adjust their behaviour to different situations and take changes of routine in their stride.	• Know some ways to manage their feelings and begin to use these to maintain control. • Listen to each other's suggestions and plan how to achieve an outcome without adult help. • Know when and how to stand up for themselves appropriately. • Stop and think before acting and wait for things they want.
8. Managing relationships	• Play cooperatively, taking turns with others. • Take account of one another's ideas about how to organise their activity. • Show sensitivity to others' needs and feelings, and form positive relationships with adults and other children.	• Play group games with rules. • Understand someone else's point of view and that it can be different from theirs. • Resolve minor disagreements through listening to each other to come up with a fair solution. • Understand what bullying is and that it is unacceptable behaviour.

9. Reading	• Read and understand simple sentences. • Use phonic knowledge to decode regular words and read them aloud accurately. • Also read some common irregular words. • Show understanding when talking to others about what they have read.	• Read phonically regular words of more than one syllable as well as many common, irregular words. • Use phonic, semantic and syntactic knowledge to understand unfamiliar words. • Describe the main events in the simple stories they have read.
10. Writing	• Use their phonic knowledge to write words in ways which match their spoken sounds. • Also write some irregular words. • Write simple sentences which can be read by themselves and others. Some words are spelt correctly, and some are phonetically plausible.	• Spell phonically regular words of more than one syllable as well as many irregular but high frequency words. • Use key features of narrative in their own writing.
11. Numbers	• Count reliably with numbers 1–20, place them in order and say which number is one more or one less than a given number. • Using quantities and objects, add and subtract 2-digit numbers and count on or back to find the answer. • Solve problems. Including doubling, halving and sharing.	• Estimate a number of objects and check quantities by counting up to 20. • Solve practical problems that involve combining groups of 2, 5 or 10 and sharing into equal groups.
12. Shapes, space and measures	• Use everyday language to talk about size, weight, capacity, position, distance, time and money to compare quantities and objects and to solve problems. • Recognise, create and describe patterns. • Explore characteristics of everyday objects and shapes and use mathematical language to describe them.	• Estimate, measure, weigh and compare and order objects. • Talk about properties, position and time.

cont.

	By the age of five, children should be able to:	What would they be doing if exceeding the targets? Then, children by the age of five would be able to:
13. People and communities	• Talk about past and present events in their own lives and in the lives of family members. • Know that other children do not always enjoy the same things and are sensitive to this. • Know about similarities and differences between themselves and others, and among families, communities and traditions.	• Know the difference between past and present events in their own lives and some reasons why people's lives were different in the past. • Know that other children have different likes and dislikes and that they are good at different things. • Understand that different people have different beliefs, attitudes, customs and traditions and why it is important to treat them with respect.
14. The world	• Know about similarities and differences in relation to places, objects, materials and living things. • Talk about the features of their own immediate environment and how environments might vary from one another. • Make observations of animals and plants and explain why some things occur, and talk about changes.	• Know that the environment and living things are influenced by human activity. • Describe some actions, which people in their own community do, that help to maintain the area they live in. • Know the properties of some materials and can suggest some of the purposes they are used for. • Be familiar with basic scientific concepts like floating, sinking, experimentation.
15. Technology	• Recognise that a range of technology is used in places such as homes and schools. • Select and use technology for particular purposes.	• Find out about and use a range of everyday technology. • Select appropriate applications that support an identified need, e.g., in deciding how to make a record of a special event in their lives, such as a train journey on a steam train.
16. Exploring and using media and materials	• Sing songs, make music and dance and experiment with ways of changing them. • Safely use and explore a variety of materials, tools and techniques, experimenting with colour, design, texture, form and function.	• Develop their own ideas through selecting and using materials and working on processes that interest them. • Through exploration, find out how to make decisions about how media and materials can be combined and changed.

17. Being imaginative	• Use what they have learnt about media and materials in original ways, thinking about uses and purpose. • Represent their own ideas, thoughts and feelings through design, technology, art, music, role-play and stories.	• Talk about the ideas and processes, which have led them to make music, designs or images or products. • Talk about features of their own and others' work, recognising the differences between them and the strengths of others.

Source: Drawn from Department for Education (2021, pp.27–31, 51–54)

So, another item in your action plan for your child with DME in the early years may be to help them develop the skills they will need. We do not mean you should teach them how to write or read or do maths (although some children with DME, even at this age, will want to do some of these). Rather, your action plan should be about helping them to develop the skills to underpin what they will be expected to do in future.

While this will be different for every child, our top 10 skills for development, in no particular order, would probably look like this:

Top 10 skills you could help teach your child when they are ready	How this will help in the future
1. Threading buttons or pieces of pasta to make a necklace	Helps improve fine motor skills, which are useful for writing, tying shoelaces, etc.
2. Painting and drawing big shapes on an A3 piece of paper	Helps improve pencil grip, which can help writing skills
3. Inviting friends or family over to play with them	Sharing, playing with other children, speaking and listening
4. Playing board games	Counting, sharing, playing with other people
5. Playing with sponge letters in the bath	Helps with the alphabet
6. Cooking cakes together	Weighing and measuring, quantities, numbers, experimentation, telling the time
7. Reading together	Listening, speaking, understanding
8. Painting with fingers, brushes, with potato prints, in fact anything you can think of!	Skills to help with writing, colour recognition, shapes
9. Dressing up	Imagination, speaking, understanding
10. Singing songs and nursery rhymes	Singing, love of music

This list could go on. While your child (and you!) may not like the thought of any of these, which is fine, we have simply tried to show you the kinds of fun things that you could do that may help your child later on, without even leaving the house!

Next, consider what else you could do with your child. This could include exploring exhibits in museums or art galleries and walks in the town or countryside. What about local groups offering activities to develop exercise and balance, or music, or a range of other inventive activities happening in your community? The next element in your action plan should be to help your child explore their passions. As you may know, this could take a lifetime, so starting early is good! An excellent book by C.J. Simister, called *The Bright Stuff*, is full of activities that will help spark your child's curious mind and boost their creativity and passion for learning.

Arguably, the pre-school years are the most enjoyable for your child and for you. So, along with addressing any behavioural concerns that may have begun to surface (action 4 in the plan below) and laying the foundations for your child's love of learning, the final stage of your action plan when they are this age should be to enjoy being with them!

ACTION PLAN FOR YOUR PRE-SCHOOL CHILD

1. Decide when and where (if at all) your child will go to school.
2. Help with the underpinning skills they will need in the future.
3. Help them explore their passions and to love learning.
4. Address any behavioural or other concerns that have started to emerge.
5. Enjoy your time with them!

DEVELOPING AN ACTION PLAN FOR YOUR 5- TO 11-YEAR-OLD (PRIMARY/EARLY SECONDARY SCHOOL) WITH DME

> Between the ages of 5–11, as parents we needed help to support our child's rapid pace of learning. The school curriculum for Years 1–6 were already known by our child when they were six years old. Now that our child is 12+ years old they have other needs in school. They need more emotional support as they feel different from other children around them. (Parent)

Ideally, you will have already developed and implemented your action plan for the family. If not, don't worry – you can start it now.

At this age, your child will begin to receive formal education. At the core of the National Curriculum for state schools in England during this time are compulsory subjects such as English, maths, science, design and technology, history, geography, art and design, music, physical education (PE), computing and ancient and modern foreign languages. Some schools also teach subjects like citizenship and personal, social and health education (PSHE), and other schools (such as public schools) may offer additional or different subjects.

Chapter 6 will help you to work positively with your child's school or learning environment to help ensure their needs are understood and met. Unless it is crucial that they are addressed now (in which case, go straight to Chapter 6), make a note of:

- What your child is saying about school, when they go in the morning and come home later
- Their behaviour before and after school
- Any specific concerns you might have
- Any feedback you receive from their teacher.

Your child may have started school once they were five years old. We recognise they may look and behave very differently at eleven going on twelve years old. What has helped to shape them are their experiences at school, with learning, friendships and how they have been nurtured. However, in this chapter we are not going to focus on your child's direct school experiences (see Chapters 5 and 6). At this stage, we are more concerned with what happens at home and how school can impact on this.

Common concerns raised by parents and carers when their child with DME is this age include:

- Changes in behaviour at home. These can happen for many reasons, such as learning new ways to behave (and even language to use) at school; trying to fit in – it is not unknown for children, especially in late primary/early secondary school, to develop new hobbies that do not particularly interest them, but that do help them 'fit in with the crowd'; and becoming more disruptive at home as they seek to 'shake off' the pressures of school.
- A growing sense of self-awareness of themselves and their place in the world. Sometimes this can lead to problems such as the child's increasing recognition of their loneliness; or awareness that they are 'different' from others in their class or school and that they have no, or few, friends like them. Sometimes, negative experiences linked to this growing self-awareness can lead to social, emotional, mental health and other problems.
- Difficulties in coping with their DME. How these show themselves depends on a range of factors, both personal to the child (their personality, their resilience, how they cope) and to the school and individual teacher, and sometimes to you. For example, a school that celebrates diversity and recognises and nurtures a child with DME will mean a greater chance of your child having a positive school experience, but one that doesn't recognise your child's DME or supports their needs

inappropriately, or where your child is bullied by classmates because of their differences, may mean they have a totally different experience. All of this can spill over into their life at home.

Parents and carers report a variety of different behaviours they experience with their child with DME at primary or early secondary school. On the positive side, their child may be energised and feel a renewed sense of purpose in their learning, loving their maths teaching, for example, or they may be racing through books on the reading list so that the school has to buy new selections of publications for them to read. This can be a positive time for the family (although one where it can be difficult to keep up!). But during this time, some parents and carers can also report a range of concerns about their child, such as their reducing self-esteem, negative behaviour, high intensity and extremes of emotion and battles over homework.

These concerns may fluctuate depending on trigger points. Finding a close, like-minded friend, for example, may remove some of the problems. How a teacher works with them, learning that inspires them, moving between classes, subjects or schools and a variety of other experiences can have a positive or negative impact on your child at home. Observe their behaviour. Listen to what they say, and work with them on finding out how best to respond to any difficulties they experience if it bothers them.

For a child with DME, during this time parents and carers and/or professionals may start to question and then explore what might be causing any difficulties experienced. This could come from a variety of different directions, as suggested by your child, by yourself or by a professional.

If you have already been through this stage, you might have spent hours looking for answers about why your child was struggling with their homework or at school or in their behaviour. Or why they were frustrated that the pace of work was too slow. Nothing seems to fit or to explain what is going on. Until, bingo! You come across one of the support groups for DME or you read a book and you experience a light bulb moment!

Many of us have been there and can only sympathise. All we can say is that you are not on your own and there is help available – we have provided details in Chapter 8 of some of the national and international organisations that will be able to support you. Don't be frightened to contact them. Almost all have experience of being in your situation.

If you are worried that you might be wrong, you are not. Many parents and carers exploring these kinds of concerns about their child are in the right place.

So what does your action plan look like at this stage? Many of the topics raised in this book will help you with this action plan. Remember to be consistent and persevere with the support you are providing. Also remember your child's strengths.

ACTION PLAN FOR CHILDREN AGED 5–11

1. Decide on your child's learning environment.
2. Keep an eye on them (their behaviour, what they are saying, any difficulties they are having) and deal with any concerns that arise.
3. Identify and help them with trigger points (such as the transition between schools and even classes, growing self-awareness).
4. Be their biggest advocate.
5. Decide on your views and approach to any SEND and HLP process and with their DME.
6. Research as much as you can about their needs.
7. Get help from others who understand what is happening and what you need.
8. Recognise that they will be a different child at twelve years old than they were at five years old.

DEVELOPING AN ACTION PLAN WITH YOUR TEENAGER WITH DME

Your child has made it to secondary school (or equivalent) and has become a teenager. They go to bed one night and, when they get up, it seems as if you have a different child:

- They have different opinions from you (and are sometimes forceful in telling you how wrong you are!).
- They are inconsistent – one minute they are arguing for something and the next minute they are arguing against it. There seems to be no logic.

- They slam doors, cause arguments between different family members and do a variety of other things such as coming in late (beyond the time you told them) or going to parties and staying out all night.
- Or they stop talking to you altogether and treat you as if you are some kind of alien.

If you are reading this and wondering what this is all about, fantastic news! You may be one of the lucky ones who sails through their child's teenage years with them without a problem. Either that, or you haven't got teenagers yet, so make the most of it!

The good news is that many teenagers with DME are content with their nose stuck in a book or with doing their homework. If anything, these teenagers can often struggle through a lack of cognitive, creative challenge with the right level of complexity for their strengths.

> When my child was this age, I needed more support for them at school, socially and academically, so they were challenged and engaged. Instead, I had to get support for their growing mental health problems. This involved me paying for a private psychiatrist for a diagnosis and a review of the medication my child was on for ADHD. (Parent)

In addition, if they are in a school environment where they don't 'fit in' or where they lack social interaction with teenagers who have similar interests, you may have concerns about friendships. Such concerns, if not dealt with effectively, may also be the cause of social, emotional and mental health problems.

Finally, even if they are well adjusted and happy at school, parents and carers need to look out for signs of perfectionism and anxiety, especially around exam time. These children can sometimes be on a knife-edge to get the highest grades, come top of the class, or even to get everything right.

> I never failed anything at school. Then, in my first year at university, I failed something for the first time. I can still remember it now, that feeling in the pit of my stomach. Why didn't I pass the exam? I would have to retake it in the next year. The embarrassment. During that summer, I got a job. I was going to stay with the company and stop going to university. Then one of the bosses met with me and said I should return to my course and I would be more resilient for my experience. I did go back, and he was right; I did feel stronger. (Parent who was a child with DME)

However, if they are in a school where DME is not recognised or valued, this may be causing growing problems for them and either their school, you at home, or both. For some children, this can erupt into behaviour problems in the classroom or 'fold in on itself' in terms of mental health problems such as depression. These are then seen as SEND and your child may finally appear on someone's radar.

These problems can carry on unless someone recognises and nurtures the child's abilities, including giving them the cognitive challenge that was missing and was part of the problem in the first place. When that is done, when they are nurtured effectively, when they find like-minded peers, the concerns contributing towards their social, emotional and mental health difficulties can diminish, if not disappear altogether. But often, by then, it can be too late, and alternative school arrangements have been made, or the child has been excluded or taken themselves out of school through stress or anxiety or both.

The bad news is that a child with DME can sometimes start behaving like a teenager early on, sometimes even in late primary school. This is due to their asynchronous development (read about this in Chapter 1). If their DME is not recognised and the whole child is not supported (both their HLP and their SEND), a child with DME may, yet again, struggle with their behaviour, or experience social, emotional and mental health problems.

The good news is that, once they leave their teenage years – particularly with your help and support – they often become their wonderful, bright and quirky selves again!

> Puberty is killing me! The hormones combined with the advanced thinking skills along with an immature understanding of social skills and logic rather than empathy means too much arguing in the family. I will be glad when it's over! (Parent)

None of this is intended to be negative – far from it. It is designed to give you suggestions about why your child may be acting as they are, and what they might need. Let's assume that you are a current or potential parent or carer who is or will be experiencing your child's teenage years. You may be exhausted fighting both with your child with DME and with a system that may not understand your child or support them effectively.

Your child's hormones are racing around their system; they want to be in control of their own life and want to break free from yours. So far, perfectly normal (we have all been through it!). However, your child is bright and intense. Every crisis seems to be bigger and more earthshattering and the solutions seem more extreme. You may be struggling, and little you do seems to work. Your child with DME may have all sorts of things looming that may make life more stressful, including work that gets even harder, exams and new people with whom to make friends and new potential friendship groups.

In primary school, lots of accommodations may have been made for your child, 'informally', with one class teacher who possibly 'just gets them'. Now your child is at secondary school. There are more subjects, more teachers and more formal structures to navigate, and more approaches to teaching your child with DME and people to convince how to support them appropriately.

> Over time, the gap between our child and their classmates widened. Schoolwork became less and less adequate until it was inadequate. The longer this carried on, the more unstimulating school became. Our child grew lazy and lost motivation and resilience. They also lost their joy of learning. (Parent)

Is it any wonder that young people with DME can experience worsening social, emotional and mental health issues as they grow older? Feedback from these young people and adults with DME reporting back on their childhood suggests that a parent's or carer's non-judgemental, unconditional love is what helps to sustain them during this potentially difficult time. Never underestimate the power of love, even if it doesn't feel as if they care (or are sometimes even listening!).

As well as the action plan you have developed and consistently applied as they have grown older (if you haven't, you could start now), you might want to build in strategies that slowly transfer elements of control over to your child, such as letting them go out shopping on their own or organising friends to come round or with whom to go out. Don't forget, though – eventually your child may be leaving home altogether, and so they will need to develop independent living skills. Developing these skills slowly can give them growing confidence and help ensure living independently is not such a shock to them when they finally do it.

We recognise that, despite all this, there may be setbacks, problems or surprises you never thought you would have to deal with as well as anxiety and upset along the way. Remember:

- Be there for your child.
- Be consistent in what you put in place (so that they know the rules of the household).
- Don't 'sweat the small stuff'. Does it really matter if your child's bedroom is untidy? If you think it does, it could be one of the rules of your household (and so deal with the problem). However, if you think it doesn't, or if you can close the door on the mess to make the problem 'disappear', 'don't sweat it', but do make it their responsibility to find their jeans so they can go out or their homework book for school (which is buried under piles of washing!).

And just as important – whatever happens with your teenager with DME, don't be too hard on yourself. Remember that every setback or failure is a way to learn how to improve the next time.

When my child was 13 years old, they really struggled with the onset of puberty. As a family, we bore the brunt of the mood swings, daily tears and increased sensitivity. When they were at home, we had to walk around them on eggshells all the time. I spoke to other parents and I

> concluded that their outbursts were far more intense and frequent than those of their children who were going through puberty as well. This was a dreadful experience for all of us. (Parent)

There are lots of books on the market both for you and for your teenager, and one that is worth looking at is *Be Your Best Self* by Danielle Brown, a double Paralympic gold medallist. If you think your child won't read anything you recommend, leave one of the books you buy or borrow lying around without saying anything. There may be more chance of it being read that way!

Of course, your child may be nothing like our description so far. Many teenagers are extremely hardworking and have good relationships with others. In Chapter 1 we have provided information for you to download about different kinds of children with HLP. They may be perfectly fine. However, you still need to keep your eye on them to make sure that they have positive mental health and feel able to talk to you if things are not going well or if they are concerned or anxious.

At this age, friendships and 'fitting in' can have a huge impact on some children, and the power of the 'school friendship structure' should not be underestimated. You can be in the 'in crowd' one minute and out the next, for no apparent reason. If you are worried about things like this, a good book to read is *Queen Bees and Wannabes* by Rosalind Wiseman. While every young person in the school or even group (if they are not educated at school) will be part of 'a structure', this could be inside with the 'popular' young people, outside, or (if the young person has enough confidence to do it) even forming their own group altogether of 'bright and quirky kids' who don't care about being part of the mainstream.

A particularly anxious child (one who overthinks everything), or one who finds it more difficult, for whatever reason, to fit in (as can happen with a young person with DME), may be particularly negatively affected by knowing where they fit into a structure.

> When I was at school all the girls were into makeup, fashion and boys. They each wanted to fit in and there was a standard for that. I wasn't interested in any of these things, so I didn't meet their 'standards'. They ignored me in conversations and, basically, I was ostracised from everyone. All because they were concerned with their image and were

worried about how I'd affect this. The school system can turn friends into strangers and can warp minds until you don't know what's true any more. In my case, the social side of school did more harm than all the education it provided. (Young person with DME)

Finding like-minded peers can so easily make the difference between a positive or a negative experience for your child at school, at home or elsewhere. Helping your child to find like-minded peers should be an important part of your action plan, if welcomed by your child (you don't want them to think you are choosing their friends for them!).

In terms of DME itself, in most cases, by the time your child is a teenager, their DME will have surfaced and some sort of investigation started or action plan put in place by you or the professional with whom you are dealing. However, this is not always the case. Sometimes, by this age, your child may have become so skilled at hiding their HLP or SEND that no one has identified the complexity of their learning needs.

This lack of DME identification can go on indefinitely until something happens – their exam results come in, they cannot hide their DME any longer, and their work performance is noticed. It may even be that it is not until they are an adult when they are having their own child assessed that they realise what has been happening with themselves over the years.

In the meantime, it is vital to listen to your child, to be sensitive to what they are saying (and what they are not saying), and how they are acting. Then stand up for them and advocate for them. Better still, teach them how to advocate for themselves.

Of course, as they move towards school-leaving age and beyond, you will need to help them to make their own decisions on a range of subjects. Giving them the skills and confidence to do this wisely (and not judging them when they don't) will help them to become independent, self-reliant adults in the future.

ACTION PLAN FOR YOUR TEENAGER

1. Listen to your child and help them to discover what they want (and need) for themselves.
2. Help them start to take control of their own life.
3. Help to support their needs.

4. Ensure the action plan in place to support their DME is appropriate and effective.
5. Help them address any behavioural and other problems.
6. Help them to advocate for themselves, but advocate for them yourself when needed.
7. Help them to find like-minded peers.
8. Help them with their transition to their future choices.

CONCLUSION

This chapter has been a mammoth run-through of some of the concerns parents and carers sometimes have about their children with DME. However:

- You may have no concerns about your child or their DME. In which case, enjoy!
- You may have other concerns. The ones we have outlined are by no means the only ones raised by parents and carers. No book could hope to cover every single area for every individual child with DME.
- There is support out there for you and your child with DME (see the list of organisations provided in Chapter 8).

Whatever your situation, the age of your child or your circumstances, we hope that we have given you some practical support on at least one or two topics that concern you currently or you feel you are likely to face in the future.

As we shall see in the next chapter, it is vital for you to be able to stand up confidently for your child to secure the most effective learning for them within the most appropriate learning environment. By doing this you will help to ensure your child will be supported to be the best version of themselves they can be.

Exploring your role as a parent or carer is our next topic covered, in Chapter 5.

Want to know more? Further information can be found at www.jkp.com/catalogue/book/9781787758100

FURTHER READING AND RESOURCES
Support for specific challenges
The questioning child

Carol Bainbridge (2020) 'How to deal with gifted kids that ask many questions.' *Verywell Family*, 4 December: www.verywellfamily.com/dealing-with-never-ending-questions-1449272

Bright Horizons (no date) 'Answering children's toughest questions': www.brighthorizons.com/family-resources/answering-childrens-toughest-questions

Randall Monroe (2015) *What If? Serious Scientific Answers to Absurd Hypothetical Questions*. John Murray.

Miriam Stoppard (2016) *Questions Children Ask and How to Answer Them*. Vermilion.

The bossy child

Kimberly Abraham, Marney Studaker-Cordner and Kathryn O'Dea (2003) *The Whipped Parent: Hope for Parents Raising an Out-of-Control Teen*. Rainbow Books Incorporated.

Rex Forehand and Nicholas Long (2010) *Parenting the Strong-Willed Child: The Clinically Proven Five-Week Program for Parents of Two- to Six-Year-Olds*. McGraw-Hill Education; 3rd edition.

Robert Mackenzie (2013) *Setting Limits with Your Strong-Willed Child: Eliminating Conflict by Establishing Clear, Firm and Respectful Boundaries*. Three Rivers Press; 2nd edition.

Philippa Perry (2020) *The Book You Wish Your Parents Had Read (and Your Children Will Be Glad that You Did)*. Penguin Life.

The child who finds change difficult

Amanda Seyderhelm (2019) *Helping Children Cope with Loss and Change: A Guide for Professionals and Parents*. Routledge.

David Trickey (forthcoming) *Helping Your Child with Loss, Change and Trauma: A Self-Help Guide for Parents*. Robinson.

The angry child

Ross Greene (2014) *The Explosive Child: A New Approach for Understanding and Parenting Easily Frustrated, Chronically Inflexible Children*. Harper PB; 5th edition.

Eliane Whitehouse and Warwick Pudney (1998) *A Volcano in My Tummy: Helping Children to Handle Anger*. New Society Publishers; illustrated edition.

The intense, sensitive child

Susan Daniels and Michael Piechowski (eds) (2009) *Living with Intensity: Understanding the Sensitivity, Excitability, and the Emotional Development of Gifted Children, Adolescents, and Adults*. Great Potential Press Inc.; illustrated edition.

Mary Sheedy Kurcinka (2016) *Raising Your Spirited Child: A Guide for Parents Whose Child Is More Intense, Sensitive, Perceptive, Persistent and Energetic*. W.M. Morrow PB; 3rd edition.

The child who has problems sleeping

Richard Ferber (2013) *Solve Your Child's Sleep Problems*. Vermilion.

Stephanie Modell (2015) *The Baby Sleep Guide: Practical Advice to Establish Good Sleep Habits*. Vie.

The child who has problems with eating

American Speech-Language-Hearing Association, 'Feeding and swallowing disorders in children': www.asha.org/public/speech/swallowing/feeding-and-swallowing-disorders-in-children

Ciara Attwell (2018) *My Fussy Eater*. Lagom.

Gina Ford (2010) *Top Tips for Fussy Eaters*. Vermilion.

Gillian Harris and Elizabeth Shea (2018) *Food Refusal and Avoidant Eating Including Those with Autistic Spectrum Conditions: A Practical Guide for Parents and Professionals*. Jessica Kingsley Publishers.

Annabel Karmel (2007) *The Fussy Eaters' Recipe Book*. Ebury Press.

Annabel Karmel (2018) *Real Food Kids Will Love*. Bluebird.

NHS, 'Dysphagia (swallowing problems)': www.nhs.uk/conditions/swallowing-problems-dysphagia

Melanie Potock and Stacey Moore (2019) *You Are Not an Otter: The Story of How Kids Become Adventurous Eaters*. Independently published.

The anxious child

John Duffy (2019) *Parenting the New Teen in the Age of Anxiety: A Complete Guide to Your Child's Stressed, Depressed, Expanded, Amazing Adolescence*. Mango.

Diane Peters Meyers (2008) *Overcoming School Anxiety: How to Help Your Child with Separation, Tests, Homework, Bullies, Maths Phobia and Other Worries*. Amacom.

Dan Peters (2013) *Make Your Worrier a Warrior: A Guide to Conquering Your Child's Fears*. Great Potential Press Inc.; illustrated edition.

The child who seems to 'daydream'

David George (2011) *Young, Gifted and Bored*. Crown House Publishing.

The lonely child

Bernardo Carducci (2007) *Shyness: A Bold New Approach*. HarperCollins; reprint edition.

Tanith Carey (2019) *The Friendship Maze: How to Help Your Child Navigate Their Way to Positive and Happier Friendships*. Vie.

Liz Dawes, Nicola Gorringe, Katherine Hodson, Lucy Russell, Jennifer Swanston and Susan Wimshurst (2018) *Brighter Futures: A Parents' Guide to Raising Happy, Confident Children in the Primary School Years*. Free Association Books.

Rosalind Wiseman (2016) *Queen Bees and Wannabes: Helping Your Daughter Survive Cliques, Gossip, Boys and the New Realities of Girl World*. Harmony; 3rd edition.

The child who is a perfectionist

Jill Adelson and Hope Wilson (2021) *Letting Go of Perfect: Empower Children to Overcome Perfectionism*. Prufrock Press; 2nd edition.

The child who is obsessed

Per Hove Thomsen (1999) *From Thoughts to Obsessions: Obsessive Compulsive Disorder in Children and Adolescents*. Jessica Kingsley Publishers.

The child who struggles with writing

Nathan Brant (2014) *Dysgraphia: A Parent's Guide to Understanding Dysgraphia and Helping a Dysgraphic Child*. CreateSpace Independent Publishing Platform.

Diane Montgomery (2006) *Spelling, Handwriting and Dyslexia: Overcoming Barriers to Learning*. Taylor Francis Ltd.

Diane Montgomery (2018) *Report on Handwriting and Achievement*: www.potentialplusuk. org/wp-content/uploads/2018/01/Diane-Montgomery-Handwriting-Report.pdf

The child who is disorganised

Peg Dawson and Richard Guare (2008) *Smart but Scattered: The Revolutionary 'Executive Skills' Approach to Helping Kids Reach Their Potential*. Guilford Press.

Richard Guare, Peg Dawson and Colin Guare (2013) *Smart but Scattered Teens: The 'Executive Skills' Program for Helping Teens Reach Their Potential*. Guilford Press.

Brian Tracy (2013) *Eat That Frog: Get More of the Important Things Done Today*. Hodder Paperbacks.

The child who dislikes homework

Daniel Siegel and Tina Payne Bryson (2018) *The Yes Brain Child: Helping Your Child Be More Resilient, Independent and Creative*. Simon & Schuster UK.

On mindfulness and meditation for children and families

Christian Bergstrom (2019) *Ultimate Mindfulness Activity Book: 150 Playful Mindfulness Activities for Kids and Teens (and Grown-Ups Too!)*. Suomen ISBN Keskus; illustrated edition.

Cory Cochiolo (2020) *Bedtime Meditation for Kids: Quick, Calming Exercises to Help Kids Go to Sleep*. Rockridge Press.

Mindful, 'Mindfulness for kids': www.mindful.org/mindfulness-for-kids

Eline Snel (2014) *Sitting Still Like a Frog: Mindfulness Exercises for Kids (and Their Parents)*. Shambhala Publications Inc.

Rayna Zara (2020) *Meditation for Kids: 10 Guided Meditation Scripts for Kids*. Independently published.

Star charts and other resources for executive functioning

Charts 4 kids, free downloadable star charts for children: www.rewardcharts4kids.com

SuperStickers: www.superstickers.com

Support organisations in the UK to support individuals with BDD

Body Dysmorphic Disorder Foundation: https://bddfoundation.org

Support organisations in the UK to support individuals with eating disorders

Anorexia & Bulimia Care (ABC): www.anorexiabulimiacare.org.uk
Beat: www.beateatingdisorders.org.uk
National Centre for Eating Disorders: https://eating-disorders.org.uk

On hair pulling disorder (trichotillomania)

Lucinda Ellery™: www.lucindaellery-hairloss.co.uk/trich-treatments.php
Ruth Goldfinger Golomb and Sherrie Mansfield Vavrichek (2019) *The Hair Pulling 'Habit' and You: How to Solve the Trichotillomania Puzzle*. Independently published.
Douglas Woods and Michael Twohig (2008) *Trichotillomania: An ACT-Enhanced Behavior Therapy Approach Workbook (Treatments That Work)*. Oxford University Press.

Support relevant for parents and carers of children of different age groups
Children across the age groups (as appropriate)

Tony Buzan (2003) *Mind Maps for Kids: An Introduction*. Thorsons.
Tony Buzan (2005) *Mind Maps for Kids: Max Your Memory and Concentration*. Ted Smart.
Tony Buzan (2008) *Mind Maps for Kids: Rev Up for Revision*. Harper Thorsons.
J. Matthews (2020) *How to Write a 5-Paragraph Essay Step-by-Step*. Independently published.

Toddlers and pre-school children

Charlotte Dane (2020) *The Anxious Elephant: A Children's Book About Overthinking, Being Realistic and Managing Your Emotions*. Independently published.
Lara David-Odufuwa (2020) *Why Do We Have to Move?* KidzAspire.
Department for Education (2021) *Early Years Foundation Stage Profile: 2021 Handbook*. Available at: https://assets.publishing.service.gov.uk/government/uploads/system/uploads/attachment_data/file/942421/EYFSP_Handbook_2021.pdf
Aleks Harrison (2020) *I Feel Angry: Children's Picture Book About Anger Management*. Independently published.
Steve Herman (2019) *How a Unicorn Made Me Stop Worrying*. DG Books Publishing.
Steve Herman (2019) *Help Your Dragon Deal with Change*. DG Books Publishing.
Tim Hopgood (2020) *Cyril the Lonely Cloud*. Oxford University Press.
Stephanie O'Connor (2020) *The Lonely Spider*. Independently published.
Mark Pett and Gary Rubinstein (2012) *The Girl Who Never Made Mistakes*. Sourcebooks Jabberwocky; illustrated edition.
Barney Salzberg (2010) *Beautiful OOPS*. Workman Publishing; illustrated edition.

Primary school-age children

Ellen Flanagan Burns (2008) *Nobody's Perfect: A Story for Children About Perfectionism*. Magination Press; illustrated edition.
Elizabeth Cole (2020) *I Am Stronger Than Anger*. Independently published.

Patti Kelley Criswell (2013) *A Smart Girl's Guide: Friendship Troubles: Dealing with Fights, Being Left Out, and the Whole Popularity Thing.* American Girls Publishing Inc.; illustrated edition.

The HappySelf® Journal: Daily Journal for Kids. HappySelf Ltd.

Dawn Huebner (2005) *What to Do When You Worry Too Much: A Kid's Guide to Overcoming Anxiety.* Magination Press; illustrated edition.

Dawn Huebner (2007) *What to Do When Your Brain Gets Stuck: A Kid's Guide to Overcoming OCD (Obsessive Compulsive Disorder).* Magination Press; illustrated edition.

David Kim (2020) *A Kids Book about Change.* A Kids Book About (Kindle edition).

My Emotions Journal: Feelings and Journal for Kids and Teens. Independently published.

Daniel Peters, Lisa Reid and Stephanie Davis (2017) *The Warrior Workbook: A Guide for Conquering Your Worry Monster.* Gifted Unlimited, LLC; illustrated edition.

Merriam Sarcia Saunders (2019) *My Whirling, Twirling Motor.* Magination Press; illustrated edition.

Merriam Sarcia Saunders and Tammie Lyon (2020) *My Wandering, Dreaming Mind.* Magination Press; illustrated edition.

The School of Life (2018) *Big Ideas for Curious Minds: An Introduction to Philosophy.* The School of Life Press; illustrated edition.

Libby Scott and Rebecca Westcott (2019) *Can You See Me?* Scholastic.

Samantha Snowden (2018) *Anger Management Workbook for Kids: 50 Fun Activities to Help Children Stay Calm and Make Better Choices.* Althea Press.

Judith Woodburn (2016) *A Smart Girl's Guide: Worry: How to Feel Less Stressed and Have More Fun.* American Girls Publishing Inc.; illustrated edition.

For parents and carers of teenagers

Suzanne Franks and Tony Wolf (2020) *Get Out of My Life: The Bestselling Guide to the Twenty-First Century Teenager.* Profile Books; main edition.

Graham Ramsden (2019) *The Teenager in the Greenhouse: A Psychologist's Guide to Parenting Your Teenager.* John Catt Educational Ltd.

For teenagers

The 6-Minute Diary for More Mindfulness, Happiness and Productivity. UrBestSelf.[3]

Dean Burnett (2019) *Why Your Parents Are Driving You up the Wall and What to DO About It.* Penguin.

Michael Cooper (2020) *SAD. The Social Anxiety Disorder Solution: How to Overcome Shyness, Prevent Panic Attacks and Find Self-Confidence.* Independently published.

Andy Cope (2014) *The Art of Being a Brilliant Teenager.* Capstone.

Raychelle Cassada Lohmann (2019) *The Anger Workbook for Teens: Activities to Help You Deal with Anger and Frustration.* New Harbinger; 2nd edition, revised.

Nicola Morgan (2018) *Positively Teenage: A Positively Brilliant Guide to Teenage Well-Being.* Franklin Watts.

Nicola Morgan (2017) *The Teenage Guide to Friends.* Walker Books.

Lisa Rivero (2010) *The Smart Teens Guide to Living with Intensity: How to Get More Out of Life and Learning.* Great Potential Press Inc.

---

3   http://createurbestself.com

YOUR ACTION PLAN

1. Make a list of any concerns you have at present.
2. Talk to your child and, without making them worried, add their concerns to your list in a different colour (put a mark or asterisk next to anything where your child feels the same).
3. If you can remember, also make a list of those problems or concerns you have had in the past and how you dealt with them. This may help you to understand what went right (and what you learned).
4. Contact the relevant organisations suggested in this book for help if you feel able. Add to your list any other information you have found out about your child and their characteristics.
5. Remember to love your child, support them and speak up for them.

CHAPTER 5

I Know Parents and Carers Are Important, But What Can We Do?

INTRODUCTION

Your role as a parent or carer and the work you do to support your child with Dual or Multiple Exceptionality (DME) is critical to their wellbeing and happiness. Providing them with appropriate support will encourage your child to be the best version of themselves that they can be. This is especially important as you lay the foundations for your child's early years, and it is also important as they grow up and eventually leave home. However, parents and carers can also present problems for a child with DME. In this chapter we explore what we mean by this and the kinds of problems that may be encountered. We also offer some suggestions for how to overcome them. Running through this are the decisions that every family needs to make and how to go about them in the best possible way.

Finally, in all this support and decision-making, many parents and carers forget about the importance of looking after themselves. We look at why you need to do this and outline some suggestions for where you can find support so that you realise that you are not on your own.

THE IMPORTANCE OF PARENTS AND CARERS

Just like with every child with DME, each parent, carer and family is unique, with their own ways of doing things. What works for one family may fail with another, and vice versa. However, across the world, researchers agree that parents (and carers) are important, and where families work well, they can have a positive impact on every aspect of a child's learning and behaviour at home, at school and elsewhere.

In their *Review of Best Practice in Parental Engagement*, Goodall and Vorhaus quote Desforges (2003), who said:

> Parental involvement in the form of 'at home good parenting' has a significant positive effect on children's achievement and adjustment, even after all other factors shaping their attainment have been taken out of the equation. In the primary age range the impact caused by different levels of parental involvement is much bigger than differences associated with variations in the quality of schools. The scale of the impact is evident across all social classes and ethnic groups. (Desforges 2003, quoted in Goodall and Vorhaus 2011, p.2)

In other words, parents and carers matter. Research has shown time and time again that family support, interest, involvement and engagement have an impact on lots of things, such as a child or young person's positive feelings about themselves, their self-confidence and self-belief, attendance at school, achievement levels, relationships with others and their ability to make friends.

While it is sometimes more difficult for parents and carers to see the impact that they can have on the life of their child with DME, research in 2020 (funded by The Potential Trust) showed the important place that children and young people specifically with DME hold family in making their lives a more positive experience.

> My family loves me just the way I am. That's important to me. (Child with DME)

> I value my family supporting me and ensuring I can make the most of my superpowers. (Child with DME)

In Chapter 6 we will touch on the kinds of things you can do to help support your child in school. What about an action plan for your life at home and how *you* personally help to nurture your child? Here are some things you might want to consider in supporting your child with DME at home. You will need to decide which apply to you or which are not relevant at present.

Behave positively

> Be the best you can be – model and show the behaviour you want your child to copy. (Parent)

Behaviour is a form of communication between you and your child, and vice versa, so treat it as such. What are you trying to say through *your* behaviour? That you're angry with them? Tell them why, and don't shout at them. Upset at something they've done? Why? What are you trying to say?

This doesn't mean that your behaviour must be perfect. If you are angry, show your child how you deal positively with anger; if you are sad, it's okay to show your child how you deal with sadness; if you make a mistake, demonstrate how you cope with setbacks or even failure. But if you can't cope with an emotion, walk away. Take time out to recover or practise any of the behaviour management techniques you may have taught your child, such as counting down slowly from 10, or slowly breathing in and out for a minute or two.

Being positive is important in nurturing your child, so try and be more positive than negative with and about them. Celebrate the progress they make in an area of concern. No matter how small, their effort may be huge. Use more positive language – 'do this' and 'do that' rather than 'don't do this' and 'don't do that'. How many times have you said to your child 'don't do that' for them to go right ahead and do it anyway!

Central to your behaviour is treating your child with respect. If you treat them with respect and talk about them as if they are already the best version of themselves that they can be (even when the going may seem tough), there is a higher chance of them being that child.

> I am a teacher as well as a parent. I remember that I used to tell off one particular child who I felt was noisy in class all the time. I think I used to call them 'the noisy one' and soon so did their classmates. One day, the class was being particularly loud and I shouted at this child, something like 'Why is it that you are always the noisy one in class?' Then I realised, this child hadn't been in school that day. (Parent)

Give your child the time to be with you. What are you saying to your child if they can't even have 5 minutes of your undivided attention each day? We recognise this is easier said than done – we all lead busy lives. Many parents and carers work part- or full-time (or may have more than one job as well as their role at home) so they are able to house, feed and clothe their family. Some have other children to look after who may have needs that are greater than the needs of the child with DME. Still others are part of families where parents are separated and where one parent spends one day a fortnight or less with their child with DME.

> I think it is important to try and give your child the gift of time. I found that difficult when my children were younger, and I still feel guilty about that. I would come home from work exhausted and my partner would spend time with our child including reading with them before bed. After all these years, I wonder if I could have done anything different. So, if I had one thing to pass on to other parents just starting out, it would be that you may be busy in your life now, but you will never get back again those precious moments you can have with your child. (Parent)

Adapt the activity to fit the time you can spend with your child with DME (and how you can do it). Look at imaginative ways in which you can communicate with them. A regular phone call or a project you work on together or 5 minutes of your undivided attention listening to them before they go to sleep can communicate to your child that you have made the effort and that they are important. That said, you should not feel guilty about what you can't do. Instead, celebrate what you *can* do and work with your child with DME to come up with imaginative ways to do it!

Finally, it is important that you don't shy away from any tough stuff you may have to deal with but tackle it with your child with DME – and others – as soon as possible. Be assertive and give your child a clear and age-appropriate framework they can work within (no wriggle room for either of you!), and make sure you stick to it (especially if your child has a strong sense of justice and fairness).

Many of the organisations highlighted in Chapter 8 offer training for parents and carers of children with DME. If you need something more general, positive parenting information is provided by organisations such as

NSPCC Learning,[1] Childcare UK[2] and Family Lives.[3] Although these organisations are not specialists in DME, they may help you to adapt information and advice accordingly.

Advocate confidently

One of the most important roles you may have is speaking up for your child with others, whether they are family, friends or teachers. Make sure they see your child's strengths. As your child becomes more independent, they will need to speak up for themselves, so you should also consider slowly teaching them how to self-advocate so that they can put their own point of view across with confidence.

Many children with DME have no problem speaking out. In fact, this is what sometimes gets them into trouble – for interrupting when someone is talking or telling a teacher a piece of information they have given the class is incorrect, or even shouting out the answer impulsively.

> When my child was about eight years old, the class was learning about the Tudors. The lesson was about Mary Queen of Scots, but the teacher was talking about Mary, Queen of England. She described the wrong person. My child with DME had been taught to speak up for themselves respectfully. However, my child was still told they were wrong and got in trouble! The teacher apologised to them the next day. My child was right! (Parent)

Start to help your child to speak up for themselves appropriately from an early age by doing things like:

- Talking about a topic in the news and encouraging everyone to give their opinions about it (be careful which topic you choose, though – some children with DME may become upset about certain current affairs)
- Showing your child what good communication skills should look like when *you* talk to others and want to put over your point of view (such as not interrupting, being respectful, listening, etc.)

---

1   https://learning.nspcc.org.uk/research-resources/leaflets/positive-parenting
2   www.childcare.co.uk/information/parenting-guides
3   www.familylives.org.uk/how-we-can-help/online-parenting-courses

- Showing your child what these skills do *not* look like. This could include acting out different situations and then asking your child how they felt. You could interrupt your child or blurt things out, and then afterwards explore how your child felt. Your child may then be able to work with you on devising an approach that works for them (and other people!).

Be careful comparing your child with DME to any other children you may have, their friends or indeed to other children you know. Even if you are doing this without realising, your comparisons can be particularly hurtful to a child with DME, and help lay the foundations for sibling rivalry, inferiority complexes and much more.

Every child is unique. Instead of comparing them to their siblings (for example), consider comparing any progress to itself. Alternatively, you could say something such as: 'Both of my children have strengths. Child A is passionate about X and has strengths in Y, while Child B is passionate about L and has strengths in M' (fill in the letters for yourself!). If you find yourself comparing your child with DME to others (especially their siblings), stop and try this approach, and see if it works for you.

Communicate sensitively

We have spoken several times about the importance of listening to your child and what they are saying as well as helping them to say what they think and to do this respectfully. However, not everything is a two-way conversation with your child. Sometimes they may just want to 'offload' their day or their worries or successes. Knowing when to be quiet is as important a skill for parents and carers to have as knowing when to talk.

Spending some time each day just listening to your child if they want to 'offload' can help some children and young people with DME to structure their thoughts and their concerns, and to verbalise any worries. This can be particularly useful for teenagers with DME who are often intense, who overthink, and who want someone to listen when their mind is going into overdrive.

However, choose your moment to do this. Many parents and carers have reported grilling their child as soon as they leave the school gates with a barrage of questions about their day. The resulting silence then causes them to worry that their child isn't talking to them! Some children prefer to talk later, when they have had time to relax. Others may prefer to talk when they are just about to go to bed (which may not help their overthinking and sleeplessness, so work out a method for stopping both of these).

If you drive them to school, children sometimes prefer to talk to the back of your seat about issues as it is easier and less personal for them. Parents and carers have reported driving for miles, as their child is comfortable with talking in this way. Similarly, other children prefer talking when doing other activities with a parent or carer, such as shopping or walking. Experiment with different approaches that work for you and for your family.

Listening can be a hard skill to learn for some of us (as I know!). As soon as we hear a problem, we wade in with our size 5 boots and try to solve it for our child. Instead, consider holding back, even if the silence drags on. A child with DME who has lots of thoughts going round in their head or intense emotions they need to explain or process, or for a variety of other reasons, may need time to think before they can talk.

Problem-solve wisely

Linked with the listening skills you require, you also need to be able to help your child with DME to find a way to solve problems that works for them. This needs to be done carefully so that your child can find their own solution rather than just being given answers. This will help them to learn the skills of effective problem-solving, as well as helping improve their resilience as they realise they have solved the problem themselves.

Strategies to evaluate how to problem-solve are helpful and can be done in different ways depending on your child's age. For example, when they are younger, you may not use the formal name of a particular technique but play games, or better still, do real-life activities that teach things like critical skills and creative thinking skills. As your child grows older, if they have not learned different problem-solving techniques at school or elsewhere, you could give them a book to read or teach them some of the techniques mentioned here or any other approaches you have found useful. Help to teach them these critical and creative problem-solving skills to cope with life's challenges.

■ Tips and hints: A few problem-solving techniques

Socratic questioning: This form of questioning can help your child get to the bottom of a problem. It is about using open questions, such as 'Why did you say that?' 'What would be the alternative?' 'What is another way of looking at it?' 'What does this mean?' Ask questions until the problem has been identified or even solved.

Critical thinking: This is all about identifying the problem, analysing it and evaluating it to come up with the most appropriate option(s) at the time. Most of us think like this all the time – 'Should we take this job or that one?' 'What should we have for dinner?' – and dozens of other decisions – large and small – every day. Giving your child the skills to evaluate critically will help a child with DME who overthinks everything and may hesitate in making any kind of decision. They could make a list of the reasons why they should do something, giving each a score out of, say, 10 about how important each individual topic is for them. Then do the same for the reasons why they shouldn't do something. Add the two scores up separately, the option with the highest score being the one they choose.

Creative thinking: This is a way of identifying new ideas and solutions to a problem. Thinking of unique ways of coming at a problem from another angle uses your child's brain to identify solutions you may not yet have thought of. Lateral thinking puzzles that don't seem solvable at first glance are popular, but with a little creativity, they are great for families to discuss and to solve. Have a look at something like *Lateral Thinking Puzzles* by Paul Sloane. He also produces a range of other publications on creative thinking.

Dilemmas: Exploring dilemmas with your child can help to improve a range of skills, including critical thinking skills. The Philosophy Man[4] has some free resources for children and young people of different ages that are worth exploring. Although they are normally provided for teachers to use with their class, look at them for ideas or sign up for the resources – for example, playing 'Would You Rather...?' (...be a

---

4   www.thephilosophyman.com

carrot than a potato?) and then exploring why is a fun way to stretch the thinking skills of younger children, or for older children, having to make decisions about hypothetical scenarios (e.g., astronauts stuck in space with limited food and having to prioritise who stays). Obviously, if your child is sensitive and intense, be careful with the topics explored in your dilemmas!

Analysing, evaluating and creating are all important skills to have in school (and in life), and are what are called 'higher order thinking skills' (or HOTS). These are based on how a child learns. For example, a child may start with remembering something (such as how to spell a word) even if they don't understand it. They then understand it, after which they can apply their knowledge. When they gain more skills, they can analyse what they have learned and evaluate it. Finally, they can create something totally different through what they have learned. Learning HOTS is important for all children, but essential for children with DME (and High Learning Potential, HLP), because of the skills it gives them to think on a higher level.[5]

Helping your child to see the whole picture – the pros and cons of every decision to be made or problem to solve – before they decide what to do about it is a useful skill for parents and carers to pass on. It is also important to give your child the skills they need to contain any overthinking, anxiety and worry, which is easier said than done, especially if their anxiety is your greatest source of anxiety.

Tackling your own anxiety positively

In Chapter 4 we looked at ways to support your child with DME who is anxious. How do you control your own anxiety? As an adult, you may already have identified what makes you anxious. You may already know how you can help to reduce your worries (and you may even have applied your ideas about what works to your own child). If not, think about:

- Whether you have always been an anxious, intense, overthinking

---

5   Potential Plus UK has produced a School Advice Sheet on higher order thinking skills. This advice sheet is free for members, while there is a small charge for non-members: https://potentialplusuk.org/index.php/product/s306-higher-order-thinking-skills

person. If so, what can you do to reduce those feelings? You don't want your child to pick up on this anxiety – your feelings could bounce off each other, like a mirror reflecting each other's emotions back and forth. How can both you and your child calm down together? Could you practise meditation techniques together each morning or evening?

- Whether your anxiety is caused by specific things going on in your life. According to the results of a study of the stress levels of 4619 respondents in 2018 by the Mental Health Foundation (summarised on their website),[6] the top causes of stress were:
  - Long-term health conditions (either an individual's own or a friend's or relative's): 36% of all adults in the study who reported stress in their life said this was a factor
  - Debt: 22% of those who reported high levels of stress said that financial difficulties were a cause of their stress
  - Expectations placed on them: 12% said they were stressed because of feeling that they needed to respond to messages instantly (e.g., for work)
  - Comparing themselves to others: 36% of women related their stress to how comfortable they were with their appearance and body image
  - Housing worries: 32% of 18- to 24-year-olds and 22% of 45- to 54-year-olds mentioned worries about housing as a key source of stress
  - The pressure to succeed: 60% of 18- to 24-year-olds, 41% of 25- to 34-year-olds and 17% of 45- to 54-year-olds reported higher stress levels due to the pressure to succeed.

Is this where your anxiety lies? For some of these (like debt and housing) you may want to consider going to talk to an organisation like Citizens Advice[7] or their equivalent. Citizens Advice provides free, confidential advice in all four countries of the UK. Alternatively, talk your problems through with someone you trust and explore with them the options open to you to solve your concerns.

---

6   www.mentalhealth.org.uk/statistics/mental-health-statistics-stress
7   www.citizensadvice.org.uk

If any more personal reasons are causing you stress or are affecting your mental health, talking to your doctor may help you to obtain the information or advice you need. This could include a referral to an organisation or specialist for further support.

Many parents and carers of children with DME report high levels of stress or anxiety relating to their child. They may be worried about how to nurture and develop their child effectively, either before their child has been identified with DME (when parents and carers may not understand what is happening to their child) or when they need to convince their child's school to support both their HLP as well as their Special Educational Needs and Disabilities (SEND).

Organisations that understand about DME should be able to give parents and carers the support they need for themselves and their child, and they can put parents and carers in touch with other families who have faced similar challenges and who may have the same concerns.

Encourage successfully

We have already spoken about the importance of treating your child as if they already were the best version of themselves. Although there is a danger that you will be ambitious for them, keep your expectations realistic. While the bar may be high, try to ensure that it is always within their reach. Be honest with your child about any failures and celebrate the effort of success.

> From a young age, I taught my child with DME to 'always have a Plan B'. This was an alternative solution for when things didn't go according to plan. Whenever they planned on doing anything I would say 'What's your Plan B?' For example, if they had planned to go out with friends, I'd say something like 'What's your Plan B if it gets cancelled?' It came into good use when my child didn't do well in their exams when they were 16 years old. They found out they couldn't take English Literature any further, as they had hoped. Without thinking I said, 'What's your Plan B?' Instead of a meltdown, my child developed an action plan for what they would do next. Job done! (Parent)

As far as you are able, try and notice the positive things your child does and thank them whenever you see them done, however small they are.

It is often natural to try and correct the mistakes they make or their negative behaviour, and we can easily forget to praise what is positive about our child – the acts of kindness they show or the behaviour of which we approve. At its most extreme, if we only engage with our child to tell them off for doing something and never notice what is positive about them, some children and young people may deliberately engage in activities that force their parents or carers to notice them (even if it is for the wrong reasons!).

Many years ago, a challenge was set for parent and carer members of Potential Plus UK who were asked to spend a week noticing and thanking their child for the positive things they did and ignoring the negatives. Could you do a similar challenge?

Develop them effectively

In Chapter 1 we spoke about a growth mindset and what it means. Could you put in place a growth mindset for yourself as well as for your child with DME? This could include things like using any mistakes you make as learning opportunities, praising your own effort, not just your achievement, and giving specific and realistic praise to yourself and not 'over the top' praise that no one (especially you!) believes.

It is also important for your child and for you (and other family members) to find their passion. None of you may know what it is immediately, and you may need to search for it. Help your child – and yourself – to find their passion in life. But remember that your child with DME's passion may not be the same as yours. Their passion will be whatever makes them happy, fulfilled and more content, whatever that looks like for them. Your passion should be this as well. Your child's life is their own, so don't map it out for them. Following their passion may lead to a life vastly different from the one you had thought they would have. Accept this and help them follow their dream.

I always assumed that my child with DME would go to university. I never spoke about any other options with them, or what they wanted. I was shocked and even a bit upset if I'm honest when they said they didn't want to go. They chose their own path and seem to be happy with the path they chose. It was me who had to adjust my thinking in the end. (Parent)

In helping them to look at options for the future (whatever age they are), encourage your child to understand their strengths and any challenges they face. Build on the first and support the second.

THE PROBLEM WITH PARENTS AND CARERS

We all have our own strengths and challenges, and we also come with our own history – our 'baggage', if you like – which can help shape the relationships we have. There will be many of these for each parent and carer, and here are just a few examples:

- Our own childhood experiences growing up, and how these shape how we raise our own children.
- Our relationships – now and in the past – with individual family members – and how these support (or otherwise) our child's relationships with them.
- How we came to parent or care for our child, and how this impacts on our relationship with our child.
- Our own experiences of school and how these affect how we approach our child's own schooling.

Let's explore how parents and carers honestly view their past experiences and what this can mean for their relationship with their own child and how they bring them up:

> I was brought up in a family where education and hard work was important as a way of getting on in life. This approach worked for me; I enjoyed school, got into a good university and had a good career. I honestly found it difficult that my child didn't want all of this. It took me a long time to see that their path might be different and that this doesn't mean it is any less important. (Parent of a child with DME)

> I left school as soon as I could, I couldn't wait to get out of the door. I've worked hard all my life and I'm not sure how I feel about my child doing anything different. For a start, university is so expensive. I wouldn't want them to be saddled with debt before they even get a job. (Parent)

> I went straight from college into university and after that I got a job. When my child is old enough, I would love them to have a year out and to do some travelling. I wish I'd had the courage to do that at their age. (Parent)

> If I'm honest, I hated school. I can hardly bring myself to even go in the place without breaking into a cold sweat. I would never go in the building if I didn't have to. (Parent)

While there is nothing you can do to change the past, you need to have a good understanding about who you are and why you might act in the way you do, ideally before you have or care for a child. Some of this may be positive and you might want to use what you have learned to help shape your experiences with your own child. However, some of your experiences may not be so good, in which case you may benefit from support so that you don't face these feelings alone. This could involve talking to people you trust about your concerns or seeking professional advice or counselling to help you deal with your thoughts and feelings and the impact these may have on your life and that of your child's.

When we turn our attention to children with DME, one of the most common realisations for parents and carers is that they may also have DME, and that this might have shaped their experiences or what has happened to them in the past. This can lead to both positive and negative reactions. On the positive side, finding out that they have DME or HLP or SEND, all of which were previously hidden, can be like finding a missing piece of the jigsaw – everything finally falls into place. They may have had the same characteristics as their child with DME but these hadn't been identified before. Their abilities and strengths may have been masked by their SEND (or vice versa) and they may have gone through life never quite being understood or failing to understand why they couldn't achieve higher grades or even 'fit in'. Identifying that they may have DME or even putting a name to their hidden HLP or SEND can be a release that puts everything else into context.

> I felt a failure at school. In my head I thought I was bright, but when I tried to organise what I thought, the words wouldn't seem to go down in the right order. It took me a long time to read anything or write anything down. Nobody mentioned anything to me, and I struggled with my work and my exams. I never felt I achieved what I could have. Years later, I took my child for an assessment. When I was getting feedback, the penny dropped. I had the same issues they did. I got an assessment for myself. It's such a relief to know that I was clever all along and had a disability. (Parent)

Sometimes a parent or carer identifying they have DME can be a negative experience. It might expose memories – sometimes buried – and past experiences in school or at home they would rather not remember. They might feel resentment that their DME hadn't been identified in the past, or that they had been punished in some way for being 'lazy', or even 'stupid'. They may begrudge the fact that their past experiences or resulting lack of self-confidence meant that they took lower-paid or unskilled jobs or developed a 'chip on their shoulder' or mental health difficulties as a result. So, while discovering a reason for their past experiences may be positive, the emotional impact of it may still be quite negative.

> I was called a 'dunce' or worse at school and couldn't wait to get out. I went from job to job, all low-paid and dead-end. When my child was assessed I realised that the very issue I was concerned about with them was the same as the one I'd had when I was a child. I had my own

> assessment which showed I was bright but with a disability. I feel so angry and really do believe that my life would have been so different if someone had identified my needs. All those wasted years. (Parent)

Parents and carers don't often bring up children in isolation. Even if they are lone parents by choice or otherwise, many have partners and are part of families. What is a 'normal' family? It is what is 'normal' for that family and the list is endless: lone parents, two parents of different genders, two parents of the same gender, adopted parents, foster carers, stepparents, grandparents, or a vast number of different combinations of parents and carers. Added to this are all the different relatives there could be within the wider family, many of whom may have different views about how a child with DME should behave and how they should be raised. So, as well as getting to grips with your own feelings, beliefs and views, you may have a whole host of other people – each with their own feelings, beliefs and views – to talk to, involve or help to understand the best way to bring up your child with DME. Their understanding and (ideally) support are important for many reasons, including that it will help:

- To reduce the number of potential differences between you in how to bring up your child with DME
- To minimise any arguments that may result from your child's behaviour
- To see and celebrate your child for who they are and not what they want them to be
- To reduce any comparisons between your child and other children.

Different families have different ways of communicating with each other, and you may have different ways of putting across the DME message to them. Starting with simple explanations may be the best way, either by drawing out the DME diagram shown in Chapter 3, or by drawing a 'bell curve' (see the one outlined below) and explaining what that means. Then you can answer any questions that may arise, such as those included below. We have added some suggested answers, but you could put these into your own words or create your own individual list of topics related to your child.

■ Tips and hints: Explaining your child's DME, example questions and suggested answers

Some suggested questions others might have about DME (after you have explained what DME is)	Some suggested answers to their questions (but you may come up with your own based on your own child with DME)
Is DME a recognised SEND?	No. It is not yet recognised as a SEND in its own right, at least not in the UK (although it is recognised by Government as an area of concern). However, my child has both gifts and talents *and* a SEND, which is [name the SEND that has been identified, if it has]
How do we treat your child?	Like any other child. However, we need to recognise that my child has strengths that need nurturing and they have certain challenges that need to be supported
What are your child's strengths?	At the moment, these are [outline or list them; we have provided examples, but outline your own]. They: • Are really good at maths • Like to be challenged with crosswords or anagrams • Know a lot of words • Read a lot of books • Enjoy playing with jigsaws on their own.
What are your child's challenges?	[Outline or list your child's challenges] For our child, at the moment this means they: • Get overwhelmed in crowds • Can't stand loud noises • Need quiet space when they feel anxious • Like structure to their day • Only like a limited number of foods [list foods] • Can seem to behave badly [describe how and when].
What should we do if your child does something wrong?	Our child is extremely sensitive and will have a meltdown if you shout at them. We find the following works well [list what you do that works, such as]: • Saying 'time out' and giving them a quiet space to go to and cool down • Asking them to clear up any mess they make or to apologise (when they are calm) • After they have calmed down, asking them what happened and how they can stop it happening in the future • Letting me know what happened before the incident, during what went on and afterwards. Our child earns time on the computer for good behaviour, so let me know how much time they spent behaving well with you

cont.

Some suggested questions others might have about DME (after you have explained what DME is)	Some suggested answers to their questions (but you may come up with your own based on your own child with DME)
Your child seems to be much further behind than their sibling?	I love both my children. They both have a unique set of strengths and things that they struggle with. I don't compare them, and I hope you won't either
What will your child's future be like?	With love and appropriate understanding and support from their family and friends and from their learning environment, there is no reason why they can't grow up to be a happy, contented adult who is the best version of themselves they can be

THE BELL CURVE

The bell curve is used in maths to look at the distribution of a set of figures. It is also known as 'normal distribution'. It was first used in 1994 by psychologist Richard Herrnstein and political scientist Charles Murray in *The Bell Curve: Intelligence and Class Structure in American Life*. This book was seen as controversial by some people. Even though it's not perfect, the bell curve itself is a useful diagram to explain the concept of DME.

When IQ scores are plotted on a graph, they typically follow a bell-shaped curve. The peak of the 'bell' occurs where the majority of the scores lie. The bell then slopes down to each side; one side represents lower than average scores and the other side represents scores that are above average.

To illustrate DME, a child with HLP (gifts and talents) might be on the right-hand side. Traditionally, to be identified as 'Gifted', they would fall in the top 2% of the population or with an IQ of 130+. If a SEND affects their cognitive functioning, this might mean that their IQ moves down the bell curve towards the centre, which is average. Therefore, a child who has DME may be in both the central band *and* the band on the right, which can make identifying them as having DME more difficult. These children are said to have a 'spiky profile' when plotting the results of any assessment test.

Getting the relationships right with all those involved in your child's life can be a challenge for any parent and carer in bringing up their child with DME. It can be further complicated by the behaviour (which is itself shaped – in part at least – by their own experiences) of any of the adults involved and the behaviour of the child with DME, shaped by the child's individual personality and behaviour.

Where a parent's and carer's (or other individuals involved in the child's life) behaviour and personality is the same or similar to those of their child, they both understand each other and know how they will behave and what to expect, even when there are problems. For example, a child who has a meltdown about somebody shouting at them unfairly may be upset about it and want to take themselves off to their room and be on their own. They don't want to talk about it or analyse it; they want to get lost in a book and calm down. A parent or carer may understand exactly what is going on – they may even feel the same way themselves – and know how their child will behave and what they need. However, another person – perhaps a partner or other relative – may think and feel totally differently. They may go into the child's room and want to talk about what has happened. They may even 'demand' to know why it happened in the first place or to point out what the child has done wrong. The child feels threatened. They don't understand why someone is 'invading' their space like this. The result is another argument, the child has another meltdown, and everything collapses into chaos.

The differences and similarities in behaviour and personality are summarised in Figure 5.1. Which box would you sit in? What about other family members or even your child's teacher?

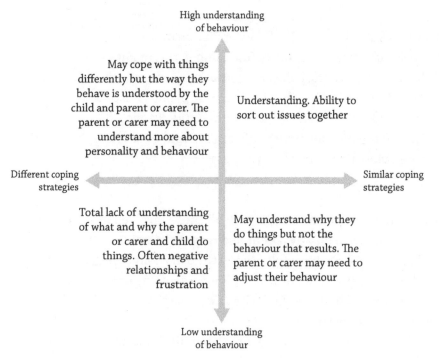

Figure 5.1. The behaviour matrix

We could not hope to list all of the ways in which you and your child might 'get' each other, or the ways in which you differ or clash. Make a list of these for yourself when you observe them.

◼ Tips and hints: You and your child, how are you the same and how do you differ?

Make a list of ways in which your child's personality and behaviour is different from yours (allowing for age).

Include in the list how you handle situations. What is good about this, what is not so good and what are you not sure about? Ask your child, if you feel able. Make your own suggestions about what needs to change in a situation you previously dealt with and how you could have improved the way you handled it.

If your child is old enough you could try problem-solving after an argument when things have calmed down again. This analysis and understanding will enable you to help each other handle situations like this in a better way in future.

> I work full-time and I'm usually still pretty wound up with what's happened at work that day and how to solve the problems I've had. All I want to do when I get home is have a cup of tea and read the paper. I just need some peace before I'm ready to wind down for the evening. Yet, every night I come in through the door and my child rushes up to me to play. Or I walk into the middle of an argument or a fight. Every night I find myself shouting at them or my other child or even my partner. (Parent)

This situation is not unique and can sometimes happen when a parent or carer moves quickly from one environment to another without time to 'switch gear'. Identifying the trigger points and developing a successful strategy to address them will enable the child to see the absolute best version of their parent or carer when they walk through the door.

If this is the kind of situation you recognise, would it help to give yourself space to change environments? Could you sit in your car, wind down and read the newspaper before going into the house? Could you go to the gym or grab a cup of tea in a local cafe to relax for a short while? If something like this isn't possible, could you arrange for your child to do some quiet(ish!) activities in which you can participate when you walk through the door?

With a child with DME who may be so excited about seeing you, perhaps you could tell them to put on their shoes when you come home so that they can get rid of some of that excess emotion by playing in the garden or in the park or going out with you for a jog? These activities may also help you shift from one environment to another and to relax. Thinking creatively to solve problems such as this can help to show you that there are solutions to many of the problems you may face.

In general, it is up to you to amend your own behaviour. The point is not that we change who we are and how we behave, but as the adult it is our responsibility to make these changes and not our child's. We are the ones who need to adapt and problem-solve any clashes between our own behaviour or personality and those of our child's.

When you have a child who is always on the go mentally, sharing their care with other family members or with friends to give you a break and to recharge your batteries is good for everyone. This may mean your child going to different people to fulfil different needs. This teamworking is fine, as long as it is open and honest (without disclosing any non-relevant confidentiality) and there is no resentment between different people for the different relationships experienced by your child.

> Every Friday from when I was 4 to 15 years old, I spent the weekend with my relatives to give my parents a break and to enable them to focus on their other children. I did lots of things – go to the theatre and the ballet and activities I wouldn't have otherwise done. My parents never said anything, but I wonder how they felt given that they couldn't afford to do these things with me themselves. (Adult who was a child with DME)

If Person A spends time reading with your child and Person B cooks with them and Person C takes them to the park, you need to make sure that they are all happy doing this (and ideally have volunteered for it!) and not wish they were doing something else. In addition, if your child says something to Person B, Person B should not tell anyone else (unless it would put your child at risk, in which case they should tell you), as this may lead to relationship difficulties. Getting the ground rules right for support like this is extremely important from the outset in case there are any problems in the future or growing resentment by one individual or another about the arrangements.

While there can be lots of personality and behaviour-related problems or situations that could impact on your relationship with your child, here are a few that parents and carers with children with DME specifically mention. And don't forget – we have provided a list of organisations that can provide you with specific support to address these and any other challenges you face related to DME and HLP within your family.

BUILDING ON YOUR PERFECTIONISM POSITIVELY

Expecting everything to be perfect and 'closing down', having a tantrum or meltdown if it is not, is a common trait for children and young people with both DME and HLP. Encourage your child to develop a growth mindset, which includes seeing mistakes as learning opportunities and a way to improve what they do, giving specific praise and not praise that is unrealistic and praising for effort, not achievement. But as this chapter is actually about *you*, how do *you* cope with perfectionism? You might not have any concerns about your child's perfectionism. Your first reaction may be to say it doesn't matter. You may be a perfectionist yourself. Perfectionism is not a bad thing in itself. What can be a problem is the way you respond to striving for perfection for yourself and for your own child. Given that many parents and carers of children with DME and HLP say they are perfectionists, let's look at some of its downsides:

- It can lead to something called 'imposter syndrome', where you feel like an imposter for getting that fantastic job, receiving that amazing award or being praised for something you have achieved. You feel as if you have gained these under false pretences. Do you want your child to grow up similarly?
- It can cause you potentially unwarranted stress and anxiety when tasks don't go according to plan.
- It can cause you to push your child to get the best grades, work that bit harder, do all those activities (even if they don't want to do them) as you believe they will 'reach perfection'. Ask yourself honestly – do you want your child to push themselves as far as they want to go or as far as you think they should go?
- It can mean that you (and your child) fail to take risks or act 'out of the box'. This is because if you do accept a challenge, go that bit further or try something new, you may make mistakes or come last, or even fail altogether. This may be something you find difficult to do if you need to be perfect. But always avoiding any kind of challenge may hold you back in life, from applying for that job or putting yourself forward for that promotion. It may also mean that this is the kind of behaviour you model to your child.

Why not learn to challenge yourself every now and then with something where you are not sure you will be perfect? Better still, do something together with your child or as a family and see how it feels!

WHEN IS GOOD ENOUGH, ENOUGH?

Many people are perfectionists. You may want the best for your child, and think that your child's best is getting the highest grades in their exams or top marks in their tests, even when you know your child has DME and may struggle with achieving this. You still push them to achieve and to get those grades, receive those awards or hand in the best assignments. The problem is, sometimes this may not be what your child wants. They may not be interested in the subject or motivated by the same things as you. They may even be struggling more than you know. So what do you do? And more importantly, when is good enough, enough?

First, take a deep breath – you are in it for the long haul.

Adjust your timeline. Perhaps your aim should be to support your child to become a confident, capable adult who is able to look after themselves in the world. Perhaps your role is to help them become the best version of themselves they can be.

Does it matter if they get a lower grade in their SATs exam? What about their GCSEs? Their A-levels? As a bottom line, it's up to them.

Some people think of life as a ladder. We achieve something on one rung and use it to go up to the next. In the real world, though, it's more like a spider's web than a ladder. If the centre is our goal, we may go up towards the centre of the web but then spiral back and find a new path – a new set of experiences, interests or passions – and use that to get to the centre.

By adopting a similar approach (both in your own life and your child's life), there is no such thing as absolute failure; just a redirection to achieve new goals. It may even bring its own rewards in attributes such as patience, resilience and determination.

I struggled with my child at school. They were 'written off' by the second year at primary school, even though I felt they had a remarkable creative talent. Secondary school was a nightmare for my child, even when their special educational needs and disability were recognised. GCSEs were a battleground; my child was just not interested in revising. They thought they could 'wing it', so their low grades came as a shock, especially to my child. It meant they couldn't do the A-level subject they had chosen, which disappointed them.

At A-level, my child couldn't find the right fit between their practical skills and intellectual ability. However, my child persevered and, even though their grades were lower, went to university to study a subject they loved. The fact that my child finished with a First, in a course that also tested their written ability (the thing they had struggled with at school), just shows what happens when the 'fit' is right and a child follows their passion. (Parent)

BUILDING ON THE POSITIVES OF *YOUR* INTROVERSION OR EXTROVERSION

Many parents and carers of children with DME identify with being introverts or shy. For a child with DME – particularly one who is also intense or hypersensitive or overthinks everything – being an introvert can be extremely difficult. The same can be true for their parents or carers.

There seems to be a great deal of misunderstanding about what being an introvert means. Are they shy? Do they just not want to be with people? Or don't they like them? Added complications arise as the world is often based on the extrovert, people who are seen as outgoing, sociable, expressive, communicative. The introvert is seen as the opposite – more reserved and quieter. Given that all our institutions – school, college, university, work – are often based on the extrovert, introverts can often feel as if they disappear in the classroom, that they fail to have their skills and abilities recognised, are overlooked for jobs or promotion and are generally seen to be unhappy. In an article by Kaufman in *Beautiful Minds* in 2018, the personality neuroscientist Colin de Young put forward the following:

> People who score low in extraversion are not necessarily turned inward; rather, they are less engaged, motivated, and energised by the possibilities for reward that surround them. Hence, they talk less, are less driven, and experience less enthusiasm. They may also find levels of stimulation that are rewarding and energising for someone high in extraversion merely annoying or tiring (or even overwhelming, depending on their level of Neuroticism). (cited in Kaufman 2018)

In other words, they are no better or worse than extroverts; they are simply different, and are energised and motivated by different things. If you are an introvert (or experience some of the traits of an introvert), you may recognise this. You are happy to go to a party, but when you have had enough, you have had enough and want to go home and read a book or be by yourself. If you are an introvert (and even if you are an extrovert and want to learn more), it is worth reading some of Susan Cain's books to help you to understand the power of introverts. She also did an excellent TED Talk in March 2012 on the power of the introvert.[8]

One of the things that interested Kaufman was whether an introvert could be happy in an extrovert world, especially when it would be easy to think of introverts as misfits. The conclusion he came to, after reviewing some of the research, was that:

> All of this research suggests that perhaps the biggest key to being a happy introvert is simply self-acceptance; not forcing oneself to repeatedly act out of character, or to think of oneself as merely deviations from an 'ideal' personality. (Kaufman 2018)

Where then does that leave you as a parent or carer who is or has a child who is an introvert?

- Perhaps you are an introvert yourself and have no problem either with this or with what your child will face in the future. That's fine. Encourage your child to accept and be proud of who they are.
- Perhaps you are an introvert who realises that being an introvert in an extrovert's world may require some support or changes in behaviour, both your own and your child's. Certainly, an article published in 2019 by Lawn and colleagues in the *Journal of Happiness Studies* suggested 82.2% of the people sampled for a study felt they wanted to become more of an extrovert to better go about their daily lives.
- If you are an introvert who has learned or wants to take on more extrovert characteristics to get on in an extrovert world, perhaps you should consider learning the skills needed to do this and pass these on to your introvert child, however difficult.
- Perhaps you are an extrovert who cannot understand why your child cannot be more like you. You might even be worried that they are not.

---

8   www.youtube.com/watch?v=c0KYU2j0TM4

- Perhaps you need to understand a little more about your child's personality and adjust your behaviour and expectations to match their needs. You then have a choice of either encouraging their – and your – acceptance for who they are or helping to provide them with the skills they need to be comfortable in an extrovert world.

I worked in finance but found office work boring. I decided to work in retail for a while to see what this was like. I am shy and a classic 'introvert'. I am also intense and overthink everything that happens to me. I force myself to go into work every day. The customers are fine. However, some days the other staff don't talk to me at all. I then get really stressed and anxious, and when I go home, I start overthinking things. 'Do they like me?' 'Am I boring?' 'What is wrong with me?' I've tried everything but nothing works. I've come to realise that this is not the right job for me. (Young person with DME)

SHOWING YOUR CHILD HOW TO MAKE FRIENDS

Perhaps the most obvious area of concern for parents and carers is with their own child's friendships. Many worry about this when their child is any age, asking questions like: are they happy, why does no one talk to them, are they lonely, are they being bullied, what should I do? However, this section is about you and how your behaviour and actions can support your child. How can you show your child how to make friends and the power of friendships and positive relationships?

For example, in work, many parents and carers who are introverts may find they gravitate towards the kinds of jobs where the skills of an introvert are valued, such as accountancy, engineering, librarianship, IT or web development. Finding the right 'fit' (the 'square peg in the square hole') can help introverts to thrive. Being a 'square peg in a round hole' can take more work.

I am in a sales job and I talk to people all day. My child with DME went to university and I went to visit them. They were just sitting in their room reading a book. I asked my child if they had been to many parties since October, but they hadn't. I asked them how many friends they had but they said one or two. I asked my child what hobbies they had taken up or clubs they had joined but they said they were happy to read in their room. Should I encourage my child to leave university or get them some counselling? (Parent)

When you think your child has no friends, is this concern coming from them or from you? Talk to your child to find out what they want; if you do, their view might be different. For example, if you are an extrovert, do not merely assume that your child will think in the same way as you, especially if they are an introvert who prefers their own company or one or two close friends rather than the many 'acquaintances' you may have yourself.

This is where listening to your child is vital. Make sure you put your personality or way of doing things to the side. Then you have a choice. You are not trying to change them or make them into someone they are not. But if they feel some of their personality traits or ways of behaving are not useful to them or are holding them back, you could teach them the skills and confidence they feel they lack. If you feel you lack these skills yourself, learning how to develop them (once you gain understanding and confidence in using them) and then finding ways of passing them on to your child may help.

If you are a natural extrovert, thinking about the skills you already have and how you use them could be useful. If your child is an introvert, you can then pass on your knowledge and these skills to your child – that's if they want them, of course!

Nobody is saying this is easy, but by listening to your child and modelling what you do, these skills can be learned. Friends – finding them, keeping them and understanding them – are complicated, especially if you are 'differently wired'. Sometimes learning all these skills might help you (and your child) to survive in an extrovert world. But being on a different wavelength to everybody else may always be difficult for your child (or for you both if you are both neurodiverse!) in a world dominated by 'neurotypical' people. The answer may be to find others who just understand you and accept you for who you are. Then you can feel free to celebrate your child's wonderful quirky ways of thinking!

Joining organisations that provide access to a whole community of people who just understand what is happening because they, too, have children with DME or HLP is important. These are the places where you can post a message saying your child has done X or share a question or concern. Almost immediately, your message box will be full of responses from others saying they've experienced that before, and this is what they did. Or simply understanding what you mean without needing to explain further. Or celebrating with you every success and commiserating when things go wrong.

> Parenting is a beautifully challenging journey, especially when your children are more wonderfully complex like this. Being supported by such compassionate and helpful people is incredible and makes the journey easier for us all. (Parent)

Finding the same kind of support for your child can literally be a life-changer for them.

REGULATE YOUR EMOTIONS

Regulating how you behave in certain situations or when certain things happen is an important skill you will be teaching your child. Their behaviour will, in part, be based on what they see you do and how you act. How good are *your* emotional self-regulation skills?

As an adult, most of the time, your ability to self-regulate your emotions when something happens should be almost perfect. However, there are situations where people (including our own children) just 'push our buttons' to tip us over the edge. In addition, we may suffer from stress, anxiety or depression, which – even if we don't realise it – can cause changes in our behaviour or even outbursts of behaviour that we may fail to keep under control.

> I went with my partner on a parent training course about anger. It was supposed to be about helping to support our child with their angry outbursts. However, we both realised that it was my inability to control my own anger that was part of my child's problem. Since that course I have tried to understand my anger and to do more to keep it in check. (Parent)

Once you have decided you need to self-regulate your emotions, developing the skills you need, either on your own or as a whole family, can help. Many non-specialist organisations offer online training courses that may help if self-regulation is a problem for you. For example, The British Association of Anger Management provides information and courses that are both online and face-to-face as well as things like anger management and counselling for couples and coaching.[9] Other options include going to your doctor to see if your local NHS Trust provides courses.

YOUR ROLE WITHIN THE FAMILY AND HOW THIS CHANGES

As your child gets older, their needs will change. From being a baby who is totally dependent on you to keep them healthy, in what seems like a moment they will be flying the nest into work, university or their next big adventure. They will move from total dependence to independence. Then you will be lucky to get a message from them once a week (usually because they need something) or a dirty bag of washing whenever they come home.

You will hopefully have been able to understand and support your child and been a reliable advocate with family, schools and others they have met along the way. What about now, when you might be near the start of your child's journey into adulthood? Are you ready to grow and develop along with your child? The kinds of decisions you may need to make in your own life as your child moves closer to independence include:

- Whether to go back to work or be a stay-at-home parent
- How to balance work and home life
- Whether to gain new skills by taking courses or qualifications
- How you are going to spend any free time you may have
- Whether your child can live independently and the impact this may have on you (financially, or with respect to things like housing and employment)
- When your child leaves home, what this will mean for you in terms of the house you live in (would you downsize?), how you spend any free time, and even when you will retire
- What you will do with your finances
- How (if at all) you will support your child's future needs (possibly with money, help with housing, etc.).

---

9   See www.angermanage.co.uk/online-anger-management and www.angermanage.co.uk

Many (if not all) of these may pass you by as problems, and you may have other challenges that need to be solved first. You may feel that your need to make decisions about any of them are so far into the future that they are not worth thinking about now. You may not be able or be prepared to address any of them, for a variety of reasons. Alternatively, you may be ultra-organised and have thought about, decided and allocated the resources to them already, even though your child has just been born!

Think about this list of dilemmas. How you prepare the ground rules now with your child (and family) will have an impact on your (and their) future self. If your child relies on you to support them financially, or for any housework you do for them, will this continue as they go through life, or will you try to make them resilient and independent? We are not talking here about not driving them to their music lesson when they are six years old. What about when they are 15 years old and can't be bothered walking to their friend's house? We are not talking about paying for their school trip (although you may have views about that). What about when they have left home and you seem to fund all their requests for cash, urgent or non-urgent?

There is no right or wrong approach to any of this, but when you think about the kind of adult you would like your child to become, how will you help them get there?

> I went ice skating with friends once when I was a teenager quite a long way from where I lived. I didn't know the area, didn't know how to get there (or back) and my friends lived in a different part of my hometown. I asked my parents for a lift to get there and back, and they refused. I still remember how angry I felt and how unfair it seemed. I had to find my way there and home using several buses, but I made it. I never understood what my parents were doing with that episode and others like it. It wasn't until I had children of my own and realised that, through my parents' actions, they had encouraged me to develop independence and resilience and to try and solve problems for myself. I think that is so important. (Parent who was a child with DME)

Few families sail through life without experiencing problems of any kind. Some problems may be comparatively small. Others may be so huge that you cannot see how you are going to solve them. What is important is to start with a positive mindset. No matter how difficult a problem might look, start from the view that there is a solution to everything. This will help you to work on what you *could* do to address the challenge, even if you don't like the solution.

Draw on the skills you have been reading about in this book including creative and critical thinking. Use the skills of others at your disposal – your child with DME or your family, trusted friends or relatives. Don't forget, there are lots of organisations in the UK and elsewhere that will have experience of dilemmas such as this. They can provide a non-judgemental, friendly and confidential ear and skills to help you problem-solve the challenges you face.

Your approach may help to give you the skills and confidence in your abilities – sometimes skills you didn't know you had – and enable you to improve how you support your own child as well as yourself. You never know, it may be you who is volunteering in the future on a helpline, giving advice to new parents and carers of children with DME!

HOW YOU CAN ENTHUSE LEARNING

Learning doesn't just happen in school. Your child's learning starts from the moment they are born and continues throughout their lives. Helping your child remain enthusiastic about learning is an essential part of being a parent and carer, but does this mean that you have to know everything your child might need to learn? Absolutely not. Does it mean that you need to:

- Make learning fun?
- Help them to explore new activities and develop new interests and passions?
- Build on their strengths and passions and use their successes – no matter how small – to support any challenges they have?
- Stand up for them when learning stops being fun?
- Help them to meet any difficulties with a positive attitude?

Absolutely!

Lots of organisations exist to provide children with different experiences that can turn into lifelong passions. Usually, the main things that can slow them down or prevent these happening are time and cost, but with a little bit of planning, both of these can be overcome. For example, learning doesn't just happen face-to-face; it can happen online, through emails or even writing and reading.

In terms of cost, some organisations offer grants or reduced fees to help lower or even remove the cost of attending activities. There are also organisations such as The Potential Trust that offer grants to families who could not otherwise afford for their child with DME (or HLP) to attend events.

ABOUT THE POTENTIAL TRUST

The Potential Trust exists to help ensure children with HLP or DME in the UK can take part in learning opportunities that enthuse them, and which enable them to make friends with like-minded children and young people.

One of the ways it achieves this is by providing Questor bursaries[10] to pay for activities that a family might not otherwise be able to afford. Over the years, these Questors have become involved in a range of activities, from science sessions to music schools to coding weeks and more. In fact, the kinds of things that the Trust will fund are restricted only by a child's imagination.

With a little imagination, learning opportunities can be completely free.

> My child was really interested in politics. I know nothing about this subject and didn't know how to proceed as my child was in primary school at the time. So I wrote to a professor of politics at our local university. The professor was flattered to be asked and gave my child some time to talk to him and answer his questions. (Parent)

Where a child is passionate about a particular subject, you could try and find a mentor for that child. If your child is in primary school, finding someone from the local sixth form, university or elsewhere to email with

---

10 www.thepotentialtrust.org.uk/questor-bursaries; to explore The Potential Trust's work in more detail or apply for a Questor grant to enthuse your child's learning, go to: www.thepotentialtrust.org.uk

questions is worth considering, providing appropriate checks and supervision are put in place. For some secondary school pupils in school, Brightside (for example) provides online mentoring to connect young people with inspirational role models.[11] You may need to convince your child's school to become a partner. Its website also has a library of regularly updated information about education, careers and student life.

Tapping into the skills of your face-to-face or online community for specific support is also a good idea. You never know, that astrophysicist who is passionate about their work may just be waiting to be asked some questions by your child who is passionate about learning more!

THE KINDS OF DECISIONS YOU WILL NEED TO MAKE

The need to make decisions about your child starts as soon as they are born and continues until they leave home (and sometimes beyond). When they are young, you will be making most of these decisions for them. However, as they grow older, they will become more and more involved in making decisions about and for themselves. This makes learning effective decision-making skills crucial. It also means that you must be comfortable with the decisions that you make, and confident with changing direction when you feel you've made a mistake or got it wrong!

We have already looked at critical and creative skills relating to your child. Could you build on these skills and use them yourself? One of the biggest areas of decision-making that many parents and carers worry about is choosing the most appropriate school for their child. Where they feel they have got things wrong, they may then agonise for weeks (or even months) about what to do about it, including changing schools or even home educating. There are very few decisions that cannot be overturned or changed if a situation is not working. Listen to what your child is saying (and sometimes what they are not saying), and work with them to solve the problem.

> My child hated secondary school. We went into school on a regular basis, but it had got to the stage where we almost had to force my child to go in. I found my child a place at a private boarding school but, after the

---

11 See https://brightside.org.uk/online-mentoring

assessment week, they refused to go back, even if the only other option open to them was to return to the secondary school in our hometown. One day, the school phoned up to say that my child was, yet again, in the medical centre. I heard a screeching sound in the background. I honestly thought it was an animal in pain. I asked about the noise and I was told it was my child. I collected them from school and they never went back. Even after all these years I feel guilty that I didn't take my child out sooner. I suppose my own experience as a child made it difficult for me to believe that school isn't the perfect fit for all children. (Parent)

So what are the kinds of decisions that parents and carers of children with DME may have to make?

■ Tips and hints: Common considerations relating to your child with DME's schooling

Before formal school age:

- Whether you need to go back to work and who will look after your child
- Whether you can afford to pay for childcare or whether you can get childcare support
- Whether your child should go to a nursery, a childminder or another relative (such as a grandparent) or a friend, or stay at home with you before school
- How old your child with DME should be before they start formal schooling
- Whether your child should go to school or whether they should be home educated
- How much involvement your child will have in making decisions about which primary school to attend
- If you send them to school, what kind of school that should be (e.g., public or online school)
- Where the school should be (e.g., local, boarding or specialist school, like a music school).

At primary school age:

- Whether you have the time, resources and confidence to get involved with your child's school
- If you have the time, whether you are going to get involved with your child's school as a class volunteer, school governor or member of the Parent Teacher Association (or equivalent) or in some other role
- How you are going to advocate for your child's strengths, challenges and needs
- How you will help your child to decide on the most appropriate secondary school for them
- If your child is being educated at home, in a non-state school or elsewhere, whether your child will attend a different type of school arrangement at secondary school age
- How far your child will be involved in this decision.

At secondary school age:

- Whether you have the time, resources and confidence and are going to get involved with your child's school as a class volunteer, school governor or member of the Parent Teacher Association (or equivalent) or in some other role
- How you are going to help your child speak up for themselves about their strengths, challenges and needs
- How you will help your child choose the best exam path for their future
- How exam arrangements will be secured and funded (e.g., for your child in home education)
- How you will advocate for their strengths, challenges and needs if you have to do this
- How you will help your child to decide on the most appropriate next steps for them (work, college, etc.).

The future:

- How you will help your child advocate for themselves if there are problems in school, college or whichever path they are on
- How you will help your child advocate for themselves wherever they are if they are not happy or if they have a grievance
- How you will help your child to choose the path they want to take next, whether that is college, an apprenticeship, university, work or another path
- How you will give effective support to your child as they make their own decisions for themselves, their own children and their family in the future.

About their DME:

- Whether you wish to have your child with DME formally assessed and how. This could be through the educational psychologist linked to the school, with a private educational psychologist or through a charity specialising in assessments for children and young people with DME or HLP or SEND
- Whether or not you decide to go for a second opinion if you disagree with the results of the assessment
- Whether you want your child to have formal statutory support (such as an EHCP or equivalent) or not, and what support you will need to achieve this
- If your child has an EHCP, how you will ensure that the progression of their strengths is included as part of the statutory framework.

The number of decisions you may need to make both for and with your child with DME may feel huge. However, facing them is not intended to make you feel overwhelmed; quite the opposite. Most of the decisions to be taken are the same as those that most parents and carers at some stage may need to make. The only additional set of dilemmas you need to consider are those that arise because of DME. Complicated? Certainly. Doable? If you believe in yourself and what you are doing, reach out for people you can trust and stick to your guns, absolutely!

Go to www.jkp.com/catalogue/book/9781787758100 if you would like help to decide about your child's schooling. If you have already made your mind up, great! If you haven't, just remember, whatever you do, the decision must be right for your child and you at this moment with all the information you have available. Also remember, this doesn't mean that you can't reverse your decision once you've made it – you might just need to decide how and when to do it.

Obviously, not every decision you make in your life or the life of your child with DME will be like this. Even with the bigger decisions, some will be easier than others. However, the more you can practise decision-making, the easier it should become to tackle some of the dilemmas you may need to address, both with and about your child with DME.

THE IMPORTANCE OF LOOKING AFTER YOU

So far, everything in this book has focused on you as the parent or carer of a child with DME. However, it is also important to ask yourself, who is taking care of *you*? Before you skip over this section as you are too busy or you don't believe that your needs are as important as your child's, or for a thousand other reasons, *stop*. Consider this: what would happen to your child with DME if you weren't there to support them? Taking care of yourself is beneficial for many reasons, not least because of:

- The improvements in your mood and behaviour because you have taken time out for yourself to relax or wind down
- The positive impact this will have on the rest of the family
- Your greater ability to deal with whatever life throws at you.

How you take care of yourself will be different for different people. It may depend on things like the time you have available, whether you go out to work or stay at home, your ability to find someone to look after your child, your income or the other resources you have. There are lots of activities that are available, free of charge, and that can be accessed even for short periods of time during the day.

The first thing you may need to do in making self-care one of your priorities is to recognise and acknowledge that you have a self-care need, which isn't easy. You may be so used to doing everything for everyone and on top of that saying 'yes' whenever you are asked to do something else. Many of us are guilty of that! Without some thought, it can be easy to forget about self-care until something happens that makes parents and carers reprioritise.

Figure 5.2 shows the kinds of symptoms that someone may have if they are stressed. How many of these do you recognise? If it's none, fantastic. If, however, you recognise one or more of these symptoms, perhaps now is the time to start thinking about how to support yourself.

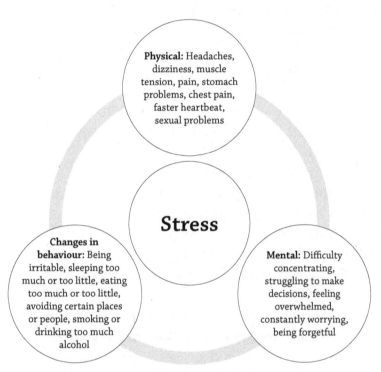

Figure 5.2. Symptoms of stress[12]

Almost 20 years ago, when my child with DME was a baby, I had a birthday gift from my partner of five days at a spa, on my own – FIVE DAYS! – where I could do what I wanted. After worrying about my child for a couple of days, I began to relax – really relax – and it was a fantastic feeling. Every now and then I think about that experience and what it felt like. I've never managed to do it since then even after all these years. (Parent)

_____

12 Adapted from www.nhs.uk

COPING WITH STRESS

- How do you respond to stress? Make a list of the kind of things that happen to you. Use Figure 5.2 to help.
- What are the three main causes of your stress at the moment?
- What activities did you enjoy doing before you had children that you are no longer able to do?
- If you could relax for:
  - 5 minutes
  - 1 hour
  - 1 evening
  - 1 day

  what would you do?
- What is stopping you each time? Spend a minute thinking about these and make a list:
  - What is stopping me taking 5 minutes out for myself?
  - What is stopping me taking 1 hour out for myself?
  - What is stopping me taking 1 evening off?
  - What is stopping me taking 1 day off?
- How can I address any difficulties I might have?
- My action plan: what am I going to do now?

Try your action plan for a week. If it works, turn your activities into a habit, something you always make time for in your life.

How do you feel?

Apart from the time it takes to bring up their child with DME (and their siblings and the rest of the family!), parents and carers highlight a variety of different sources of their own stress specifically related to having a child with DME, including:

- Loneliness – having nobody who understands their child and their DME and being unable to talk to others about this

- Being judged – others judging them and their child with DME for their actions or behaviour
- Pressure from others – from other family members or friends, all with views on 'the correct way to bring up a child with DME'
- Lack of understanding about DME – sometimes others (including the child's teacher) can see a child with DME and how they behave and believe that the child is lazy, poorly behaved or spoilt with parents or carers whose parenting skills are what is at fault
- Exhaustion – sometimes parents and carers report rushing from appointment to appointment or from crisis to crisis with a child with DME for assessments, treatment or activities to enthuse them.

This list could go on, and this is in addition to some of the other pressures in families that may cause stress (such as debt, unemployment or housing problems). Without taking time out to relax, you run the risk of burnout. Taking care of yourself is just another way to provide the best care you can for your child with DME.

WHAT SUPPORT IS OUT THERE FOR YOU?

As we have said throughout this book, you are not alone. There are parents and carers of children with DME all around the world, all experiencing similar challenges to the ones you face, all needing to make the same decisions and feeling stressed and isolated, just as you may sometimes feel. If you have no or few trusted friends locally who you can meet with face-to-face and talk to about DME and your child, and who will understand and support you, remember that there are organisations in the UK and elsewhere that provide a range of support options to parents and carers everywhere to support them with their journey, such as telephone support, training to help you cope, explore or address the dilemmas you face as well as dedicated peer-to-peer support groups online, through social media, chatrooms or face-to-face.

In Chapter 8 we have provided a list of some of the organisations that provide specialist DME-related support for parents and carers. Research the services they offer and take some time out for you to find other parents and carers who best understand your situation. You are so important.

> It's a journey of exploration and so reassuring when you realise there's a whole community out there who are in the same position as you. (Parent)

> I felt so much relief that I was talking with others who really understood my experiences with my child and were able to tell me the kinds of things I could expect bringing up my child and how to talk to them effectively. (Parent)

CONCLUSION

This chapter has been about you, your behaviour (and how this can impact on your child's), some of the skills you may need to develop (if you don't already have them), the kinds of decisions you may need to make and the common dilemmas facing parents and carers of a child with DME.

For many parents and carers, the pressures to nurture a child with DME effectively can be immense. It can sometimes be difficult to remember that your child and their quirkiness or flashes of brilliance should sometimes just be enjoyed for what they are, part of the child's wonderful, different way of looking at the world. Tomorrow, these children could be the scientists or engineers or musicians or...wherever they find their passion. They just need support to help them get there.

Hopefully, some of the challenges outlined in this chapter will be familiar to you. The most important message is, however, that as well as being responsible for your child with DME, *you must also take care of yourself*. With you to help support, guide and advocate for them, give them the skills they need for independence and to love them unconditionally, your child can have the superpower to become the best version of themselves.

> Want to know more? Further information can be found at www.jkp.com/catalogue/book/9781787758100

FURTHER READING
Understanding your child and how to support them effectively

Edward Christophersen and Susan Mortweet (2009) *Parenting that Works: Building Skills that Last a Lifetime*. APA Life Tools.

Rebecca Eanes (2016) *Positive Parenting: An Essential Guide*. Penguin Publishing Group.

Adele Faber and Elaine Mazlish (2012) *How to Talk so Kids Will Listen and Listen so Kids Will Talk*. Piccadilly Press.

Joanna Faber and Julie King (2017) *How to Talk so Little Kids Will Listen: A Survival Guide to Life with Children Aged 2–7*. Piccadilly Press.

Kimberlee Anne King (2017) *Parenting Is Hard. Suffering Is Optional. A Handbook for Parents on the Brink*. Inspired Attention Inc.

Michelle Korenfeld (2017) *Raising Creative Thinkers Guidebook: Becoming a 21st Century Educator. Igniting Children with the 5E's: Explore, Experience, Examine, Elevate and Express*. CreateSpace Independent Publishing Platforms.

Mary Reckmeyer and Jennifer Robison (2016) *Strengths-Based Parenting: Developing Your Child's Innate Talents*. Gallup Press.

Daniel Siegel and Mary Hartzell (2013) *Parenting from the Inside Out: How a Deeper Self-Understanding Can Help You Raise Children Who Thrive*. Teacher Perigee; 10th anniversary edition.

Paul Tieger and Barbara Barron-Tieger (2001) *Nurture by Nature: Understanding Your Child's Personality Type*. Little, Brown & Company.

Lea Waters (2017) *The Strength Switch: How the New Science of Strength-Based Parenting Helps Your Child and Teen Flourish*. Scribe UK.

About introversion

Susan Cain (2012) 'The Power of Introverts.' TED Talk, February: www.ted.com/talks/susan_cain_the_power_of_introverts

Susan Cain (2017) *Quiet Power: Growing Up as an Introvert in a World that Can't Stop Talking*. Penguin Life.

Susan Cain (2020) *Quiet Journal: Discover Your Secret Strengths and Unleash Your Inner Power Diary*. Clarkson Potter.

Scott Barry Kaufman (2018) 'Can introverts be happy in a world that can't stop talking?' *Beautiful Minds*, 5 October. Available at: https://blogs.scientificamerican.com/beautiful-minds/can-introverts-be-happy-in-a-world-that-cant-stop-talking

Rodney Lawn, Gavin Slemp and Dianne Vella-Brodrick (2019) 'Quiet flourishing: The authenticity and well-being of trait introverts living in the west depends on extraversion-deficit beliefs.' *Journal of Happiness Studies 20*, 2055–2075. Available at: https://link.springer.com/article/10.1007/s10902-018-0037-5

Debbie Tung (2017) *Quiet Girl in a Noisy World: An Introvert's Story*. Andrews McMeel Publishing; illustrated edition.

Your self-regulation skills

Ryan Martin (2021) *Why We Get Mad: How to Use Your Anger for Positive Change*. Watkins Publishing.

Looking after you

Scott Barry Kaufman (2020) *Transcend: The New Science of Self-Actualization*. Tarcherperigee; illustrated edition.

Kai Kermani (1996) *Autogenic Training: The Effective Holistic Way to Better Health*. Souvenir Press Ltd; new edition.

Gabor Maté (2019) *When the Body Says No: The Cost of Hidden Stress*. Vermilion; 2nd edition.

YOUR ACTION PLAN

1. Think about your own strengths, personality and behaviour. How can these help your child with DME to be the best version of themselves?
2. Think about the negative aspects of your personality, behaviour and actions. How could these prevent your child from being the best version of themselves?
3. How can you build on your strengths, and adapt or change the more negative aspects of yourself, so that you can have a positive impact on your child's behaviour and actions?
4. What scaffolding do you need to help build around your child to give them the underpinning skills they need to help with whatever they find difficult?
5. How can you make sure that you are a good role model for your child?
6. What is your plan for taking time out for yourself?
7. How do you plan to find others who understand your experiences of bringing up your child with DME?

CHAPTER 6

How Do I Build Positive Relationships with the Professionals Who Support My Child with DME's Learning?

INTRODUCTION

Every child in the UK should be receiving formal teaching by the time they are five years old. For some children, this will be in a mainstream school built of bricks and mortar. It could be in a faith-based school, a Montessori school, a special school, a forest school, an independent school or in another of the wide range of different school options on offer. For others it may be in some sort of alternative provision, home education or education in small groups in the community or even online learning. Whichever way they are taught, most parents and carers will be involved in relationships, of one form or another, with the individuals who teach their child.

This chapter begins with the assumption that most children attend school of one sort or another. Therefore, the role of professionals in their child's education is pivotal. In terms of Dual or Multiple Exceptionality (DME), this chapter outlines the ways in which these professionals can be important, including as champions for DME, advocates or mentors of a child who has DME and deliverers of inspiring education for pupils with DME.

It also highlights how important it is for parents and carers to develop positive relationships with professionals. It suggests the kinds of things that they could do to nurture these relationships, and to get involved with the school, for the benefit of their child who has DME. It also explores potential problems and pitfalls that can arise, including what to do when everything else seems to have failed.

However, we also recognise that some children and young people with DME will not be educated in a school building at all. Two of the more commonly used alternatives to mainstream schools or specialist provision are home education and online learning. These can overlap and are sometimes even used alongside mainstream schooling to supplement or support a child's learning. The challenges and opportunities that both can bring are therefore explored in this chapter.

THE IMPORTANCE OF PROFESSIONALS

> Even now, after all these years, I remember the teacher who lent me his copy of *The Complete Works of Shakespeare*. I was 11 years old, and we didn't have many books in our house. That teacher inspired a lifelong love of reading and learning and one that I wanted for my own children. (Parent who was a child with DME)

Most parents and carers can think of at least one teacher or other professional who taught them when they were younger and who, by a word or a look or an action, inspired them to be the best that they could be. You can't bottle that skill or teach it on any teacher training course. Many, if not all, of those who enter the teaching profession do so because they believe in the power of education to inspire and enthuse learning, and want to pass on their knowledge and enthusiasm to future generations. This is so vital for the skills and wellbeing of the individual, the economy and our whole society. If done effectively, their teaching and involvement in the education process will lay the foundations for a stable, forward-looking and healthy civilisation.

According to the *Teachers' Standards*,[1] in terms of their teaching, a teacher must:

- Set high expectations that inspire, motivate and challenge pupils
- Promote good progress and outcomes by pupils

---

1   www.gov.uk/government/publications/teachers-standards

- Demonstrate good subject and curriculum knowledge
- Plan and teach well-structured lessons
- Adapt teaching to respond to the strengths and needs of all pupils
- Make accurate and productive use of assessment
- Manage behaviour effectively to ensure a good and safe learning environment
- Fulfil wider and professional responsibilities.

Teachers are also expected to demonstrate consistently high standards of personal and professional conduct, including things like:

- Upholding public trust in the profession and maintaining high standards of ethics and behaviour, within and outside school, by things like:
  - Treating pupils with dignity, building relationships rooted in mutual respect, and always observing proper boundaries appropriate to a teacher's professional position
  - Having regard for the need to safeguard pupils' wellbeing, in accordance with statutory provisions
  - Showing tolerance of and respect for the rights of others
  - Not undermining fundamental British values, including democracy, the rule of law, individual liberty and mutual respect, and tolerance of those with different faiths and beliefs
  - Ensuring that personal beliefs are not expressed in ways that exploit pupils' vulnerability or might lead them to break the law.
- Having proper and professional regard for the ethos, policies and practices of the school in which they teach and maintaining high standards in their own attendance and punctuality.
- Having an understanding of, and always acting within, the statutory frameworks that set out their professional duties and responsibilities. (Department for Education 2011, pp.10–14)

This list is a tall order for any individual, and many teachers reach and achieve more than is expected of them – working long hours to enable all pupils – including those with DME – to be the best versions of themselves they can be. Other professionals whose job is to support those children and young people referred to them meet similar high standards.

THE PROBLEM WITH PROFESSIONALS

However, just as with parents and carers, where pupils, parents and carers experience problems with teachers and other professionals, this can have a negative impact on the outcomes achieved. Some of the challenges that can be encountered include:

For the pupil
There is a clash of personalities and/or behaviour

In the last chapter we outlined what happens when a parent or carer has a clash of personality or behaviour with their child. The same thing is true of teachers. Some teachers just 'get' the child with DME; they know how to motivate them, how to inspire them to learn and how to encourage their strengths and abilities, while supporting their Special Educational Needs and Disabilities (SEND) appropriately.

There are some professionals who have the opposite effect. Their personalities clash with their pupil's and, unless they actively change their behaviour when dealing with the child or young person with DME (in a way that the child or young person understands), they will not get the best from them. Clashes may even cause a pupil to develop behavioural problems leading to their reprimand and sometimes temporary or permanent exclusion.

While these clashes could occur with any pupil, pupils with DME may have more difficulty keeping their behaviour in check. The outcome can include exhibitions of their strong feelings of justice and fairness, or situations arising from the intensity or depth of their emotions. Such extreme outbursts can mean that, when there is a clash of personality (or the pupil feels they are not treated fairly), the results can be explosive.

There is a lack of understanding by the teacher
or other professional about DME

Most general teacher training courses in the UK provide little training on recognising pupils with SEND in the classroom, and they provide virtually none on recognising pupils with High Learning Potential (HLP), let alone DME, even though this concept has been recognised for a long time in schools and within Government. For example, the Department for Education first published a book in 2008 called *Gifted and Talented Education: Helping to Find and Support Children with Dual or Multiple Exceptionalities*.

This has since been archived but it was a concept that was both recognised and supported by Government. There is currently no mandatory teacher training to help professionals recognise pupils with DME in the classroom, and as a concept it is barely considered at all.

Notwithstanding, specialist teachers such as SENCos (Special Educational Needs coordinators), those responsible for More Able pupils and inclusion managers (or equivalent) may have received additional training in all these topic areas, including DME. In addition, individual teachers may have done training courses under their own steam, driven by a passion for supporting these pupils or personal experience of them at home or in the classroom.

As there is relatively little understanding in schools about how to recognise and support pupils who have DME, when a pupil with DME starts to show typical DME characteristics (such as flashes of brilliance that are not backed up with written work, or meltdowns in the classroom that could be signs that the pace of work might not be sufficiently challenging for them), the identification of potential causes – and the solutions – may be misguided.

> We didn't get any help at all in school for years. Whenever we raised the issue of 'adequate challenge' we were informed about approaches such as 'greater depth' and 'mastery'. Over the years we were left with a child who had developed severe mental health difficulties due to chronic underchallenge. School really needed to understand the consequences of their actions. The best these children can often expect is being used as extra teaching assistants. I think that is inappropriate when all they want is harder work. (Parent)

Lack of appropriate identification or effective teaching strategies to support these children can have a long-term detrimental impact on their anxiety levels, mental health and behaviour. It can also lead to the growing inability of the child or young person with DME to be able to attend school altogether, or to be excluded from school or their learning environment.

> I think schools need to do more to recognise DME. They need to be encouraged to think of simple ways to support DME in the classroom. A good place to start would be making sure they have work available to

> really stretch and challenge these children effectively. Some teachers seem to do this easily. Others seem to struggle with the idea. Then they have to deal with the behavioural fall out that results. Whereas, if they had kept the child busy and stimulated in the first place, none of these problems would have happened! (Parent)

There is often a similar lack of understanding about DME among other professionals who may work with a child or young person such as the educational psychologist used by a school to assess a child's needs. This can result in misdiagnosis or treatment plans that are not as effective as they would be if the child or young person with DME were properly identified and understood.

This lack of awareness about how to identify and support DME makes specialist training in this area for teachers and other professionals in school (or supporting the pupil with DME) critical. Without this, many pupils with DME may go undetected for years or professionals may not understand why teaching programmes for those with SEND are not working as well as they could be, if at all.

The teacher or other professional does not know how to support children and young people with DME

However, it is not enough to identify children and young people with DME. Teachers and professionals need to know how to support them effectively. Taking an 'off the peg' solution from either the SEND or the HLP world to support them may simply not work. They do not often inspire the child or young person to use their intelligence to learn. What is needed is a method, approach or programme that uses the individual's HLP to overcome their SEND or learning difficulties. For example, forcing a pupil with DME to achieve the basic building blocks before they can progress to more complex concepts can be a recipe for disaster. 'More of the same' (MOTS) can frustrate a child with DME at best. It can be much easier to tackle the problem in reverse, giving them the higher-level work and using it as a hook to put the basic building blocks in place.

We spoke earlier in the book about the positive impact that higher order thinking skills (HOTS) could have on children with DME and HLP. In such children's education we should be encouraging *HOTS*, not *MOTS*!

Sometimes, encouraging teachers and other professionals to explain the 'how' and the 'why' to a pupil with DME can help them to understand the context within which they are working. This theoretical knowledge can then be used to understand what is happening or why they have a difficulty that stops them from learning. This idea can be used with many concepts. For example, explaining how someone learns in a way that is age-appropriate to a child with DME can be an effective way for them to learn that making mistakes (and learning from these!) is positive for brain development and a growth mindset.

In addition to the suggestions for how to do this outlined below, there are also lots of clips on social media that a parent and carer (or professional) can access if a child with DME needs something more visual.

EXPLAINING THE IMPORTANCE OF MAKING MISTAKES: NEUROPLASTICITY

Neuroplasticity (or brain plasticity) is the ability of networks in the brain to change through growth and reorganisation. One of the ways this can happen is by making mistakes and learning from these. A simple way of putting this across to a child with DME (although every child would probably benefit from this) is outlined in an article by Cullins for *Big Life Journal* (2020). *Big Life Journal* itself provides lots of free printable materials about growth mindset. It also provides journals to support children (for which there is a charge). We also like the regular blogs about topics connected with growth mindset. We think the site is well worth signing up for.

How would you teach about neuroplasticity to your child with DME?

Teach them about their brain. Depending on their age, you could go into quite a lot of detail about the brain. Although there are clips on platforms such as YouTube that can help with this, some parents and carers of younger children use visual effects, ranging from a sponge to a set of wires or even stories to illustrate the point. In the case of the latter, Cullins writes:

> Imagine that you're in a big field filled with tall, overgrown grass. Your job is to get to the other side. The first time, crossing the field

will be difficult, you will have to fight your way through the big, tall grass. But if you keep trying, you will get there. The next time, it'll be a little easier. Every time you cross the field, it'll get easier and easier. Eventually, you'll create a new path in the grass from going over it again and again.

This gives a simple image of how we learn.

Then explain to your child how mistakes make the brain grow. The brain cannot grow if it keeps getting the answer right; it doesn't form new pathways. To find and strengthen new pathways, your child must challenge themselves, take themselves out of their comfort zone, and keep going to the next level of difficulty. Eventually this will involve making mistakes. However, explain to your child that this should be celebrated as mistakes mean brain growth.

As well as celebrating their mistakes, helping children to think about what they learned from their mistakes (and what they would try next time) also helps them to grow.

This kind of approach is part of the theory of growth mindset, first explored by Carol Dweck in the US. In the UK, advocates like Barry Hymer (who co-wrote the *Growth Mindset Pocketbook*) have been champions of this kind of approach to learning that is still actively being used in schools across the country as a way of dealing with the problems resulting from perfectionism and making mistakes in the classroom.

Source: Adapted from Cullins (2020)

There are lots of resources available to support teachers and professionals in understanding and nurturing DME. There are also resources that have been developed to help lay the foundations for the support children and young people with DME need. Many of these can be used both at school (or the chosen learning environment) and at home to develop the child's confidence in their abilities.

A lack of understanding about the kind of support a pupil with DME needs can make their progress through education a difficult one. Improving the skills of professionals in how to support their pupils with DME (through training and other resources) is critical. It is also important for the right resources and approaches to be used with the pupil with DME. This means that – in the UK at least – we need more and better resources and approaches to be developed and good practice to be shared so we can learn from the successes of others.

For UK professionals (and also pupils, parents and carers), it is worth looking at schools in the US to see what the elements of good practice look like in supporting pupils with DME. Although approaches would have to be adapted for the UK system (and culture), one example of this is the Bridges Academy. Based in California, this school is exclusively for Twice-Exceptional (2e) pupils aged between 9 and 18. Bridges has also recently established Bridges Academy Online, building on the school's strengths-based, talent-focused model to support Twice-Exceptional students.

The teacher or other professional does not believe that DME exists

There is worrying evidence both from parents and carers (and also professionals) that there may be some professionals who simply do not believe that DME exists. Reasons given include things along the lines of:

> I've never heard of it and I have been qualified for X number of years, and if I've never heard of it, it can't exist.

To such things as:

> This is just a new-fangled idea to cover up for a child who is lazy, badly behaved or where parents [or carers] are the problem.

While these may be quite negative attitudes, let us assume for a moment that they are right, that there is no such thing as DME. Treating children and young people as if they *did* have DME and supporting them in a strengths-based approach may still be no bad thing, especially if it motivated them to be their best version of themselves. In fact, identifying the strengths and talents of every child in the classroom and using these to support the areas in which they struggle can help improve the wellbeing, happiness and achievement of all pupils, including those pupils who do (or could) have DME.

Let us now assume that DME *does* exist. Which system has more chance of working for the benefit of the child with DME?

- Option A, a system that overcompensates for the number of DME pupils, or
- Option B, a system that doesn't identify them at all?

Of a choice of these two extremes, it is expected that most people would choose Option A, especially if it cost no more money than Option B (and could actually save some). Therefore, even if a professional (or parent and carer or even a pupil) does not personally believe that DME exists, would it not be better to treat the child who might have it as if they *do*? At least until further investigations have taken place to provide more accurate evidence. While this negative attitude may be unfair to professionals (and some parents and carers), where it does exist in a school it needs to be questioned and challenged. Once again, training in DME as well as exposure to children and young people with DME can help.

Tom Ropelewski (an American screenwriter, producer and director) was responsible for two films in the US about Twice-Exceptionality: *2E: Twice Exceptional*, which focuses on children and young people with DME and their journeys, and *2e: Teaching the Twice Exceptional*, which focuses on how to teach pupils with DME. Although there may be a small charge for renting or buying each film, it may be worth it (although you may need to watch both of them through the lens of your own culture or country).

For the parent and carer
There are differences in perspective between the professional and the parent (or carer)

Once again, differences between your personality, behaviour and perspective and those of the professional you are meeting about your child with DME can be important. They can contribute to solving problems or making them worse. You wouldn't be human if you didn't find that some professionals get 'right up your nose'. They patronise or talk down to you. They have a different way of getting things done. They seem cold and clinical when you just need some support for your child. They don't accept when they have made a mistake or got something wrong. Somebody's behaviour needs to adapt.

As a result, many parents and carers report feeling anxious about going into school, and it is common for them to let their concerns build up until they reach the point when they become emotional or explode when they have their first school meeting and act and say things that they probably shouldn't. This situation can be made worse by their own past experiences. For example, as a child you might have hated school or been bullied or told off for your behaviour or what you couldn't do. Many years later, you have your own child, and they may have similar problems to the ones you experienced when you were a child. How do you feel about going into school? You know you should go in to address your concern before something bad happens, but you just can't do it.

Finally, the situation has built up so much that you have to go into school. Or, worse still, you are asked to go to a formal meeting. Just walking through the school gates brings you out in a cold sweat. It brings back memories of when you were at school. Then you think 'This is my child they are talking about and I want the best for them'. You go to the meeting. You have had to take time off from work to attend on a day you told the school was not ideal. Your partner cannot join you as they work shifts. You get to the meeting and there are three people there from the school and you are on your own. The meeting starts and the professionals use abbreviations and don't explain what they mean. You don't ask. By now you are starting to feel emotional, undermined and angry. Put all that together and this could be a recipe for disaster and one that does not help to meet the needs of your child.

While we hope this is an extreme description, and certainly does not seek to patronise either you or your child's teacher, elements of this may ring true of some situations some of the time. However, before we make suggestions about how to support you in situations like this, let's look at it from the professional's point of view.

Many professionals do not understand how to deal with parents and carers appropriately. They find it hard to change their behaviour to fit the circumstances and they do not know how to make it easier for parents and carers to deal with them or the school. When they became a teacher, they may have felt that they immediately had to know the answer to everything, and anything less would mean that they had failed. With some teachers, perspectives like this can make dealing with parents and carers something to be avoided at all costs. When they must do it, they may be stressed and say things they don't mean.

Sound familiar?

A perfect illustration of this is, in some schools – especially secondary schools or equivalent – where it can be difficult to even find the name or details of the right person to contact. Why?

Professionals must work within the rules set (such as the way information evenings are run or the way in which information is sent out), whereas others may be more flexible in meeting the needs of parents and carers and support them appropriately. If either parents and carers or professionals (or both) also adapt their behaviour and perspective on the topic being discussed, this can make a real difference to solving any problems in school, and in the long run can help both parties to feel more supported.

Every parent and carer (and what they need and want) will be different and every learning environment will be unique. Here are some suggestions for how parents and carers can be made to feel welcome when going in to discuss their child. This (or something similar) could be used by the school or other setting. It would ideally be drawn up with the involvement of parents and carers in the school. A similar list could be written down for parents and carers to follow with professionals.

A SCHOOL CHARTER FOR SUPPORTING PARENTS AND CARERS

1. All parents and carers will be treated with respect, and their concerns taken seriously, no matter what they want to discuss about their child.

2. We (the school or other setting) have an open-door policy for parents and carers and can make an appointment at a convenient time for them to discuss their child.

3. We are a parent-friendly school and will work with parents and carers to regularly review our approach, and will make changes to it if we need to do so.

4. We understand that parents and carers sometimes work shifts and may have childcare responsibilities and transport difficulties. When we arrange to meet a parent or carer, we will work

with them to try and overcome these problems, including using new technology or meeting at their home or another suitable location.

5. We will always refrain from using jargon. If this is not possible, we will give a clear explanation of what it means and check it is understood by everyone.

6. We understand that behaviour can sometimes appear negative, either in tone or in what is said. We believe that behaviour is a form of communication and we will work to keep our own behaviour as open and positive as possible, as well as understanding that the behaviour of parents and carers may be affected by concern for their child.

7. In meetings, if parents and carers would find it useful, we will provide a person to take notes of any agreed points of action. We will send these out using a method agreed with the parents and carers within five working days.

8. Any agreed action points will have a clear date for delivery and also who is responsible for doing it.

9. We recognise that a parent or carer's concerns about their child (including their child's activities or behaviour at home) may not be the same as our concerns at school. We will therefore work together honestly to develop a strategy for everything related to the child. This will identify concerns both at home and at school and what is seen in both settings.

10. We will develop honest relationships with parents and carers and work in a positive partnership in the best interests of the child. This includes being open and honest when we cannot deliver what the parent or carer feels their child needs. This is the case even if we disagree with the choices that pupils, parents and carers are making.

It cannot be emphasised enough that there are some excellent examples of best practice around the country and of schools that go 'the extra mile' to support their pupils, parents and carers. If your child goes to one of them (or perhaps you teach in one yourself), that's fantastic news. It is worth its weight in gold.

There is a lack of understanding that DME can present differently between school and home

The challenges in the relationship between parents and carers and professionals that we have outlined so far could apply to any parent or carer with any professional. In fact, strategies that achieve positive relationships between parents and carers of children and young people with DME and professionals are positive strategies to support all children and young people.

However, there are also some differences in how a child or young person with DME presents at home and in other, formal, environments. It is especially important for professionals to understand what these can be and to support parents and carers who raise such concerns, especially where they impact on the child with DME's school experience.

Some children and young people can be well behaved and quiet in a formal environment (usually school or equivalent). Yet, once they leave that environment, the emotions they have bottled up may be released. If there is no channel for these, their behaviour can change. Parents and carers report a range of emotions in their child, ranging from tears to anger, biting, kicking and hitting those who live with them (including parents and carers, friends and others), even destroying furniture. This kind of behaviour will continue until, often exhausted, the child calms down.

Alternatively, a child or young person with DME can have behavioural issues at school (or other environments), where they 'hit out' in frustration as a response to the situation they find themselves in and may be punished in some way. Yet, as soon as they leave that environment, and go home, their behaviour changes. Left to themselves (where they can follow their own hobbies and interests and do things at their own pace or even just relax), they become a different child – quiet, absorbed, pleasant.

> We could not convince the school that our child needed to be stretched and this was the reason for their poor behaviour at school. They were like a different child as soon as they got home. They love reading and at home they could read as many books a week as they wanted, whenever they wanted. From the school's description it was like we were talking about two different children. (Parent)

Of course, it is often not as simple as this. For example, pupils with DME may act differently in different subjects at school. At home, their behaviour may be affected by your actions and expectations. For example, some parents and carers may take their children to the park or local playground before going home or encourage them to play in the garden. Others may begin a strict routine of 'homework before play' as soon as they get home. There is no right or wrong answer to this as every child will have different needs. It is worth keeping a diary to describe your child's actions following different approaches or after activities in different environments. Then you can see if there are any patterns or explanations for their different behaviour. Using this information, you could try and develop solutions to what you find.

As well as making notes, try and look for low-level solutions to what you can see. For example, some children are tired when they leave school (or other formal setting) and just need to rest. Some children are hungry and just need something to eat. Giving them something like a banana often works (rather than a biscuit, which gives them energy quickly but can wear off quickly as well). You know your child best and are best placed to solve any difficulties you face.

Armed with the knowledge about your child at home (especially if you have explored some of the low-level solutions and still face a problem), you can now work with your child's teacher or the other professionals who support your child. Both you and the professional need to work together positively to describe what you are seeing at home *and* school (or elsewhere), and to map out a picture of your whole child with DME.

This means that you both need to believe each other about what you are seeing, and you need to come up with solutions together and then test them out in the different environments. Then you can give each other feedback about what is working and what is not (although you may both need to give it time to see what happens).

This does not have to be done through a formal meeting (although regular face-to-face meetings are often useful). It could be done, for example, through a home school book where messages are passed from parent or carer to professional and back again. As this can be time-consuming, not all teachers will be able to do this, but if the class or pupil has a teaching assistant (or equivalent), perhaps this is something they can help with.

Although a home school diary can work for younger pupils, if you have access to technology, a regular email diary might be easier, so that notes are not also read by the child (and so do not need to be so cautiously phrased, they do not have to be written by staff during school time when they are busy teaching children and they can be copied to the SENCo, or whoever is in charge of DME in the school), and so that any concerns or patterns can be tracked and identified.

Parent and carer knowledge about DME is not appreciated, recognised or wanted

By the time a parent or carer goes to talk to a professional about their child, especially in a school environment, they have developed varying amounts of knowledge and experience about DME – what it means, what it looks like, common concerns with DME and the support needed both for their child and more generally.

- Some parents and carers may have known about DME for a long time (or '2e' or 'GLD'…) and have read everything they could about it over the years.
- Other parents and carers may have recently been reading an article about DME and experienced a 'light bulb moment', realising that their child fitted the DME description.
- A few may have just been recommended a book to read by their local doctor or health visitor or a friend.
- Others may not have thought about DME until reading this book, and are now looking for some answers to help them better understand their child.

Wherever you are on your path to learning about DME, the chances are that, by the time you go in to school to share what you know with the professional, you will have already heard of DME (or whatever you have chosen to call it) and have some understanding about what it means.

Things are starting to change in the UK, as organisations supporting children and young people with DME work hard to raise awareness with schools, although there is still a high likelihood that your child's class teacher or other professional in school may not yet be aware of DME. This is fine if the professional listens to what you have to say about DME and how it applies to your child (or, if you do not yet feel confident yourself, are willing to talk to one of the specialist organisations supporting DME). However, what happens if they do not want to listen to you?

While working positively with professionals is important for parents and carers and is in the best interests of the child (and that is more important than anything), a minority of professionals may not want to hear what you have to say. This could be for several reasons, including their lack of time, stress in coming to grips with a new concept, lack of belief that DME exists or that it applies to your child, wanting to be the professional who knows 'everything' and the need for them to process what you are saying, to think about it (and what it means) and to do some research themselves on DME. These are all understandable, and you need to make allowances for them. While you may not know which of these reasons apply to your child's professional, it is important that you make it as easy as possible for them to understand what you want to explain.

One suggestion for doing this is sharing the explanation of DME that is provided in the downloadable material at www.jkp.com/catalogue/book/9781787758100. You could print these off and give them over to your child's professional.

Parent or carer involvement is not understood or wanted

More generally, while this is far less common, there are still some professionals who do not understand or want parent or carer involvement in the school environment. As a result, it is not made easy (or doesn't feel like it) for any parent or carer (including those who have children with DME) to go into school.

To try and understand why, let's focus on the school environment. A school is an extremely busy place. In a primary school, a class teacher has upwards of 27 children to support (and their parents or carers), each with their own individual needs and concerns. A SENCo may have lots of cases to support. They may also teach in a class or may even be the headteacher with the pressures that brings. Whoever coordinates support for More Able pupils may combine their duties with class teaching or, again, may be the headteacher.

Other professionals may include learning support assistants (LSAs) (or teaching assistants, TAs) who may be responsible for the day-to-day support of pupils within a school. That's before we talk about a range of other professionals – educational psychologists, occupational therapists, speech and language therapists – whose time may be limited and even rationed.

Schools have different structures and people doing different job roles (with different titles!) within them. Therefore, any list provided can only give examples of the kinds of jobs you may come across. In addition, how the school may use individuals in different job roles may change slightly from school to school. If you do not understand who is or could support your child in the school, ask. Alternatively, sometimes the main job roles are identified on the school's website.

SOME OF THE PROFESSIONALS WHO MAY SUPPORT YOUR CHILD'S LEARNING[2]
Teaching and related staff

- Class teacher: The person (or even sometimes more than one person, if they share the job) who teaches a class in school.
- Inclusion manager: Sometimes the role of SENCo and More Able coordinator (or equivalent) is overseen by or merged into this role that focuses on ensuring every pupil in the school receives appropriate provision to meet their needs to make sure they are included within the classroom and teaching provided.
- Learning support assistant (LSA): Likely to support one or more children, looking after their needs.
- More Able coordinator, Gifted and Talented coordinator, or equivalent: Unlike with SEND (which has a statutory framework) there is no statutory framework for DME or HLP in the UK. In England at least, schools have different titles for the people coordinating support for their pupils with HLP and some do not have a role at all. However, as originally devised, this coordinator would essentially do the same work as the SENCo but targeted at pupils with HLP. This happens rarely, though, and schools focus on their More Able pupils or even their high achievers (and ability is not necessarily the same as achievement!).
- Special Educational Needs coordinator (SENCo): Responsible for developing and coordinating a school's strategy for pupils with SEND. This could include (among many other things) managing provision, meeting with teachers and other

---

2   Taken from www.gov.uk and www.nhs.uk

professions, parents, carers and others to ensure effective support is put in place and progress updated.

- Specialist teacher: Teachers who specialise in teaching one subject (e.g., music) or in supporting a specific group of pupils (e.g., teacher of the Deaf).
- Teaching assistant (TA): May concentrate more on academic support for a child and may be less likely to have a permanent one-to-one role with an individual child.

Specialist staff

- Audiologist: Routine hearing tests are provided in the UK by an audiologist from within a few weeks of birth to when a child is about four or five years old. The latter hearing test may be conducted at school. If any hearing problems are identified, a referral may be made to an audiologist at the school, in the community or at a hospital. Some parents and carers prefer to go to a private audiologist and there will be a fee for this service.
- Educational psychologist: Carries out a range of different tasks including the assessment and support of children who have a range of social, emotional or learning difficulties.
- Mental health professional: Some schools in the UK have developed triage systems to support pupils with mental health problems. This could include:
  - Mental health support teams, announced by the Westminster Government in 2017 and intended to provide early intervention to tackle some mental health and wellbeing problems such as mild to moderate anxiety.
  - Partnerships with or referrals to Child and Adolescent Mental Health Services (CAMHS) (or equivalent). Unless it is an emergency, professionals may first assess a child with mental health and related difficulties before recommending support.
  - Qualified mental health first aiders (who may also be professionals doing other jobs in the school).

- Music or drama therapist: Uses music or drama to help children explore personal, behavioural and social problems.
- Occupational therapist: Works with children who have problems carrying out activities. For example, they may have extreme sensory difficulties or balance or handwriting problems. The occupational therapist would work with them to assess what is going on and seek to address the problems they are having.
- Social worker: May work in or with the school to spot signs of abuse and neglect and works with teachers to support children at risk, for whatever reason.
- Specialist optician: Free eye tests are available in the UK through the NHS. If anything more serious is suspected, a child may be referred to hospital. Some parents and carers may take their child to a specialist optician privately, and there will be a fee for this service.
- Speech and language therapist: Works with children with speech, language and communication difficulties, helping them to communicate to the best of their abilities.
- Youth worker: Usually does things like organising and running programmes in the community aimed at young people. However, schools in some parts of the UK may have youth work programmes.

A secondary school is usually much larger than a primary school and it can therefore sometimes be more difficult to develop individual relationships with teachers or to go into school about your child. Added to the list above will be your child's form tutor, who is often responsible for their general wellbeing. Sometimes, there will be a head of year who takes on the responsibility for the whole year with regards to welfare, attendance and discipline. Then there is likely to be a multitude of subject teachers. You may only see these people at information evenings.

As in primary schools, there are then the specialist staff, from SENCos and More Able and Talented coordinators, More Able lead teachers, inclusion lead teachers (or whoever supports the school's strategy for HLP and

DME) to educational psychologists and others, depending on the school's needs and approach. This is in the state sector, where education is free in the UK. Even then, however, schools will differ in the kind of structures they have, especially as they relate to DME. The structures and services may be different again in other schools such as public schools (which are privately run and where there is a fee to attend).

This still only scratches the surface of the school system. If you are interested in finding out more about the different kinds of schools, at least in England, the UK Government's website may be of some interest.[3]

Anecdotal evidence suggests that many teachers arrive at school at about 7.30am and finish their working day long into the evening, after they have prepared for the next day's lessons. Is it any wonder that more than 33,500 professionals actively left teaching in state-funded schools in England in 2019?[4] These figures do not include people who retired or died in service.

It is likely that schools in other countries face similar pressures.

So what does this mean for parent or carer involvement? Or, to put it another way, what should you expect? The 'Tips and hints' in this section outline some of the points parents and carers often raise about school involvement (and suggestions, if any, about what to do). Every child and school and situation is different. If in doubt, ask questions and get the answers from the professionals themselves. Alternatively, information may be provided on the school's website.

■ Tips and hints: Common questions from parents and carers on engaging with school and some suggestions

I don't know who the best person is to contact about my child:

- In a primary school. The best place to start is usually with your child's class teacher. Arrange an appointment with them at the end of the school day or through the school office.

---

3   www.gov.uk/types-of-school
4   https://explore-education-statistics.service.gov.uk/find-statistics/school-workforce-in-england

- In a secondary school. This can be a bit trickier, especially if the school is large. If it is, there may be more formal systems in place and more people to see. A good place to start is with your child's form tutor or their head of year. If you don't know who they are (and even if you do), phone the school office and ask. They should have a system for passing on messages or even making appointments.

I don't know the best time to meet with the professional:

- If you want to meet them in person, you may need to make time for this. If you work or it would be difficult for some reason, try and explain this to whoever is making the appointment for you and they may be able to come up with another solution.
- After school (once children have been collected) is often the best time in a primary school. If you need it, ask if the school can offer childcare support so that you can discuss your concerns about your child without them listening. Otherwise, you might have to arrange for them to be picked up by a friend or relative.
- In a secondary school, you will usually be told the best time to meet. This could be before school, during the school day or after school has ended. You may still need to tell the person making the appointment about work or other responsibilities and childcare (and although this may get easier as your child gets older, you may have other, younger children).
- Most schools can make use of remote meetings, although you need to tell them if you don't have access to the internet or a suitable computer.

How often should I meet with them?

- This depends on your child and your concerns. Generally, however, asking for a meeting once a term with the professional working with you to review progress on something of concern is reasonable. Meetings with specialists may be less often.
- If you are worried, you could ask the professional how often they think you should meet with them.

Can I take someone with me to the meeting?

- Having a meeting with a professional can be a daunting experience for anyone, especially if you are not used to meetings like this or if you are on your own. If you want to take someone with you for support, ask them to help you by taking notes, but make sure you tell them what the meeting is about beforehand and what you hope to achieve, so that they can understand what is going on. It is also a good idea to tell whoever is organising the meeting so that the professional knows they are coming. Go to www.jkp.com/catalogue/book/9781787758100 if you want to know more about how to prepare for a more formal meeting.
- Sometimes organisations are available at a local level that can provide someone to accompany you if needed. Check this out with your local authority (or equivalent). Schools themselves may also have parent support workers on site.

Should I take notes?

- It is useful to ask someone to take notes so that you don't forget anything, and especially to summarise the action that is agreed at the end of the meeting. You need to agree with the professional either before or right at the start of the meeting who will take these and when they will be available. It is also useful to have timescales against each action point and the name of the person responsible for the action.
- The advantage of the professional taking the notes is that they should be typed up by the school. Also (providing you agree with the notes – and go back to them if you don't) by writing them, the professional will be committing to what they have written. The disadvantage is that it may take time for the notes to be sent to you, and you also have less control over what is written. Making notes may also prevent the professional from listening to you, although they could get round this by arranging for someone else to take the notes for them (so be prepared for this).
- The advantage of you taking the notes is that you have more control over what is written (but if it will prevent you from listening, get someone to take these for you). The disadvantage is that you

may have to get these typed up (and you may be just as busy), although you can see immediately what you both agreed.

What if I want to see other professionals? I want to have my child assessed or identified as having SEND or DME:

- Having the professional on your side will mean you work together to have your child's needs investigated and met. However, sometimes this isn't possible (e.g., through lack of resources), in which case the professional should tell you. Although this may not seem a positive outcome at the time, complete honesty between both you and the professional is the best way forward for everyone, as it means that alternative solutions can be sought (including changing schools).
- Sometimes the teacher or other professional you see may simply not support what you want. In the case of an assessment to identify SEND, it may be because they do not feel that your child needs it (because, for example, they are performing at an 'age-appropriate level'). In such cases, there are options for parents and carers including going to the local authority directly or finding an approved specialist through the local doctor or even going privately and paying for an assessment. Go to www.jkp.com/catalogue/book/9781787758100 if you want to know more about this.

I am not happy with the support my child is getting – who should I see?

If you have had one (or even several) meeting(s) and you are still not happy with the support your child is receiving, you have several options open to you, including:

- Going back to the professional you saw and asking for updates and discussing how best to move things forward. Schools can often work slowly, and the problem may be one of different expectations about what will happen and when. It could also be a simple lack of communication between you and the professional. Find out what the stumbling block is and then you can decide what to do next.
- Going to another, more senior, professional in the school for support. In a primary school, this could be the headteacher. In a secondary school it could be the head of year or a member of the

senior management team. Ask in the school office or see if there is any relevant information on the school website if you don't know.

- In any case, as this stage it may be useful to ask for a copy of the school's complaints procedure, which should be available on the school's website. If you can't find it, phone the school office and ask them to send you a copy. This should outline the procedures that the school has said it will follow if a complaint is made. It may help you to understand who to go to if you feel your child is not getting the support they need.

- Depending on what the complaints procedure says, going to the headteacher or deputy head, and finally, the committee responsible for governing the school, may be an option open to you.

Do I have any other options if I feel I am getting nowhere with my child's school?

- If you believe that you have tried but are getting nowhere with your child's school in obtaining the support needed, start thinking about alternative approaches. This could include moving schools in the area or even finding alternative types of education more suited to your child's needs.

- Before taking this option any further, consult with your child about what they want to do. They may have clear ideas of what they need and what might help them but not feel able to articulate this to teachers.

- If you then feel able to speak up on behalf of your child in this way, meet with the school to present their request. The SENCo may be receptive to your approach as this is the underlying principle of the Ofsted framework (and the SEND Code of Practice).

- However, if you cannot get any further, you may feel that leaving the school is the only realistic option open to you, especially if you know your child's views on this and they are supportive of such action.

Research the next steps by:

- Exploring other options open to you such as other schools in your area, alternative types of schooling, home educating or other ideas.

- Looking at which of these options, if any, will be in the best interests of your child. For example, if the school your child attends is the only school that is suitable for them, you may look at how your child's needs can be met in different ways beyond the school gate such as through tutoring or paying for professional support yourself.
- Talking to other parents and carers and other specialists such as experts in the local authority can also help.
- Moving to a new house. While this may be a more extreme solution to finding a suitable school that your child likes, some parents and carers do choose to do this, and it could be an option you are prepared to consider.
- Taking a break from formal education altogether.

Whatever you decide, your child's health and wellbeing should come first. Many parents and carers decide that everything else (such as exams and school achievement) can take a backseat as long as their child is happy.

WHAT DOES EFFECTIVE DME EDUCATION LOOK LIKE?

Individual parents and carers may have different views on DME and what they are looking for in terms of 'effective DME education' at different stages of their child's education. The result is a complex patchwork of provision for children and young people with DME that will appeal to different individuals in different ways (and which, by definition, may not be suited to everyone at any one time). That said, there are some underpinning characteristics that should be common to all DME education, regardless of the setting or what is offered to nurture and inspire these children and young people.

According to Yates and Boddison (2020), effective DME education doesn't just happen in the classroom. Getting DME right takes place on several levels, including for national Governments and policymakers, for the whole school, for the classroom and in working with families. Go to www.jkp.com/catalogue/book/9781787758100 if you would like to read the list of suggested actions under each heading.

In addition, *Twice-Exceptional Gifted Children* by Beverly Trail shows how teachers and others can harness the strengths of the pupil with DME to ensure that they thrive in the classroom. She identifies a three-tier approach to DME education:

- **Tier 1: Universal support** – what is happening in the classroom in general. This includes things like supporting academic achievement, nurturing gifts and talent, encouraging interpersonal relationships and promoting understanding about themselves (intrapersonal relationships).

  The important point with all this is that it is done by everyone in the class. Although it might be done in slightly different ways (such as putting children on different tables or streaming), everyone will be in the same, inclusive, classroom. This low-level kind of support for your child with DME shouldn't cost any more than it would for any other child. Differentiation is something teachers should already be doing as a normal part of their job. Sometimes, this is all it takes in terms of the support your child with DME needs, and should be easy for the teacher to understand. However, if your child is not making the progress you think they should in the class, or if you feel that they need more challenge in their work or they are experiencing problems (such as social, emotional and mental health difficulties or behavioural challenges), you might need to try and get more targeted support for them.
- **Tier 2: Targeted support** – providing more intensive support for your child, such as working in small groups on specific topics (for example, anxiety) outside the mainstream classroom. This could include short-term tutoring for individuals or small groups that focus on specific topics such as how to tackle exam questions or how to plan. It could also include things like subject groups that are put together to enable children to learn at the stage they are and not

their age. It could include encouraging friendships, teaching skills to empower the child or young person, encouraging them to join school initiatives or to set up after-school or lunchtime groups themselves (such as Minecraft® groups).

Again, if your child has progressed onto some of these kinds of activities in Tier 2, and you feel they are still not making the progress you think they should, or if you feel that they need more challenge or they are experiencing problems, you might need to try and obtain more intensive support for them.

- **Tier 3: Intensive support.** Under Beverly Trail's model (and a structure that is common in many schools in the UK, even if the DME focus is different), Tier 3 is the highest level of support provided for the pupil with DME in school. Intensive support means just what it says – ideally it would be support involving one or more professionals diagnosing what is going on and providing an individualised programme of intervention to meet all the needs of your child with DME.

  The reality of this, of course, hinges on whether the school or educational environment has the resources (both in terms of money and time) to fund this, and whether they see all aspects of what may be needed as a priority. If, by this stage, you have developed an open and honest relationship with your child's teacher, you may get a clear signal about what the school can afford. Certainly, by this stage (and probably much earlier on), you may have had an assessment for your child. The school may even be talking about an EHCP (or equivalent).

  Examples of the kinds of things that may be put in place in Tier 3 to support your child with DME include individual support for specific areas such as in a subject, or to support behavioural or mental health difficulties (such as specialised counselling), moving up one or more classes (known as acceleration) or studying at a higher level in one or more subjects. It could also mean moving to a school that supports pupils with DME, early entry to college or university, apprenticeships or real-world experience, or mentoring by professionals in areas of interest. It could also include teaching coping methods and approaches for the individual to tackle their emotions.

Many children with DME will start to achieve once their needs have been recognised and they are receiving Tier 1 support. Others may need to go all the way to Tier 3 and this may take time and a lot of meetings between you and the professionals supporting them. However, what happens after Tier 3? If Tier 3 is not having the desired effect and, most importantly, if your child is miserable, depressed or their health or wellbeing is suffering, it may be time to think about moving schools or into alternative provision.

Unless your child's school is the only option available (which may be the case for some families), the reality is that you may already have been considering changing schools for your child even before the various options in the different tiers were pursued by the school. We will explore this in more detail later in this chapter.

BUILDING POSITIVE RELATIONSHIPS WITH PROFESSIONALS AS A PARENT OR CARER

Before we look at the options open to you if your child is unhappy at their current school, let's look at the importance for parents and carers of building positive relationships with professionals. Despite all of the concerns we have spoken about in this chapter, despite potential difficulties and problems, despite potential clashes of perspective and potential lack of recognition of DME or the support that is needed for your child with DME, building positive relationships with the professionals supporting your child is absolutely essential.

A positive relationship can make your life easier and, more importantly, can help your child to become the best version of themselves they can be. Even when you face challenges with your child or the setting they are in, a positive relationship can go a long way towards finding a solution. This doesn't mean that you fail to stand your ground when you want something to change, but having a positive attitude (even if you hated your own schooldays), asking questions in a supportive way, delivering your side of the bargain and getting involved in the school can all help to break down any barriers and build the positive relationships you need.

> When I first started having problems with my child at school, I decided to try and understand a bit more about how the school operated. So, I volunteered to go in and be attached to a class to listen to children read. Although it wasn't my own child's class, it was a real eye-opener in terms of seeing how the school worked. Later I joined the PTA [Parent Teacher Association] and helped organise things like Summer Fayres, fundraising events and other things. The teachers (including my child's class teacher) got to know me. I didn't do this to get any special treatment, but I found it much easier to go into school after that to discuss with them any concerns I had about my child. About two years before my child left the school, I was asked to stand as a Parent Governor, and I got elected. I found out about the school's education strategy and the amount of juggling they had to do to meet every pupil's needs. It taught me a lot, and I think my practical knowledge from being at the 'sharp end' with my child was useful to them too. (Parent)

Apart from getting involved with the school or educational setting, what else can help to build positive relationships between you and the professionals for the benefit of your child?

Being positive with your child about the professionals who support them

This doesn't mean that you are dishonest with your child. However, if you have a negative opinion about the professional, keep it to yourself and don't share it with your child. If your child has a bad opinion about them, ask them why this is, what it is they don't like about the person, what the professional does exactly, when they do it and other similar questions.

You can then ask them how they would prefer to be treated or spoken to (for example), and how the professional should be encouraged to do this. This gives your child a voice without you having given your own opinion about the professional.

Obviously, this may only work so far. For example, your child may ask for your opinion, in which case you could say that, while you hear them and their view is important, you don't know the professional well enough or have sufficient evidence to form your own opinion. An approach like this is more important for your child's self-confidence than one that contradicts their opinion or puts them down or tells them something like 'don't be silly'. Also, by questioning your child about their experiences with the professional, you will be able to collect valuable information to use if you really need it at some point (such as taking your child out of school).

Dealing with your concerns as soon as possible

If you do not address your concerns as soon as you feel able, there is a chance that they will grow into massive problems that then become more difficult to address. There is also a chance that by then you may be so emotional or tense that being able to solve the problem positively is significantly reduced. Even if you hate the thought of going to meet with a professional to sort out a problem, do not put it off. It is much better to have a discussion with the professional *before* it becomes something that cannot be easily sorted out or before your child takes matters into their own hands, such as being too anxious to go to school. An effective school will have an open-door policy. Don't be frightened to use it because you think that professional will not make time to see you.

Knowing your rights

Speaking to organisations first that can explain your rights and the school's responsibilities can be helpful. In addition, don't forget the specialist organisations that support DME that can help you prepare for your meeting.

> We did things a bit back-to-front and let the school lead us down the wrong route. Going into a meeting armed with facts, an understanding of what's possible and legitimate requests rather than feeling you are asking for special privileges can help to reduce frustration levels. (Parent)

Remaining calm (for as long as you can)

Try not to explode, especially at the first sign that the professional does not understand or says there is nothing they can do to help. Being calm and putting across your point of view is the best way to be able to get the problem resolved. Being angry, shouting and making personal remarks about the professional to their face is not the best way of forming a positive relationship for the benefit of your child. This applies even if any concerns you and your child have are not being heard, listened to or acted on. In situations like this, you may come to realise that the professional, you and your child are so far apart that there will never be a solution to the challenges you face. Perhaps you may also come to the conclusion that moving school or finding a different professional outside school to support your child are the only alternatives.

In the past, parents and carers have shared numerous stories about differences they have experienced with the professional supporting their child, such as being told that their extremely sensitive child 'just needs to toughen up', a teacher not accepting that a child had dyslexia, even after a professional assessment, a professional believing that a child's severe mental health difficulties were solely because of the way they had been brought up, and a carer having to move their child's school five times to get the right understanding and support.

Raising concerns positively

There is an excellent leaflet for parents and carers on the Whole School SEND Gateway (2021) coordinated by nasen.[5] This is part of the 'Ask. Listen. Do.' Series and is called 'Understanding SEN Support: Questions to support young people with SEND and families in conversations with schools'. The SEND Gateway is free to join, although you have to register first before you download the leaflet. As part of the same series, NHS England have produced a booklet on *Top Tips for Families and Carers* that may help you with providing feedback or raising complaints or concerns at school or elsewhere.[6]

Rather than becoming angry or emotional in difficult situations at school, being assertive in a positive way is more likely to help you to achieve your goal. This includes:

---

5   https://sendgateway.org.uk
6   www.england.nhs.uk/wp-content/uploads/2018/06/Ask-Listen-Do.pdf

- Using a positive tone that sounds confident and assertive rather than aggressive
- Being knowledgeable about your rights, the law and the relevant policies in the school or within your country
- Knowing what you are seeking to achieve from the discussion, and thinking about what a positive outcome of a meeting would look like
- Reflecting with the professional what is working well
- Being polite, clearly stating your case and what you are looking to achieve
- Asking what the school or professional can do to support you and your child with DME. If the answer is not as positive as you had hoped it would be, ask what the difficulties or problems are and how these could be solved
- If possible, negotiating towards something achievable for everyone. This could mean agreeing to a staged approach to support your child so that everyone could see what works
- Summarising what has been agreed, and thanking the individual for their time.

If, after you do all this, you are still no further with addressing your concerns (and do not know what the stumbling blocks to obtaining a compromise could be), anger is still not the answer to resolving your problems. You may need to walk away and look for an alternative solution, which could include:

- Obtaining a second opinion or approach to solving your dilemma
- Exploring an alternative way of addressing your concerns or finding alternative provision such as a different school or another type of education setting altogether
- Solving the problems relating to your child's DME in some other way. You may need to think more imaginatively about how to solve your concern, and this is where talking to or meeting (virtually or face-to-face) other parents and carers can give you the inspiration and ideas you may need.

Working hard to have positive meetings with professionals is vital not only in building good working relationships with professionals but also in helping to ensure your child's long-term wellbeing in a school that is effective at meeting their needs.

Want to know more? Go to www.jkp.com/catalogue/book/9781787758100 for some useful, practical tips for you if you have a formal meeting with professionals. These are for a meeting in school, but they could also be relevant in other environments.

Obviously not every meeting you have in school will need to be structured. Some will be far more informal or shorter. However, it is useful to be prepared, and the basic structure is often similar whatever kind of meeting is held.

PARENTAL INVOLVEMENT, ENGAGEMENT AND COPRODUCTION IN SCHOOLS

In the past, parents and carers were told what was going to happen to their child in school. Then they were consulted. Then, a few years ago, we had parental engagement (where parents and carers were even more involved with schools and had a say about how their child's education and support needs would be recognised and met effectively). The latest phrase is *coproduction*, which came out of the Children and Families Act in 2014. Its emphasis is on placing children, young people and their parents and carers at the centre of the decision-making process.

With coproduction, the school needs to ensure it develops clear policies and practice about how parents and carers and pupils will have a voice in making decisions about subjects such as how their child's SEND will be supported.

While coproduction may have been thought of in terms of SEND, for a child or young person with DME, the important thing is how their HLP interacts with their SEND. Merely being involved to help guide and influence how your child's SEND will be supported is only half the equation. Stretching and challenging their HLP must also be part of the coproduction process and delivered within the context of their SEND. If this does not happen, there is a real danger that a child's behavioural, social, emotional and mental health will worsen. This may result in a range of outcomes including inability to attend school, school exclusion and worse.

Schools themselves are starting to develop good practice to meet the challenges of coproduction, including using language and writing documents that can be understood by everyone, writing documents in age-appropriate language for children and young people and encouraging active involvement in evaluating whether an approach has worked.

Ultimately, meaningful coproduction happens for DME when parents and carers, professionals and pupils work together to:

- Make decisions about subjects such as the best ways to support DME in terms of the activities or approaches or professionals put in place
- Customise the support provided to meet both the HLP and SEND needs of the individual child or young person
- Involve all the relevant professionals who are (or who should or will be) supporting the child or young person with DME
- Identify funding needs (and the total budgets for support)
- Identify any training needs that professionals and others may have so they can have an in-depth understanding of DME and how to support it (and how this will be delivered)
- Agree how success will be measured and how and when it will be evaluated
- Identify any barriers to working in partnership and address these. This could include barriers to participation (such as parents and carers not having a computer or internet access or being unable to meet during the day because of work or childcare constraints or lack of time during the school day for the professional).

These kinds of requirements will be relevant for families and professionals no matter the kind of school or where it is located.

Underpinning these are the relationships between parent or carer, child or young person and professionals, which must be based on:

- The acceptance of and respect for everyone's feelings, wishes and concerns
- An open and honest discussion about what is wanted, what can be delivered and any problems in delivering it
- All members being equal and (in the case of children and young people) being involved in the discussion and any decisions made in an age-appropriate way

- Everyone's understanding of DME and the importance of a strengths-based approach towards meeting need
- An understanding of the type of environment that can best deliver what is agreed and any difficulties within the existing setting that would need to be addressed.

The school could write this up in a charter or commitment either for DME, SEND or HLP, or for all children and young people within the school.

Figure 6.1 shows the 'zone of coproduction' when everything is considered and real partnership takes place.

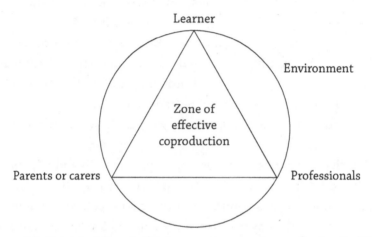

Figure 6.1. The principles of effective person-centred coproduction for DME
Source: Yates and Boddison (2020, p.45)

There are many advantages to everyone working like this, including everyone's increased confidence, a reduction in problems (or a speedier resolution to any problems that arise), greater ownership of solutions by everyone, better joint problem-solving skills rather than just relying on one person for their solution and changes in behaviour including more self-help by families and fewer incidents of professionals feeling they must provide all the answers. In the end, it is hoped that this work will have a positive impact on the child or young person's mental health, wellbeing and achievement levels.

If you are interested in finding out more about coproduction for DME, *The School Handbook of Dual and Multiple Exceptionality* (Yates and Boddison 2020) has a chapter on coproduction for teachers of pupils with DME.

WHEN SHOULD I EXPLORE ALTERNATIVE ARRANGEMENTS FOR MY CHILD'S EDUCATION?

If your child is unhappy, whatever their reasons, they are all valid. Listen to your child. Let them help you to problem-solve solutions to what is happening with them and that you feel could be delivered for them, either in school or elsewhere.

So far, we have talked about formal education being done in schools. While this is not the only way to deliver education, in the UK it is still the most popular education option (at least in the first instance) chosen by parents and carers. The question is, when should you explore alternatives to this for your child with DME if you are having challenges in the school they are currently attending? In other words, when is enough, enough?

Many parents and carers agonise over this. Changing schools or taking their child out of school altogether to try another kind of learning is often, quite rightly, seen as a big decision and not one that should ever be taken lightly. However, when all avenues have been followed within the school, when all other options have been considered (and tried), and if your child is still unhappy, it may be the only other option available.

How long should you wait before acting – six months? A year? It is difficult to be precise because all situations are unique. However, as a rough rule of thumb, consider the following:

- Your child's physical, emotional and mental health and wellbeing.
- Whether the school will ever be able to offer what you feel your child with DME needs.
- Whether any other professionals you have seen and trust agree that other solutions need to be found to support your child's DME.
- Whether you feel the professionals are listening to you.
- Whether you understand why your child's needs cannot be met. For example, is the problem due to lack of school resources or lack of understanding about or support for DME or some other problem?
- Whether any other options to support your child's learning exist or are suitable for your child and that you (and they) can support.

Of all these considerations, we believe that your child's health and well-being is always the most important consideration. If you feel that their current education setting is making this worse, trying to get this back on track should be your primary concern.

It is up to you how you define this. You know your child. For some children, one major incident may be all it takes. Other children will be resilient and will not want to leave their current school, even if their learning or other needs are not being met. There could be any number of reasons for this, from them not wanting to leave friendship groups to disliking change. It could also include their 'relief' at being left to coast in class without having to work too hard or to be pressurised in any way. 'Just being good enough' may be acceptable to them and even welcomed. It would mean they could carry on out of the 'achievement spotlight' and enjoy doing the things in which they are really interested.

Parents and carers sometimes mention that they have accepted that their child goes to school for social reasons and that their real learning takes place outside the classroom. In such situations, achievement may need to take a back seat in favour of a school where your child is happy in all other aspects of their learning. While some parents and carers may find this difficult to accept, it may be the only solution at the time.

> Once our child's initial needs for 'harder' maths were met, we then had to focus on the areas they struggled with to decide which ones mattered and which could be left. We had to gently support those areas that needed it, social skills, finding like-minded peers. This was a challenge but was met by the school enrolling our child in the Maths Olympiad and other maths competitions. For us, it was recognising that supporting our child's social and behavioural needs was more important than meeting their intellectual needs. We realised that our child couldn't learn if they weren't in a safe/happy place. This meant finding the right school and accepting a place in a special school. Academically, it wasn't that great, but it was right for our child at that time. Actually, our child taught me that having good emotional and social skills including resilience, patience and empathy are more important than gaining an A*!
> (Parent)

If parents and carers focus on the long term, preparing their child for life beyond school, this might put current achievement goals at school into context. It may mean helping with their child's self-confidence or self-esteem and using learning in school or outside as a way of finding their passion. In the long term, this can be just as valuable (if not more so). Exams and courses can be taken at any stage in someone's life. Physical and mental health, once gone, may be lost forever.

You may struggle with this approach. However, whatever your views on school and achievement, make sure your child's wellbeing is supported now, first and foremost. In doing this, love them unconditionally, do not judge their decisions, give them the skills they need for the long term, and wait.

Once you feel confident of your child's current health and wellbeing (or you have determined it is not so damaged that you need to take immediate action), you might then want to consider whether the school is able – in your opinion and that of the professionals who have been working with your child and whom you trust – to recognise and support your child's DME effectively.

Remember that a school may simply lack sufficient resources to support your child's DME appropriately. A good school will be honest about this or suggest ways in which the support could be provided, including paying for it yourself. Although this may not seem like a positive result (especially if you cannot afford to pay for the support needed), as an outcome it may be an honest one and one that you can build into your plans about what to do next. Honesty is always a better option than leaving a child or family wondering if the right support will be offered.

Some schools are experts at using pots of money effectively and using the latest schemes to support children and young people in a variety of different ways. These schemes change all the time and so it is worth asking your child's school if they have access to one that could be used to meet your child's needs. For example, some schools have made use of the Pupil Premium[7] and equivalent schemes to fund imaginative approaches to learning in school for specific groups of children (such as those eligible for free school meals, children adopted from care or those who have left care). Many schools have used this scheme to pay for additional support for high-achieving (or potentially high-achieving) pupils within the eligible categories.

---

7   www.gov.uk/government/publications/pupil-premium-allocations-and-conditions-of-grant-2020-to-2021/pupil-premium-conditions-of-grant-2020-to-2021

If your child is at school, you might then want to think about whether anyone is listening to your voice (or asking for your voice to be heard). As we have already argued, in many schools in the UK at least, knowledge and understanding about DME is low. Professionals may not know what DME is, how to identify it and, as important, how to support a pupil with DME effectively. You are your child's advocate. It is important that you speak up for them to help them thrive and to be the best version of themselves they can be in both their learning and life. Is your child's school listening?

Armed with a book to pass onto the teacher, or a fact sheet about DME, start a process to help them understand what it means to be DME and to recognise the kind of support a pupil with DME needs. Don't forget, there is summary information about DME in the downloadable resources and a free fact sheet can be downloaded from the Potential Plus UK website.[8]

If you feel that the school isn't listening (and that they will never listen), you might want to explore in detail any other options available to you and your child, and then evaluate whether you would consider any of these. For example:

- Unlike in a busy town (where there may be a good selection of primary and secondary schools), you may live in a rural area or one where there are few options (if any) other than the local primary or secondary school for your child to attend.
- You may not feel that you can afford a public school (although remember, many such schools offer bursaries or awards that provide funding for low-income families or for particular children, such as if your child were a talented musician).
- Even if such schools are within your reach, the only one on offer may require a long journey to attend it each day. Or there may be a boarding school where your child could go for education either during the week or term (although some do have day pupils). What are your views on this? You may or may not like the idea of either your child travelling long distances or leaving home for days or weeks at a time.
- If a school that charges fees is an option, it is just as important to check that your child's needs will be met. It is important to understand the rules, regulations and the structures in place to support

---

8   https://potentialplusuk.org

children with SEND, HLP and DME. These may be different between different types of school (such as private and state-funded). As with everything, there are good and not so good schools in all sectors. This means that whichever option you choose, you must ask the right questions and do your homework before making your final decision.

- Alternative models of education such as online learning can provide approaches that appeal to some young people. The Think Global School[9] even offers a travelling high school where students live in four different countries a year for three years!

- Some learning options can provide a mixture of online and face-to-face learning. For some, this 'blended' learning can provide the best of all worlds. This includes online learning in key subjects linked to classroom teaching, online schools within mainstream schools, flexi-schooling (see below) and a variety of other models that take the best from the traditional school and the best from any alternatives.

- Home education options are actively chosen by many families of children with DME either right from the start or following difficulties within school (including a child's exclusion from school or their growing anxiety about attending). Home education, however, is not for everyone. You may not be able to consider this because you work full-time and would find it difficult to fit your work around your child's needs. Alternatively, you may feel that you do not have the time, patience or skills to educate your child at home. Notwithstanding, home education models in the UK are delivered in a variety of ways such as through using tutors in different subjects, sharing the teaching between different parents or carers, bringing together groups of children for face-to-face or online learning, and a multitude of other different approaches.

WHAT IS FLEXI-SCHOOLING?

Flexi-schooling happens where a child or young person is educated for part of their day or week or for one or more specific subjects at home, and then spends the rest of the time in school. This means that they stay on the school register, will usually do any exams in

9   https://thinkglobalschool.org/about

school and will receive any benefits the school has to offer. The purpose of this is often to provide education more easily than is possible at home for certain subjects.

Parents and carers of children with DME (or HLP or SEND) may seek flexi-schooling for a variety of reasons, including the child or young person being overwhelmed or having significant meltdowns if they stay in the same classroom all day, having specific gifts or talents for which they need to train or enter competitions, such as chess or tennis competitions or theatrical performances, needing higher-level support in certain subjects than the school can provide and helping to prevent problems for the child including growing anxiety about attending school or their possible exclusion in future.

According to the Department for Education guidance for parents:

> Although children being home-educated are not normally registered at any school or college, you may choose to make arrangements for a child to receive part of his or her total education at school (flexi-schooling) or at an FE college or other provider if the child is aged 14+... Schools and colleges are under no obligation to agree to such arrangements, but some are happy to do so. (Department for Education 2019, p.5)

To obtain permission for flexi-schooling, it is worth getting the class or form teacher on board and then making a formal request to the school for the headteacher's agreement. They do not need to give this and may want to discuss this with other staff, the school's board of governors or equivalent or local authority, so approval may take some time.

Barriers to flexi-schooling that have been reported by parents and carers in the past include being told their child will miss out on topics being learned, being absent from key activities and not being able to catch up for tests and exams. However, for a child with DME it may be a positive solution to difficulties encountered at school, and a child with DME may be able to catch up with their work or do it at home with appropriate support.

If you are thinking of flexi-schooling your child and you live in

England, take a look at the article on flexi-schooling on the Home Education UK's website.[10] (It is always worth checking the Government websites (or equivalent) of your own country to obtain the latest guidance as legislation and approaches are often updated.)

Alternative options in schooling are in place, being considered or developed around the world. In the world of DME, the Bridges Academy in the US and others like it are held up as models of good practice for children with DME. In the UK, however, there does not yet seem to be a DME-focused state school that has been developed to provide free opportunities for all its pupils with DME. However, free schools in England may have the flexibility to provide this DME specialism. They are still funded by the Government, have more control over how they do things and do not have to follow the National Curriculum for educating pupils.

Despite a current lack of specialist provision, children and young people with DME may find that some of the elements of schooling outlined above may work for them. Home education (or home schooling) and online schools are explored in more detail in the next section as alternative approaches to education.

ALTERNATIVE MODELS OF EDUCATION

Home education and online schools have been growing in popularity in the UK over recent years. In this section, we explore both in a little more detail and provide more resources for you to look at if you are interested in exploring either or both options for your child.

Home education
A short history of home education

Home education has existed for centuries in the UK. However, it wasn't until the 1970s and 1980s that home education as a mass movement began in the UK, and the numbers of families who began to opt for home education – either through choice or necessity – grew, although even in

---

10 www.home-education.org.uk/articles/article-flexi-schooling.pdf

the 1980s, the numbers of children being home educated was still small in relation to the numbers in school. This changed in the 1990s, with more widespread use of the internet. Not only did this give children and young people easy access to lots of learning opportunities, which they had never had before; it also gave families the opportunity to talk to each other, to share resources and to find out about learning opportunities and ideas to deliver home education.

It is difficult to give an accurate figure for the numbers of home-educated children, as registration is voluntary, and anecdotal evidence suggests that some children do not appear on the list kept by their local authority to monitor the quality of delivery of the home education being provided in their area. These figures are also for England only, so the figure of 53,000–58,000 is likely to be an underestimate, and that is before we add in the effects of the pandemic where, for a while, all children in the UK were educated at home! It will be interesting to see how many have returned and how many have remained in home education over the next few years.

The delivery of home education

Home education is delivered in a variety of ways in England. In the home, it may be delivered face-to-face and on an individual basis by the child's parent or carer or by a tutor or other specialist or with a small group of other children or young people taught by parents or carers or by tutors. Outside the home, it may be delivered face-to-face by an external organisation (e.g., maths support organisation) in various locations (including supermarkets, coffee shops or equivalent). Online home education may be provided on an ad hoc basis to study a subject or area of interest through a course or a one-off class or in organised sessions with other children, such as Minecraft® clubs. One of the benefits of online learning is that education really does become learning without limits. Children and young people from across the globe can link up and do courses together, whether they live in Texas or Teddington, Glasgow or Gdansk.

What are my responsibilities as a home-educating parent or carer?

The latest Government guidance for parents and carers refers to *elective* home education, which is where a parent or carer proactively chooses home education as a positive way of supporting their child's education needs. Schools should do everything they can to work positively with parents and carers and pupils to ensure that those who choose home education only do so for positive reasons and not as the last resort because of problems with their school attendance, exclusion or other negative experiences.

The current legal position on home education in England is taken from *Elective Home Education* (Department for Education 2019) and is outlined below. However, before choosing to home educate your child, it is worth checking the latest guidance for your own country. If you need more information, see the websites for Schoolhouse (Scotland)[11] and Home Education Northern Ireland (HEdNI).[12]

THE CURRENT LEGAL POSITION OF HOME EDUCATION IN ENGLAND

2.1. As parents, you – not the state – are responsible for ensuring that your child, if he or she is of compulsory school age, is properly educated. Despite the term 'compulsory school age', education does not have to be undertaken through attendance at school, even though the parents of any child living in England can request a state-funded school place and the local authority is obliged to find one – or make alternative arrangements for education of your child.

2.2. There is no legislation that deals with home education as a specific approach. However, Section 7 of the Education Act 1996 provides that: The parent of every child of compulsory school age shall cause him to receive efficient full-time education suitable – (a) to his age, ability and aptitude, and (b) to any special educational needs he may have, either by regular attendance at school or otherwise. Elective home education is a form of 'education otherwise than at school' and this piece of legislation is the basis for the obligations of parents. It is also the starting point for local authorities' involvement.

2.3. A child becomes of compulsory school age from the first of the following dates (31 August, 31 December or 31 March) which occurs

---

11 www.schoolhouse.org.uk
12 www.hedni.org

after she or he becomes five years old (or if the fifth birthday falls on one of those dates, on that day). The child remains so until the last Friday of June in the academic year in which she or he becomes sixteen. Children may also be educated at home in order to participate in education and training until the age of 18.

2.4. You may also decide to exercise your right to educate your child at home from a very early stage, before he or she reaches compulsory school age. There are no requirements in that case as to the content of any home education provided – since there is no legal requirement for any education to take place at all, although state-funded places of between 15 and 30 hours a week would normally be available in early years settings for children of an appropriate age.

2.5. Unless otherwise stated, the rest of this guidance is solely concerned with the provision of home education for children who are of compulsory school age.

Source: Taken from Department for Education (2019, Section 2, p.6)

In other words, home education is a form of 'education otherwise', and is therefore legal in England.

One other type of education provision that it may be useful to mention is 'education otherwise than at school' (EOTAS). This is designed to meet the needs of children with SEND who, for whatever reason, cannot attend a mainstream or special school.

If a child or young person has an EHCP, they can still choose to home educate their child. However, the school no longer has any legal duty to secure any of the special provision outlined in their plan and parents and carers are responsible for making alternative arrangements.

If a school or college is not appropriate for your child, the local authority can arrange for any special provision they require to be delivered somewhere other than their school or college or even early years setting. In this instance, the local authority would be responsible for continuing to secure and fund that provision. This could include any therapies that would otherwise be provided in school (such as speech and language therapy). (For more information about this see the SENDIASS website.[13])

Parents and carers who choose to home educate are not required to have a set timetable for their child's education or set hours in which their education will take place. They do not even have to have set school days or terms. A child can start their formal learning before they are school age and go on past their leaving age. In other words, it is entirely flexible to meet the needs of the child or young person.

While there is no definition of a suitable education, it must be suitable for the age, aptitude, ability and special needs of the child or young person. However, there is *no* legal requirement for parents and carers to ensure that their child should do things like gain specific qualifications, be taught the National Curriculum, be given formal lessons, have any school-type socialisation with their peers or reach school-based age-specific standards.

According to Westminster guidance on elective home education, even if there is no specific link with the National Curriculum (or equivalent structure), aiming for an appropriate minimum standard may be useful. Many home-educating families will be doing some of these by choice already.

The departmental guidance for parents and carers also stresses the importance of the views of the child or young person. Many will have strong views about their own education and this may conflict with the views and opinions of their parents and carers. While the ultimate decision to educate a child or young person at home rests with their parents or legal guardians, the Westminster Government is guided by the United Nations Convention on the Rights of the Child (UN 1989). Section 12 states that:

> Parties shall assure to the child who is capable of forming his or her own views the right to express those views freely in all matters affecting the child, the views of the child being given due weight in accordance with the age and maturity of the child.

Another option for education that should be mentioned is deschooling (sometimes called 'unschooling'), which is a subset of home education. It usually happens when the child or young person has left school on a

---

13 www.sendiass4bcp.org/about-us.aspx

temporary or permanent basis. It is often suggested or put in place by parents and carers because of increased social, emotional, behavioural and mental health difficulties due to increased exam stress, school anxiety, bullying or other problems at school. Deschooling is, as the name suggests, an approach to education where there are no pressures or expectations at all to follow any kind of timetable or to do any formal learning. This does not have to mean that no learning takes place. However, if the child wants to spend all day reading a book, they can do this; if they want to go and visit the flamingos in the local bird sanctuary with their parent, nobody will stop them. They are free to follow their interests and passions or to discover new ones. Hopefully, at the same time, this approach will reduce the traumatic effects of what has happened to them and improve their resilience and future ability to cope with whatever life throws at them.

This kind of learning is often also beneficial to parents and carers who might have been under some strain in supporting their child in school. It gives both parties the chance to take a break from formal schooling and explore what they love about learning, when given the chance. Often, by removing the stress and pressure to learn, the child or young person will gradually be able to take on board learning in the subjects a school would recognise, although the speed with which they do this will depend on their experiences to date. If you are interested in learning more about deschooling, see the article on the Home Education in the UK website.[14]

As it is a subset of home education, deschooling is legal. The fact that no formal education takes place (although there may be lots of learning!) seems to put deschooling under the category of 'a settling in period for the child', but this should be checked with specialists in home education before this option is pursued and chosen for your child.

More generally, in thinking about whether you can educate your child at home in the long term, you may want to consider practical things like whether you have space in your house to do it and the skills and resources you need. If the local authority comes to evaluate the suitability of how you educate your child at home, they may also ask about these. So, discussing with them and others about what they want to do before you home educate permanently or for the long term (and think in terms of years rather than months) might help you to come to the right decision for your child and yourself.

---

14 https://home-ed.info/home_ed_articles/deschooling

An important consideration for parents and carers in deciding to home educate is the cost. According to the latest department guidance for parents in England:

> 3.6...if you choose to educate your child at home, you as parents must be prepared to assume full financial responsibility for the child's education, including bearing the cost of any public examinations (which would have to be entered via an external examinations centre, which may be some distance from your home). Some local authorities may provide financial or other assistance to home-educating families for public examinations, but this is discretionary. Other costs to consider include books, paper, IT and other equipment, and educational visits and sporting activities. Local authorities can consider giving support when special educational needs are being met through home education and additional costs are incurred because of those special needs. Even in these cases, assistance is discretionary. Some local authorities operate support groups or forums for home-educating families, or provide access to advice; but again, this is discretionary. (Department for Education 2019, p.11)

In most cases, therefore, when you choose home education you also need to be prepared to pay for it yourself, although it is worth checking what support is available from your local authority (or equivalent). While this can sound off-putting, help is sometimes at hand through organisations that support learning opportunities for those who cannot afford it through to charities and parent groups that help support those who home educate. In other words, you do not have to do this alone.

Details of some of the main national organisations supporting parents and carers who home educate are provided at www.jkp.com/catalogue/book/9781787758100. However, lots of home education activity happens at a local level. Going on to the internet, to your local library or volunteer centre (or equivalent) should help you find a local home educating group to contact. Perhaps the best known of the home educating groups in the UK is Education Otherwise (go to www.jkp.com/catalogue/book/9781787758100 for information about them).

So what do you have to do to move your child into home education? There are two main strands for parents or carers:

- Deciding to home educate if your child is not yet enrolled at school.
- Deciding to move your child into home education when they are in school.

Home education before school enrolment

Under current guidance, if your child had never been enrolled at school, you do not have to inform your local authority in England and you do not have to get anybody's consent to home educate. That said, if you want guidance or advice from the local authority, it might be worth letting them know that you have decided to home educate.

Moving into home education from school

If your child is at school and you decide to take them out to home educate them, you do not have to tell the school that you have done this, although it might be a good idea to do this so that they do not impose some kind of penalty (such as a fine) for your child's non-attendance or put your child into their system for non-school attendance.

As well as the school, you do not legally have to inform the local authority in your area, although it may be a good idea to do this as well so that you can access any advice or support from them. These rules also apply to children and young people with EHCPs. However, where your child attends a special school arranged by the local authority, you must obtain the school's permission before it can remove your child's name from the school's admissions register. If the local authority refuses its permission, you can appeal to the Secretary of State for Education (or equivalent).

In England, permission to home educate must also be obtained if your child is attending any school because of a school attendance order. This order must be removed before the authority can have your child's name taken off the admissions register.

In England, Ofsted can carry out inspections from time to time of local authorities. This may include the way in which they carry out their duties in relation to vulnerable children. Although home-educated children are not necessarily 'vulnerable', such reviews will include children missing education, and may therefore cover the work of the authority on behalf of those children who are being educated at home. Reports of local authority inspections are available on the Ofsted section of the GOV.UK website (see Ofsted 2021).

As with other kinds of regulations, it is always worth keeping up to date with the latest approaches in your own country.

What's next for home education in the UK?

Home education has been growing at a tremendous rate in the whole of the UK. At present, its future is secure. However, in England at least, there have been moves in Government for some time to tighten up the rules relating to educating a child outside school and making sure that the quality of the home education delivered is rigorously evaluated and of high quality. Many powerful Government professionals, even when they have no real knowledge of home education, seem determined to reduce the number of children receiving it. Whether this comes to pass or not will depend on – among other things – the strength of the parent and carer voice.

To turn the subject on its head and examine it through a different lens, how many children will need to leave mainstream schooling to finally encourage those in office to embrace this form of learning and to recognise that, for some children and young people, it is the best way of all to inspire their education?

Online learning

Online learning can take many forms, from doing a free taster course in a subject, to paid-for, recognised qualifications up to degree level and beyond. These can be delivered in a variety of ways, from online teaching backed up with paper-based work through to everything being done online.

In the UK, most people think of The Open University as one of the early pioneers of online learning. This was established in 1969, well before the internet was in widespread use (with the World Wide Web as we know it today being invented by Tim Berners-Lee in 1980). Since then, many adults (and some young people as well) have received Bachelor's or Master's degrees or other qualifications in a variety of different subjects. Many young people with DME have studied courses at The Open University.

■ **Tips and hints:** Applying to The Open University as a young person with DME

According to The Open University's Policy for the Admission of Applicants under the age of 18:

...a young person must normally be 16 years old or older by the start date of the module for which they wish to enrol or register. This policy sets out three exceptional admissions criteria for students under 16...

...The Open University will exceptionally consider applications to register to study with The Open University from young people who are under the age of 16. Each application will be considered on its own merits... (The Open University n.d., pp.1, 6)

This policy may change from time to time and would need to be checked with The Open University. However, in the past, this policy has led to children as young as 11 or 12 being able to start degree courses, once they met the admissions criteria. If you would like to read about one child's journey down this path, *Gifted! The Story of a Teenage Genius* by Cameron Thompson and his family may be worth looking at.

In 2012, The Open University, in partnership with Seek Ltd, set up FutureLearn,[15] a Massive Open Online Course (MOOC) learning platform. This offers free courses and taster sessions in a variety of subjects, from languages to psychology, computing and more. In 2020, FutureLearn partnerships with universities and other providers were added to help teach adults and young people in a variety of subjects. Many children and young people find this online learning experience great fun. According to FutureLearn:

You need to be over the age of 12 to access the platform. The content is university calibre but designed to be accessible to all. (FutureLearn n.d., p.3)

Some parents and carers with children younger than 12 have reported that they have registered for courses and then made their mind up about whether the learning would be suitable for their child with DME and, if so, sharing it with them.

At the time The Open University was created, some felt that there should be an alternative option for those people who wanted or needed to improve lower-level or practical skills. As a result, The Open College was created in 1987 and ran until 1991. Based on The Open University model, it was a publicly funded distance learning college that transmitted courses via television programmes on Channel 4. It offered courses below degree level,

---

15 www.futurelearn.com

in subjects ranging from basic education to vocational courses. As it was publicly funded on an open channel, anyone could watch the programmes shown, although registration and payment had to be made for things like assessments. Although it closed in 1991, it led to the development of organisations like the National Open College Network[16] and The Open College of the Arts,[17] both of which are still in existence.

As technology has become accessible to more and more people, the number of online schools and colleges for young people and adults has grown, both in the UK and around the world. There is a charge for accessing these and few specifically support children and young people with DME. While there are many online courses that will support children and young people with DME, schools that provide the 'total education experience', from initial assessment of need to packages that meet that need, groups so that relationships can be formed with like-minded peers, to someone who can take care of the welfare and achievement of the child, are much rarer. Most are within the private sector (for which there is a charge, even if grants or bursaries are available), and so state-recognised online schools are the rarest of all. Certainly, in the UK, the one that also recognises and supports the needs of pupils with DME is almost non-existent.

In terms of schools in the state sector, the only one explicitly supporting children and young people with DME is the Nisai Academy.[18]

ABOUT THE NISAI ACADEMY

While this offers a blended learning approach, online learning is at its core. The key for children and young people with DME is that in all its online learning it considers their stage in terms of their ability and not their age. Using online learning as all or part of the learning solution, Nisai offers a variety of different services, including:

- Physical schools with an online learning focus
- Schools within existing schools for pupils to access all or part of the curriculum while still within the school environment
- Home education packages.

---

16 www.nocn.org.uk
17 www.oca.ac.uk
18 www.nisai.com

Within the school environment, for example, a pupil with DME might need extra support with their writing and literacy, and would be put in an appropriate online class with Nisai Learning to do this. However, they may be more knowledgeable and advanced in their abilities in maths or science and thus be able to access teaching at a higher level.

Although Nisai normally support children with DME at secondary school age, they do make exceptions. They have also established a Skills Academy to help young people get the skills they need to move into work.

In terms of funding, while you could pay for your child to learn with Nisai, if your child has been excluded or is no longer able to attend mainstream school, in England at least, the Government has a legal obligation to provide education to all children up to the age of 16. This means that a funding option should always be available. What makes Nisai unusual in its support for pupils with DME is that it is funded and commissioned by a child's school or local authority.

By the end of 2020, Nisai had been approved by 30 local authorities, and this number is increasing. Quite often, working with a specific child or young person with DME – in partnership with parents and carers – will help support the local authority in providing a child with SEND and DME with the most appropriate education to meet their needs.

If this is not an option for you, other initiatives may be on offer within your child's school to fund all or part of their learning with Nisai. The funding available within schools changes all the time. Working in partnership with Nisai before approaching your child's school is therefore a good idea. You may also want to do this to check in advance whether your child responds well to this type of learning. There are occasionally grants available from Nisai or others to fund a short trial period for your child.

Meeting the dual needs of a child with DME is not easy. Providing work that stretches and challenges such children and provides a faster pace to their learning, yet delivered within the context of their SEND, will require imaginative approaches to learning in a variety of settings. For many of these children, online learning provides one possible solution to meeting their needs. Others may not yet have been considered or even invented.

Perhaps one day we will see the establishment of specialist education provision in the UK that combines all we know about effective education for children and young people with DME. This will require vision at the highest level and the ambition to provide education solutions nationally that work for children and young people with DME in the UK. We eagerly wait for that day to come.

CONCLUSION

This chapter has provided an overview of how to work in positive partnership with schools to help ensure they recognise and support both your child's strengths and the challenges they face, thereby enabling them to be the best versions of themselves they can be.

In many ways, it has only skimmed the surface of what is happening to support DME up and down the country, if not the world. Just as every child and young person is unique and every parent and carer different, so, too, is every teacher or professional who will support your child and every way in which they will teach. There are hundreds – if not thousands – of different educational environments and models of delivery. All of these provide the UK with a rich tapestry of learning opportunities that could benefit the child or young person with DME.

We have learned that one size definitely does not fit all. An excellent school for one family is the same one another family does everything to avoid. Also, there cannot be rules and regulations to cover how every child learns and what makes them passionate about learning.

However, education and learning is more than the building or the approach used. It is about the professional – the teacher or other person – who just 'gets' your child with DME and who inspires them to find their passion. It is about the individual who mentors them and provides them with lessons for learning that will stay with them for the rest of their life. It is about someone believing in them, who supports them through 'thick and thin', and who picks them up when they feel things have gone wrong or when they begin to doubt themselves.

The people who do this are you and the professionals and the others who live and work with your child. We hope that this chapter has helped to give you the tools to make that positive partnership happen.

> Want to know more? Further information can be found at www.jkp.com/catalogue/book/9781787758100

FURTHER READING
Resources on DME to support the teacher or other professional

Susan Baum, Robin Schader and Steven Owen (2017) *To Be Gifted and Learning Disabled: Strength-Based Strategies for Helping Twice-Exceptional Students with LD, ADHD, ASD and More*. Prufrock Press; 3rd edition.

Kelly Hirt (2018) *Boost: 12 Effective Ways to Lift Up Our Twice-Exceptional Children*. GHF Press.

Scott Barry Kaufman (2018) *Twice Exceptional: Supporting and Educating Bright and Creative Students with Learning Difficulties*. Oxford University Press.

Diane Montgomery (2003) *Gifted and Talented Children with Special Education Needs: Double Exceptionality*. Routledge.

Diane Montgomery (2015) *Teaching Gifted Children with Special Educational Needs: Supporting Dual and Multiple Exceptionality*. Routledge.

Beverly Trail (2011) *Twice Exceptional-Gifted Children: Understanding, Teaching and Counseling Gifted Students*. Prufrock Press; illustrated edition.

Belle Wallace, Sue Leyden, Diane Montgomery, Carrie Winstanley, Michael Pomerantz and Sally Fitton (2010) *Raising the Achievement of All Pupils within an Inclusive Setting: Practical Strategies for Developing Best Practice*. Routledge.

Denise Yates and Adam Boddison (2020) *The School Handbook for Dual and Multiple Exceptionality: High Learning Potential and Special Education Needs or Disabilities*. Routledge.

Real-life stories of interest to parents and carers

Elaine Halligan (2018) *My Child's Different: The Lessons Learned from One Family's Struggle to Unlock Their Son's Potential*. Crown House Publishing.

Rod Thompson, Alison Thompson, Bethany Thompson and Cameron Thompson (2012) *Gifted! The Story of a Teenage Genius*. CreateSpace Independent Publishing Platform.

About home education

Wes Beach and Sarah Wilson (2012) *Forging Paths: Beyond Traditional Schooling*. GHF Press.

Gill Hines and Alison Baverstock (2019) *The Home Education Handbook: A Comprehensive and Practical Guide to Educating Children at Home*. Piatkus; illustrated edition.

Pamela Price (2013) *How to Work and Homeschool: Practical Advice, Tips and Strategies from Parents. Vol. 5.* GHF Press.

Eloise Richman (2020) *Extraordinary Parenting: The Essential Guide to Parenting and Educating at Home.* Scribe UK.

Simon Webb (2010) *Elective Home Education in the UK.* Trentham Books.

YOUR ACTION PLAN

1. Listen to your child and value their opinion about their education.
2. Make sure that their wellbeing comes first in everything you do with their learning.
3. Try and develop positive relationships with any professionals who teach your child.
4. Advocate for your child about what they need to support their DME.
5. Don't give up if things don't go according to plan, but keep trying to get your child's DME needs met.
6. Know when alternative solutions need to be found and put in place an action plan for what to do and when.
7. Don't be afraid to explore alternative types of education, such as online learning and home education, to meet all or some of your child's learning needs.

CHAPTER 7

Where Next? The Way Forward

INTRODUCTION

At this point, hopefully, your child may be settled at school. You may have developed a positive relationship with the professionals who support them. Their teachers and other staff in their school may have started to understand and support Dual or Multiple Exceptionality (DME) in general or your child specifically. Or you may have made the decision for your child to move into other kinds of provision such as home education, online schooling or something completely different. Apart from a few problems that you can handle, you may feel that your job is done.

That's the good news.

The not so good news is that every parent and carer, no matter the age of their child, will always worry about their child.

The purpose of this chapter is to give you the hope and the belief that, no matter how you feel now, no matter the problems you face, and no matter what lies ahead, you do have the skills and the growing confidence to deal with them. You should also know that, if you need help along the way, there is a range of organisations that can provide the ongoing support and guidance you may need.

THERE ARE ALWAYS OPTIONS

No matter how difficult or hopeless you believe a situation is, you need to believe that there is a solution for everything, even if you don't like the answer. The greatest skills you need, we believe, include:

- Listening to what your child is saying

- Problem-solving to list all the possible solutions to whatever they are facing
- Negotiating with others – your child, teachers, professionals, other family members – to make the solution feasible
- Project management – making sure the option decided on is put into place and works
- Patience and impatience (whichever are needed)
- A positive attitude and the ability to recognise and praise effort and success.

You are already using these skills already every day, *every day*. You now need to apply them to the different situations you may face.

'That may be easy to write, but more difficult to put into place', you may say. Not every situation can be solved. However, if you start with a positive attitude that there is a solution for everything, there will be a way through any difficulties you face. As we have said, though, you may not like the solution, and so you, or others, may need to give a little. However, starting from the position that there is an answer, that you just need to find it, can help. Then many, if not all, problems can be solved. Let's look at a couple of examples to illustrate this.

Example 1: Your teenage child with DME develops severe behavioural difficulties at home. Your relationship with them breaks down to the point that they will not talk to you about what is going on. You ask them what is wrong, but they won't tell you. However, they do say that the only option is for them to teach themselves at home. They begin to have increased anxiety about going to school. So you meet with the school to try and sort it out. However, either the school does not recognise what is going on or they don't know how to solve it. Instead, they tell you that your child has not been attending school and you will be getting a letter about this, and possibly a fine. What can you do?

Despite your child being more than capable of getting good grades in their exams (and you being ambitious for them to do this), the obvious solution for your child is to pull them out of school to focus on ways to reduce some of their anxiety (possibly opting for deschooling for a while). You remember that this is their life and the decisions they make need to be theirs alone. They need space to find out what their interests are and to create and follow their own dreams and ambitions.

It takes 11 years of learning and exams taking a backseat. During that time, you have tried not to interfere and have learned to be patient. Until one day, your child begins to ask the question 'What am I going to do with the rest of my life?' They now need to find out that answer for themselves.

Example 2: Your child has thrived in their primary school and absolutely loved it. Teachers there understood them, and you felt a lot of accommodations had been made for their bright, quirky nature and ways of learning. Your child hates change, and you are worried that going to secondary school will make them anxious and prove a negative experience for everyone. You explore all the options for schools in your area. Everything seems so large, and you feel your child would hate it. You explore other options. Eventually, you find a small school about an hour away that you think would better meet their needs. The academic work this school provides, on paper, seems fantastic. Your child could even learn languages like Mandarin Chinese! Compared to the performance of the local school, you feel it would be much better for your child.

You decide to talk about both options with your child before filling in any school application forms. You make a list of everything you think your child needs. Then you ask your child to do the same. Their list looks nothing like yours! They want a locker and want to be with their friends. They like the idea of being able to walk to the secondary school and want a school that has a Minecraft® club they can join. You take their views on board and both of you go and visit the local school and the school an hour away. The local school impresses you. It could deliver most of the things your child (and you!) was looking for. The SEND coordinator (SENCo or SENDCo) seems willing to listen about your child's traits and their need for stretch and challenge within the context of their SEND. They outline the support programmes available, including helping those children who may be concerned about change (such as transition from primary to secondary school) and those with social, emotional and mental health difficulties. You are impressed. More importantly, so is your child. The SENCo looks at them when they talk about what they could do. Even the size of the school doesn't put your child off (once they know there is support available for them).

The smaller school an hour away does not inspire your child in the same way. The buildings look wonderful, and the exam results seem fantastic, but the teachers talk to you when you meet them and ignore your child. Their only advantage seems to be their results. The children in the school are dressed smartly and seem to be working hard, but there doesn't seem to be any room for a bright and quirky child who thinks differently, who asks strange questions, and who needs their learning to be inspired.

You talk to your child about the dilemma. Your child makes an important point to you that being happy is more important than exam results. With your child's involvement you make the application to the local secondary school. A year later, you believe you have made the right decision. Where there have been problems, someone in the school has always listened. The school's size means there are lots of specialists who can help with different areas of concern you have had. Your child has even set up a 'Bright and Quirky' club for all those who think just like them, and it even has Minecraft® sessions!

Would you have made the same decisions? Perhaps not. However, both parents problem-solved in different ways. In both, their behaviour or perspective had to change before any solutions could be found to their dilemma. Other problems may take similar changes in teachers or others. The key point is that even where problems seem hard to solve, believing you *can* find a solution is a good place to start. Then the options need to be considered and the best one chosen with the knowledge and understanding you have at the time. These are skills we have been learning throughout this book. Use them.

WHAT WOULD YOUR CHILD WITH DME NOW SAY TO OTHER CHILDREN WITH DME, WITH THE BENEFIT OF HINDSIGHT?

The Potential Trust, in partnership with other organisations, recently carried out a survey of children and young people with DME, adults with DME and parents and carers of these individuals. One of the questions asked was about the suggestions (with the benefit of hindsight) those with DME would make to their past selves (or others like them now) when they were just starting out on their DME journey. The words below are the children's, young people's and adults' own words, which speak for themselves.

The views of children and young people with DME

The support of their family was particularly important to children and young people with DME, along with having like-minded friends who 'have their back' and the support and understanding of others, particularly teachers and other professionals. In terms of what they would say to support other children with DME:

On family:

- Family support really helped me.

On friendship:

- Keep looking for someone who 'gets you'.
- Making friends with like-minded people like you really helps.
- Just be yourself and find places to go and things to do where people are like you.

On understanding yourself:

- Life might get tricky or upsetting, but just remember your strengths and happy memories really will help.
- My family helped me make the most of my superpower. Try and make the most of yours every day.
- Don't always look at the bad things; focus on the good.

On finding a champion:

- Find someone to fight your corner and, if you trust them, try to believe them when they say something nice about you.
- Describe any difficulties you have as best you can.
- Tell your parents or someone if things go wrong or things aren't working. Get them to find you a better activity or teacher.

On learning:

- Make the most of extra lessons, stretching your learning and using technology to learn.
- Think 'outside the box'.

The views of adults with DME

Adults with DME were more negative than the younger children, perhaps as they had lived longer and had to cope with DME in secondary school (which was often seen by them as a more negative experience) and beyond.

On friendship:

- Don't be anxious to keep friendships with people who mostly make you feel bad. Invest in friendships with people that are good.
- Find structured activities or a club or group that you can take part in.
- Don't stay in situations where you're being hurt by people even if at first adults don't listen to you or support you.
- Be patient and look for 'your people'.

On understanding yourself:

- Just be yourself. It is not always easy but in the end it is worth it.

Having DME may mean that many people will not judge you on two counts but will only look at one or the other. Hence, good qualities may be overlooked by people looking at your Special Educational Needs or Disabilities and those looking at these will not see your exceptionalities. (Parent)

- Keep moving forward. It's never too late to find your niche.
- Don't try and be someone you are not.

I have had many people try to put limits on what I could achieve because they saw me as a child with dyslexia and didn't look at what I had already accomplished. (Parent who has a child with DME)

- Trust yourself. There are many people who will tell you what is best for you, even if you tell them it wouldn't be beneficial.

- If life gets dark, keep pushing until you find the light.
- Your childhood doesn't have to define you, nor do any negative experiences. You are more than them.

See your weaknesses as equal to your strengths in life. Think of both before you embark on a project or goal. Then you will be in balance with yourselves. (Parent)

- Some unpleasant situations may be unavoidable, and you just have to endure them and believe that, when you grow up, you can create a good life for yourself.

On finding a champion:

- Find the support you need and lean on this when you need it.
- Ask people to support you, especially for the things you find difficult like spelling words or understanding what people are saying or mean.
- Get teachers to understand that there are different ways of communication. You don't always have to write things down.
- Find someone who knows things you want to learn and is interested in teaching you.

Ask for help if you need it. Being smart doesn't mean you don't need help. We all need help at some point. (Parent)

- Have a mentor to support you, especially if your family can't.
- Find someone who will listen to you and understand what you are going through and help you work with teachers and parents to find a solution.

You can overcome whatever difficulties you face and become successful if you can just find people who are willing to give you a chance. (Parent)

- Keep looking for someone who will listen properly and understand and help you figure it out.
- Keep trying to talk to others until someone listens. This makes you feel heard. When you find them, ask them to help you as much as they can.

> You shouldn't have to be alone but finding someone who is equipped to help can be so rare. So just keep on trying. (Parent)

On learning:

- Have as many experiences as possible. Get library books, go to museums and outside to explore nature. Let parents and carers stimulate your curiosity, but also allow yourself to be bored.
- Learn how to talk to other people, the etiquette of this and how conversations work on a theoretical basis.

On family:

> The most beneficial events in my life were due to family support. (Parent)

WHAT WOULD YOU SAY TO OTHER PARENTS AND CARERS OF CHILDREN WITH DME?

Among other things, the survey also asked parents and carers for the top three suggestions they would make to other parents and carers of children with DME who were just starting out on their journey. What kind of things do they wish that they had been told? As you might expect, this resulted in a lot of different suggestions.

About parents' and carers' relationship with their child with DME:

Really understand your child:

- Really understand your child, both their positives and negatives, and embrace and celebrate their differences.
- Try to learn and see what your child's world is like and see things from their perspective.
- Remember, it's like having two children in one body.
- Don't compare your child with others; let them be themselves.
- Take care of your child emotionally.
- Focus on your child's strengths and build their confidence.

Help your child to shine at what they are good at:

- Enable them to succeed at things they are good at rather than always trying to work on the things they find difficult.

Be their champion:

- Be your child's biggest champion, publicly support them and defend them to others (advocate for them), especially those who don't understand them.
- Love them unconditionally and believe in them.

Communicate effectively:

- Listen to your child and what they are saying, and make sure you communicate with them all the time.
- Give your child the space to be themselves and to do their own thing.
- Be honest with your child about who they are.
- Be honest with your child about yourself, what you know and when you get it wrong.

Be honest with your child. Sometimes, adults don't know everything, can be downright wrong and are quite capable of being total a**holes! (Parent)

Help them find activities and friends:

- Help your child to find hobbies that interest them and make use of these to find friends.
- Be prepared to think 'outside the box' and try different things until you find one that works.

I think as a parent or carer of a child with DME, you need to put in place a lot of structure. All days have to have some intellectual stimulation, physical activities and breaks when needed. Make a plan for during the week and also at the weekends. Unplanned time can be stressful for your child. This needs to be flexible in case they are having a bad day. (Parent)

- Keep your child active.
- Help your child to socialise with other children with DME and to find friends who just 'get them'.
- Teach your child about important things in life like morals and how to deal with others.

About parents' and carers' relationships with friends and family:

- Encourage friends, family and others to learn as much as they can about DME.
- Accept that you may lose friends who just don't understand your child or what you are doing. You will find new ones who do.

Accept that some friends don't 'get it' and you'll drift apart. Find people who do 'get it' instead. (Parent)

About parents' and carers' relationship with professionals:

Encourage greater understanding of DME:

- Make sure that teachers and other professionals (and the establishments they work for) have the right training, and make sure that your child (and others like them) is understood and supported in the right way.
- If a teaching professional keeps telling you that your child is naughty, ignore this and focus on your child's unmet needs.
- Try and make an ally of professional staff so they can help to support your child.
- Accept that professionals will look for labels to rationalise their understanding of differences. Remember that your child is more than a label when they analyse their strengths and challenges.

Find a DME champion:

- Find experts who are supportive and help champion your child and DME.

Getting the right support:

- If you need to, make sure you get a formal assessment of DME or other issues you are worried about. Don't wait until they become problems.
- Try to solve any problems as soon as they arise. Don't delay the support your child may need.
- Trust your instincts when it comes to educational settings, support or diagnoses for your child. What is your gut telling you?

Trust your instincts. You know your child better than anyone. You understand their needs and what works for them. You also probably know more about their specific conditions than many medics or educationalists with whom you'll deal. Trust these instincts. Be strong and don't allow yourself to be ignored or put down. You're almost certainly right. (Parent)

The skills that parents and carers need to develop to support their child:

- Do your own research about DME, High Learning Potential (HLP) and Special Educational Needs and Disabilities (SEND). Don't rely on experts.
- Educate other adults about your child and DME in general.
- Keep on top of the latest thinking about DME and your child's SEND.

Research and have in your mind or on paper in your pocket examples of what happens elsewhere to support DME or research on the latest thinking or even the law so you can back yourself up in a meeting with a professional. Show that you know what you are talking about and are not to be ignored! (Parent)

- You need to navigate the system, so get to understand the right activities or support packages that exist for your child.
- Remember, children with DME won't always fit into mainstream activities and a lot of SEND activities will be too basic for them. So, you will really have to look for the right things for them to do.
- The internet means that there is more information available out

there on DME and the support you and your child needs. If you can, use it to become an expert yourself.

About parents' and carers' relationship with themselves:

- Being a parent or carer with a child with DME can be lonely, so reach out to others for support.
- It can also be really, really hard, emotionally, mentally and sometimes physically. So make sure you put in place strategies for self-care and recharging your batteries so you can ride your own rollercoaster with your child.

> Remember the instructions for putting on an oxygen mask when asked to on an aeroplane? If you don't put yours on first, you will not be able to help and support your child. (Parent)

- Join as many support groups as you need to find out about DME, and get support for yourself in the process.
- Find your own peer group. Not only may this help find other peer support for your child, but it will also mean there are other parents and carers to support you.
- Understand that your child's needs and wants are not the same as yours. Try not to force them to want or be what you want them to be.

> The hardest bit can be to accept your child for who they are. (Parent)

- Progress not perfection is the aim.
- Remember, DME can be an advantage.

This survey was conducted in 2020 and the results were published in 2021 and can be found on The Potential Trust website.[1]

---

1   www.thepotentialtrust.org.uk

HELPING YOUR CHILD TO NAVIGATE THE MAZE AHEAD

As we have continually stressed throughout this book, every single child, parent, carer, family, professional, school and situation is different. And that's before we build in different cultures, views, parts of the country and all those other things that make us unique. All of this gives a rich tapestry of views and perspectives you will encounter with and about your child with DME. Some of these will be positive, some will not be so positive, and some will be major hurdles for you and your child to overcome in the months and years ahead.

As your child grows older, they will become more and more independent, until finally they will fly the nest and leave home to go to college or university or to work or travel or to take advantage of the infinite number of opportunities that will be on offer when they are ready to leave. What can you do to help them to navigate the maze ahead?

Here is a short list of some of the practical things you might want to consider. You could build on this list to meet your child's needs and DME characteristics and also their circumstances.

What kind of skills does your child need for the future?	Examples
Financial skills	Budgeting, managing bank accounts, paying bills, paying rent or buying property

cont.

What kind of skills does your child need for the future?	Examples
Practical house skills	Washing and drying clothes, making beds, cooking, cleaning
Job application skills	CVs and writing job applications, developing the skills needed for work, coping with rejection, managing documents and paperwork
Advocacy skills (speaking up for themselves)	Putting forward their own case (e.g., for support), negotiating (e.g., for a pay increase)
General welfare skills	Registering for a doctor or dentist, researching and understanding different types of support (e.g., free support or paid services) and finding insurance for items
Basic DIY skills	Changing a plug, changing a fuse, putting a screw in a wall, assembling flatpack furniture
Cooking skills	Cooking enough of their favourite meals so they can cope on their own, cooking on a budget
Accommodation skills	Looking at the accommodation options in an area, evaluating whether one is better than another, finance and contracts related to accommodation, furnishing accommodation, reading gas and electricity meters

Some of these seem obvious. Some of them may already be taught in their school. However, a number of young people – especially those who have been put into 'Gifted groups' or 'Higher Ability classes' – may not have been taught these basic skills at school and may struggle with them when they are older, unless you teach them at home. This is because their classes can often focus on theories and higher concepts rather than the practical everyday skills they may also need.

It is a good idea to help your child develop these kinds of skills as early as possible, so that they are confident in doing basic practical things before they leave home (even if they choose never to cook for themselves or make their bed after they leave you!). What can seem like a fun game when they are four or five years old will help to give them the skills they need in life. We have all had to learn these (to a greater or lesser degree), and many of us still rely on our parents or carers, even now, to help with problems we encounter. However, giving your child the basics will help them more easily navigate the maze that lies ahead.

CONFIDENCE WITH MONEY

Many children with HLP like to get their teeth into real subjects and dilemmas so they can understand the relevance of what they are doing or learning. In terms of confidence with money, some suggestions for helping with this when they are young include:

- Encouraging your child to save up small coins that they can count out and spend in a shop or save and spend later on a larger item they want.
- Helping your child to set up a bank account and then pay small amounts of money into it on a regular basis.
- Agreeing with your child what they will receive as pocket money (if anything) and then providing this for them to either save for the future or to spend now.

Pocket money is a hot topic in some families – whether to give it, at what age to start it, what to give it for, how much it should be. According to Statista (2020), the average pocket money for children in the UK in 2020 ranged from £2.78 at the age of 4 to £8.08 at the age of 14.

According to Alex Rayner, writing for RoosterMoney (2021) (a global movement that supports parents and carers to support their children to learn about money):

> The most common 'jobs' that earn pocket money are things like tidying the bedroom, making the bed, doing the washing and looking after pets.

RoosterMoney has a Rooster Card with limits set by you and which is designed to enable children to make decisions safely in the real world and a Virtual Pocket Money Tracker.

Although this is a contentious area for many (and one that might conflict with your values or beliefs), the advantages of this or similar systems are that:

- They give children and young people real-life understanding of money, finances, saving and budgeting
- They can give confidence in dealing with making financial decisions.

Often, the first time many children and young people have money of their own is when they receive grants to pay towards their education (such as at university), gain an apprenticeship or find a job. If they are not used to things like budgeting, saving and spending by then, there is a risk that they could end up in debt or make the wrong decisions. Providing sensible real-life support in a safe environment, where real decisions have to be made and lived by, helps prepare your child to navigate through the maze of adulthood.

THERE IS LIGHT AT THE END OF THE TUNNEL

This book should give parents and carers and others the belief that there *is* light at the end of the tunnel. Hopefully it will have confirmed that, with your support and the support of others around your child, they can become strong and resilient, well able to tackle whatever life throws at them.

Your role in all of this has been, is and will always be vital to their mental and physical health and wellbeing. Believe in them, help them see and really understand who they are and encourage them to believe in themselves. You are their best advocate, the person who can champion their needs and help them celebrate whatever they achieve.

However, their journey is ultimately theirs alone. All we can do is provide them with the skills they need to flourish in whatever lies ahead, the resilience to bounce back from life's setbacks, an ear to listen without judging, and any support they need. That, and your unconditional love. If we can do all this and do it to the best of our ability, we can be proud that our job is done.

BELIEVE IN YOURSELF, BELIEVE IN THEM

So what have you learned in the previous chapters? Let us summarise. You have learned that:

- A child can have *both* SEND *and* HLP. The name for this is 'dual and multiple exceptionality' (or DME). In some countries, this is known by other names, such as 'Twice-Exceptional' (or 2e) or 'Gifted with Learning Difficulties (or Disabilities)' (GLD).
- Your child may face a range of challenges in the classroom or at home as a result of their DME. These problems can be addressed appropriately by supporting both their gifts and talents and using these to build their skills and confidence in those areas they struggle with.
- A strengths-based approach that focuses on their strengths to support the challenges they face aids their health and wellbeing, and helps them to be the best version of themselves they can be.

Hopefully, you have also learned that:

- You are the most important teacher and advocate for your child.
- You can develop the skills you need to support your child in the best possible way. This includes facing and addressing those areas where you yourself might struggle as an individual and as a parent or carer.
- With effective support, you can overcome most challenges and find solutions to even the trickiest of problems.

Finally, you have also learned that:

- Developing a positive relationship with the professionals who support your child is vital to supporting them. You have the skills to help you to develop these relationships positively and with the aim of solving any problems you may come across along the way.
- Where things are not working, despite the effort you have put in, that you can and will be able to make the right decisions with and on behalf of your child, including finding alternative ways of supporting their education.
- There are solutions to every problem, and even where you do not like the solution, you can and will choose the best solution for your child's health and wellbeing. This may sometimes not be the solution you would have chosen. It may also mean that other areas of your child's life that you thought were important must take a backseat, which includes exams and academic success.

- You have also learned that the most important thing is for you to love your child unconditionally and to understand the importance of prioritising their health – including their mental health – and wellbeing above all things. At the end of the day, this is what matters the most.
- You have learned that you need to believe in yourself, in the skills you have learned and will go on to learn in the future, and also in the fact that you, of all people (either alone or with your partner or family), are the best person to support your child.
- Finally, you have learned that your own health and wellbeing are also important and that, no matter how serious or tough life looks, how hopeless the situation, you need time for yourself to recharge your own batteries. Only then will you be able to provide the support your child and family needs.

WHERE NEXT?

So what is the next chapter of your own story and that of your child's?

Reading this book may only be the first stage of your journey. From here, you may do lots of further reading or exploration on the internet and elsewhere about some of the subjects that have been raised, and that you think could be relevant for your child. Or you may have come to read this book as a way of consolidating the research you have already done. Either way, we hope that it has given you some things to think about.

However you take this forward, at whatever stage your child is at, or whatever challenges you face, remember that you are not alone. Some of the organisations listed are there – in different ways – to provide you with the help you may need or to answer any questions you might have.

On a wider scale, what about your child's own story? What does the future look like for them? This book comes with no guarantees. As we all learn on an almost daily basis, the future can often look quite different from the one we expected. But one thing we do know is that, with advancements in technology and changes in both the demand for and supply of goods and services, the world of tomorrow will be hugely different from the one we know today.

The skills that many of our children have, their ability to question, to think in the abstract and to use their gifts and talents in partnership with their SEND, could well make them extremely valuable indeed to our society. With your support to help them to lay strong foundations to underpin their DME – self-belief and self-confidence, understanding about themselves, flexibility, maximising their strengths and abilities, helping them to find their passion – they will have the opportunity to succeed whatever the future holds for them.

CONCLUSION

This chapter brings together the skills you have learned throughout this book and, in the next chapter, there is a list of organisations that you can research, join and contact as appropriate, for any problems you encounter along the way.

Although it may not seem like it, the time in which we are all currently living is an incredibly exciting one for children and young people with DME. Unlike any other, with the kinds of skills that they have, they will be more in demand than at any time before. Prepare them wisely for this future; lay the foundations for what they need; encourage the strengths-based approach to DME; and be positive about this with them and others who support them. Most of all, put their health (including their mental health) and wellbeing first and love them. And finally, believe in them.

All of this will carry them a long way through life and help them to be the best version of themselves that they can be.

FURTHER READING

Greg Orme (2019) *Human Intelligence: How Curiosity and Creativity Are Your Superpowers in the Digital Economy*. Pearson Business.

Emma Sue Prince (2019) *7 Skills for the Future: Adaptability, Critical Thinking, Empathy, Integrity, Optimistic, Being Proactive, Resilience*. Pearson Business; 2nd edition.

YOUR ACTION PLAN FOR THE WAY AHEAD

1. Believe in yourself and your own superpower.
2. Believe in your child.
3. Give your child the underpinning skills they need for the future.
4. Listen to them.
5. Be positive, and help them problem-solve whatever issues lie ahead.

CHAPTER 8

Resources for Further Support

A LIST OF ORGANISATIONS IN THE UK AND ELSEWHERE THAT SUPPORT FAMILIES OF CHILDREN AND YOUNG PEOPLE WITH DME AND OTHER LINKS

There are many organisations both in the UK and elsewhere that support children and young people with DME and their parents and carers. In making a list of some we will inevitably have left others out, for which we apologise. However, most of these have been chosen because they have gone 'the extra mile' for DME over the years, and we have certainly benefited from their services and positive 'can do' attitude. That said, we can make no guarantees about the quality of service offered or provided for you and your child, so we suggest you explore what they offer and see if it is relevant for you and your family.

A list of UK-based organisations that specifically recognise DME and support families of children with DME (including parents and carers and/or children and young people)

2eMPower
Contact details
https://www.2empoweruk.org

(Please note, the website may not show current workshops on offer.) Please contact Professor Sara Rankin for details of upcoming events and to join the mailing list: s.rankin@imperial.ac.uk

Objectives
To inspire and enable more 2e students (age 14–17) to undertake STEM (Science, Technology, Engineering & Mathematics) degrees and to become valued members of the STEM workforce in the 21st Century.

The 2eMPower Project team aims to support 2e students and their parents with the strategies and approaches needed to improve the confidence, capability and motivation of students with 2e.

Services relevant to parents/carers of children and young people with DME
Bespoke one-day STEM workshops for students with specific learning differences held online or at Imperial College London. Parent networking and support in parallel.

Three-day STEM summer schools for autistic students or students at Imperial College, with accommodation on campus for families.

Costs
Free resources on the website.

Events are free to students attending State schools.

Students from Independent schools are charged at cost.

Any other information of relevance to parents and carers
Originally established in 2017 by Professor Sara Rankin of Imperial College London and Dr Susen Smith of GERRIC, University of New South Wales, Sydney, Australia. It is now run by Professor Rankin and her team at Imperial College London.

British Mensa
Contact details
www.mensa.org.uk

Email: Services@mensa.org.uk

Twitter: https://twitter.com/BritishMensa

Facebook: https://facebook.com/BritishMensa

Objectives
A membership society for people of all ages with a high IQ.

One of Mensa's core aims is to 'identify and foster human intelligence'. They have a gifted child consultant and a Mensa Gifted and Talented Support Programme, to support young members and their families (among other things).

Services relevant to parents/carers of children and young people with DME
British Mensa has about 1700 members under the age of 18. They are full members and are offered the same range of benefits as adult members: magazines and newsletters, special interest groups and social events. They are encouraged to join their own group – Junior & Teen – and take part in Family Mensa events arranged across the country.

In addition, their gifted child consultant works with Mensa to create support programmes and events for people living and working with gifted children.

One of the programmes Mensa runs each year is its Young Mensans Future Paths conference that aims to demystify the process of applying to and studying at the Universities of Oxford or Cambridge. As well as the chance to talk directly to admissions tutors from both universities, the event includes inspirational speakers and the chance to look round one of the historic colleges.

Costs
There is an annual fee for membership and costs attached to some specific events.

Any other information of relevance to parents and carers
Although British Mensa does not say anything about including children and young people with DME in membership, many children and young people who come into membership do have a range of SEND as well as a high IQ.

Coram Tomorrow's Achievers
Contact details
www.tomorrowsachievers.co.uk

Objectives
Part of Coram children's charity. It is a provider of enrichment classes for exceptionally able and curious children aged 5–13 (including those with DME).

Services relevant to parents/carers of children and young people with DME
Face-to-face tailored enrichment masterclasses to inspire and help harness the talents of curious and exceptionally able children. These workshops cover a wide range of topics, including science, coding, maths, philosophy, literature, the arts and virtual reality.

Costs
Masterclasses are affordable for parents and schools.

Full bursaries are available for children whose parents or carers receive free school meals or universal credit.

Any other information of relevance to parents and carers
There is some information for parents and carers on their website along with information about how to apply for a grant.

GIFT
Contact details
www.giftcourses.co.uk

Email: enquiries@giftcourses.co.uk

Objectives
GIFT has been nurturing the brightest, most curious young people for 42 years, providing the best possible conditions for exceptionally able pupils – including those with DME – to thrive.

Services relevant to parents/carers of children and young people with DME
GIFT runs weekly online Zoom classes, day workshops, a summer school and other residential courses for gifted children of primary and secondary ages, from all schools and none.

Costs
There is a cost for all activities that are run, starting at low rates for Zoom philosophy, debating and improv classes.

However, for families who would struggle with this, there is a bursary scheme from The Potential Trust.

Any other information of relevance to parents and carers
Parents have sometimes found a letter of guidance for teachers from GIFT has been helpful in advocating for their children with schools. Email them if you would like a copy.

nasen (National Association for Special Educational Needs)
Contact details
www.nasen.org.uk

Tel: 01827 311500

Objectives
nasen is a charitable membership organisation that exists to support and champion those working with, and for, children and young people with SEND and learning differences.

Services relevant to parents/carers of children and young people with DME
Membership services: online resources, funded webinars, bi-monthly magazine, etc.

Costs
Membership is free.

There are some paid-for subscription services.

Any other information of relevance to parents and carers
It is worth noting that the wider nasen family includes the DME Trust and the Whole School SEND Consortium, both of which have useful information and resources about DME. More information is available on the nasen website.

Naturally Talented Me (NTM) CIC

Contact details

https://naturallytalentedme.com

Nikki Mears (co-founder): nikki@naturallytalentedme.com, 07971 476935

Nick Boothroyd (co-founder): nick@naturallytalentedme.com

If you would like to try the user platform to unlock your Talents and see a new version of yourself, register and then log in: www.naturallytalentedme.com/login.aspx

User guide: www.naturallytalentedme.com/NTM_user_guide.pdf

Facebook: Naturally Talented Me

LinkedIn: NaturallyTalentedMe

Objectives

Naturally Talented Me (NTM) is a Community Interest Company (CIC) that hosts a unique online platform that enables those who struggle in presenting their skills and abilities to be able to showcase their true potential. NTM's innovative approach helps people better understand their core natural talents and provides them with a compelling mechanism to showcase these talents to potential employers, enabling them to be seen and found.

NTM has reimagined how to find new, diverse talent pools and to provide communities with an unbiased platform to help them shine. NTM's SeeMe approach supports those who are finding current job opportunities limited to them by focusing on roles that match their talents and by giving them a new way of looking at alternative career pathways previously not considered. NTM also provides users with a lifelong career-based support mechanism and a three-dimensional SeeMe portfolio that showcases their talent and potential.

Services relevant to parents/carers of children and young people with DME

NTM was developed as a simple and effective approach to uncovering the core talents that everyone possesses, no matter their age, background or circumstance, including those with DME.

Young people and parents/carers will find the platform easy to use and an engaging way to really discover their true potential, plus an innovative mechanism for showcasing a whole range of career options.

The tool also opens wider conversations designed to reveal the attitudes and behaviours that are sometimes hidden or unknown, and gives everyone a greater understanding that there are so many avenues available when you focus on the positives young people (and their parents and carers) possess – Talent.

Costs

NTM is free to all users. Everyone is able to create a personal SeeMe portfolio, and can send it to employers to showcase personal potential. Individuals can also use the Auto-Match function to match for a lifetime their talents to all new opportunities held within the platform.

There is a commercial platform that is available for organisations and a job posting facility for any employers wishing to source and find new diverse talent for which there is a cost. Contact NTM if you are interested in this.

Any other information of relevance to parents and carers

NTM is currently developing relationships with employers, industry sectors, regional councils and UK-wide programmes to bring a whole range of new potential work-based solutions for all of its users.

This will ensure that work-based solutions continue to grow across the UK, delivering greater understanding of the huge range of talent and potential that is available across a whole range of diverse communities and groups, including for those with DME.

Nisai Group (including the Nisai Education Trust)

Contact details

www.nisai.com

Email: info@nisai.com

Twitter: https://twitter.com/@NisaiLearning

Facebook: www.facebook.com/NisaiLearningPage

YouTube: www.youtube.com/channel/UCAG5QGc091jG2_EcTIjrNJw/featured

Objectives

Nisai provides both traditional schooling with a difference and virtual schooling in the UK and overseas for students who may, for whatever reason, struggle to fit in or to achieve their best in mainstream school environments.

This includes learning opportunities for DME and high ability learners. Nisai recognises that many of these students struggle between their ability level and their level of maturity which, in mainstream school, can result in their bullying and disengagement.

Regardless of whether virtual learning is provided at school or home, Nisai offers time-tables that enable them to study at their current working level rather than their age. This enables them to study alongside different age groups of students and to be supported for both their strengths and the subjects in which they may struggle.

In addition, Nisai has set up the Nisai Education Trust, a charitable arm to explore answers to the emerging questions around maximising the potential of learning in a post-industrial age. Although a new charity, Nisai Education Trust has an ambitious goal of seeking to change the learning landscape for all those for whom education needs to work better.

Services relevant to parents/carers of children and young people with DME

Online learning programmes for children and young adults from age 8 and above (working level dependent).

Full year and long-term programmes crossing Key Stages 3, 4 and 5.

Learning booster programmes to fill gaps in your child's knowledge.

1:1 support with a mentor.

High impact, low literacy support through Units of Sound.

Costs

There is a cost to access all programmes. However, support may be available to enable parents to access funding.

Any other information of relevance to parents and carers

Parents or carers should contact Nisai at info@nisai.com if they need any help or support.

NWGT (North West Gifted and Talented)

Contact details

Aileen Hoare: aileen.hoare@northwestgiftedandtalented.org.uk

Objectives

To support schools in meeting the needs of their most able learners.

Services relevant to parents/carers of children and young people with DME

Advice and guidance for schools on how best to meet children's needs (including those with DME).

Support for individual schools and children (including pupils with DME).

Saturday Challenges.

Maths and English masterclasses (children need to be nominated by their school for these).

Costs

There is a cost to attend Saturday Challenges (although grants may be available from, for example, The Potential Trust). Other activities do not involve a cost to parents or carers.

The OT Company

Contact details

www.theotcompany.com

Facebook: theOTcompany

Twitter: @MarizaOTC

Email: Mariza@theotcompany.com

LinkedIn: www.linkedin.com/in/mariza-ferreira-21032449

Objectives

The OT Company is run by Mariza Ferreira, a specialist paediatric Occupational Therapist.

Its work involves helping children overcome the barriers they face in doing the tasks they need to or want to do. These 'tasks' can vary widely from everyday activities such as writing legibly, being able to concentrate in class or dressing themselves independently, to those of particular interest such as having the basic skills to play football with friends.

'Barriers' facing these children can be a combination of sensory and physical difficulties, as well as social and emotional difficulties. Examples include not being able to cope with noise, light and touch, hyperactivity, an intense need for movement, poor fine or gross motor coordination, difficulty relating socially to other children their age, and extreme emotional reactions if things do not go as they perceive they should.

The OT Company uses a variety of occupational therapy intervention approaches as required to ensure a comprehensive service.

Services relevant to parents/carers of children and young people with DME

The OT Company uses a unique therapy approach called DME-C that has been developed specifically to help High Learning Potential (HLP) and DME children and their families to address the difficulties related to occupational therapy they face head on.

It was the first organisation to recognise the specific needs of HLP and DME children in this way.

Services offered include:

- Direct support for DME children aged approximately 2 to 14, including: assessment and treatment sessions to address identified needs, for example sensory processing difficulties, handwriting, emotional difficulties. Normally these are in person but online options are available.

Support for parents of HLP and DME/2E children: Training and awareness including:

- A pre-recorded online course for parents of DME/2E children who struggle to cope with noise, called 'How to help your high learning potential child cope with noise'.

- A full and pre-recorded online course for parents of DME/2E children who have sensory processing difficulties that severely affect their ability to participate in relevant activities and tasks, called 'How to help your gifted child with sensory issues cope in real life'.

- Optional online live group sessions for parents who have completed the full course 'How to help your gifted child with sensory issues cope in real life'.

- Optional online live one-to-one sessions for parents who have completed the full course 'How to help your gifted child with sensory issues cope in real life'.

Costs

Some short online courses are provided free of charge.

There is a fee to do the longer courses and live sessions and also for the direct support for your child.

Any other information of relevance to parents and carers

The OT Company is seeking more OT specialists in the UK to understand how to support a child with HLP or DME. If you are interested in finding out more, contact Mariza.

A current list of specialist paediatric Occupational Therapists who have trained in the DME-C approach is also available. Please contact Mariza directly to obtain the list.

PEGY
Contact details
www.pegy.org.uk

Email: pgconferences@btinternet.com

Objectives

Taken from the PEGY website:

PEGY is a voluntary organisation with contacts around the world. Their aim is to support the issues facing exceptionally and profoundly gifted children, including:

- Influencing educational planning and strategies within the UK.
- Providing educational psychologist support.
- Supporting research in this field.

Potential Plus UK

Contact details

https://potentialplusuk.org

Email: amazingchildren@potentialplusuk.org

Tel: 01908 646433

Twitter: @PPUK_

Facebook: @PotentialPlusUk

Instagram: @potentialplus.uk

Objectives

Potential Plus UK's objectives are to:

1. Improve the quality and provision of support for young people with high learning potential, including those with DME.
2. Raise awareness about the needs of young people with high learning potential and advocate for improvements in policy and practice.
3. Create and sustain a community of mutual support among families with high learning potential young people.
4. Empower young people with high learning potential to develop self-understanding and lead change.

Services relevant to parents/carers of children and young people with DME

- Information, advice and guidance services: webchat, telephone helpline, e-advice sheets and activity packs, articles and blogs.
- Assessment services: Potential Spotter, HLP Assessment, Early Years Assessment, School Pack, Emotional and Social Profile, In-depth Sensory Profile, Handwriting Profile.
- Training: HLP and DME parents' online courses and workshops, professional development for teachers and professionals.
- Community activities: BIG Family Weekend, Be Curious Weekend, BIG Adventure Weekend, vPlus online courses, vPlus online festival, competitions, dedicated peer-to-peer support groups.

Costs

Some resources are free of charge on the website and other services and resources can be purchased individually.

Potential Plus UK is a membership organisation and this is provided at different levels called Family Essentials Membership and Family Plus Membership with different fees.

Concessionary rates are available for both Family Essentials and Family Plus memberships.

For more information about family membership: https://potentialplusuk.org/index.php/become-a-member/family-membership.

Any other information of relevance to parents and carers

Potential Plus UK fundraises to provide services at low cost or fully funded whenever possible.

They also have a Scholarship Fund to aid access to their services.

The Potential Trust

Contact details

https://www.thepotentialtrust.org.uk
Email: thepotentialtrust@clara.co.uk
Twitter: @PotentialTrust

Objectives

The Potential Trust was set up set up to provide, promote and encourage whatever makes education more interesting and exciting for children and young people (up to school leaving age) who have high learning potential (HLP) and/or DME – especially those with considerably more than the average share of curiosity, creativity, perception and persistence – and to enable them to have access to events and experiences that facilitate their personal and social development, and their creative, artistic and practical skills as well as their intellectual abilities.

Services relevant to parents/carers of children and young people with DME

The Trust offers bursaries to HLP and DME children and young people from low or lower-income UK-based families who have the potential for high attainment (possibly though not necessarily academic) but who are not achieving at the level they could reach and cannot afford to take part in UK-based activities that:

- Enable them to learn new things and to try new challenges
- Enable them to explore existing interests or mastery of skills in greater depth
- Encourage them to make new friends and have new experiences.

The Trust also champions the cause of DME by organising and funding Potential Conferences for organisations (including those set up by or for parents) and by setting up partnerships with other organisations.

Any other information of relevance to parents and carers

The Potential Trust wants to raise the profile of DME in the UK. If you have any ideas to help do that, The Potential Trust would like to hear from you.

PowerWood Project CIC
Contact details
www.powerwood.org.uk

Email: office@powerwood.org.uk

Twitter: https://twitter.com/PowerWoodUK

Facebook: www.facebook.com/PowerWoodUK (there is also a closed Facebook PowerWood group: www.facebook.com/groups/1648425685414993)

Pinterest: www.pinterest.co.uk/PowerWoodUK

Instagram: www.instagram.com/powerwood.neurodiversity

YouTube: www.youtube.com/channel/UCY4TG2kEimJ5SgJbdT0QzRQ

Objectives
PowerWood is passionately dedicated to advocating for and supporting families and individuals living with high-ability neurodiversity in a combination with intensity, sensitivity, hyper-reactivity, learning difficulties, uneven development, emotion regulation issues (including being easily overwhelmed) or mental health issues.

Despite their intelligence, such children are often distracted by their strong emotional reactions, which steer their behaviour away from directing constructively the energy associated with neurodiversity towards their self-chosen aims. Typically, overexcitable (OE), neurodiverse, more able or bright children might be easily overwhelmed by the strength of their emotional reactions, and the anxiety this creates alongside their sensitivity and intensity can be a real challenge for their family and the educational and health professionals who support them. This is particularly challenging for the people in the young person's network if they are operating without the information, tools and strategies that would support them.

PowerWood seeks to make the world a place where all more able families and individuals living with neurodiversity are welcomed and celebrated, and where they can follow their own dreams.

Services relevant to parents/carers of children and young people with DME
- Blogs and vlogs on the website.
- Online individual and family support.
- Tests.
- Children's corner.
- Ideas for activities for parents.
- Resources on Multilevel Emotional Regulation Theory (MERT).
- An emotional support crisis guide.
- Online community.
- Free membership.

Costs
Most resources are free on the site (although PowerWood asks for small financial contributions if possible).

PowerWood wants to make its consultancy and coaching services accessible to individuals and families from all walks of life in a socially justified way, therefore operating a tiered model for fees based on family income.

Any other information of relevance to parents and carers

Most families and individuals who find PowerWood have gone through a period of feeling lonely, misunderstood and judged by family, friends and professionals. They have often been unable to find the right support and are doubting themselves and their ability to cope.

PowerWood supports parents, teens, children and individuals with tips, tools and strategies in a respectful and non-judgemental way to find the way back towards being in charge of their own and/or their children's emotional reactions, enabling them to steer any situation towards self-chosen goals.

A list of useful organisations outside the UK for parents and carers of children with DME (whose services can be accessed from the UK)

Bridges Education Group (including Bridges Academy Online)

Contact details

https://bridgeseducationgroup.com

www.bridges.edu; https://2ecenter.org/bridges-academy-online-high-school

Objectives

The Bridges Education Group consists of Bridges Academy School, The 2e for Research and Professional Development, *2e News* publishing, Bridges Graduate School and Bridges Academy online High School. Bridges is dedicated to advancing the intellectual, creative and social-emotional lives of 2e students everywhere. It has a 25-year history of educating Twice-Exceptional (2e) children in the US. In 2020 it adapted its model for the online space.

Bridges advocates a strength-based, talent-focused model that develops students' intellectual, academic and social-emotional skills as they engage in creative and meaningful work that paves the way to higher education and future careers.

Services relevant to parents/carers of children and young people with DME

Bricks-and-mortar school for Grades 4–12 (ages 9–18); online school for grades 9–12 (ages 14–18); summer classes available to children outside its community; ask the 2e expert, a service for children, young people, parents and others; training summer programmes for parents and carers; free subscription to *2e News*; academic coaching; study with the Master's Summer Institute for professionals and parents; and the Bridges Graduate School of Cognitive Diversity in Education, offering a Certificate, a Master's and a Doctorate in 2e.

Costs

There are charges for most things (this varies by programme). *2e News* is a free subscription.

Any other information of relevance to parents and carers

Bridges online Academy is part of the Bridges 2e Center. The Bridges 2e Center for Research and Professional Development is a first-of-its-kind multidisciplinary hub where professionals, scholars and practitioners combine expertise to enhance understanding of the growing population of 2e students. As well as encouraging and undertaking research into

2e, it provides courses and workshops for parents and others, and shares resources about best practice for those with 2e to improve services for these children.

Bright and Quirky
Contact details
https://brightandquirky.com

Email: support@brightandquirky.com

Facebook: www.facebook.com/brightandquirky

Objectives
Bright and Quirky's mission is to ease the struggle for bright and quirky children and parents and carers, help them achieve their full potential, and inspire the hope that new ideas and possibilities bring, working with the top educators and psychologists to make this happen.

Services relevant to parents/carers of children and young people with DME
Relevant services for children and young people:

- Catalyst, an online programme for 2e children and teenagers that provides intellectual engagement and social connection with like-minded peers, guided by expert mentors who understand 'bright and quirky' children.

Relevant services for parents and carers:

- The Bright and Quirky Idea Lab, a global learning community for parents of bright children with learning, social and/or emotional challenges. It provides direct access to leaders in the field of child development, education and psychology, giving parents and carers the tools, strategies and community support to help their children thrive.
- The Bright and Quirky Summits, annual online training events on a variety of issues.
- A blog and a weekly vlog providing expert nuggets, with interview excerpts from the top experts.

Costs
No cost for blogs or vlogs and some free access to events. Bright and Quirky's Annual Summit has approximately 25 speakers over five days, and is free to the public. Other services may have a charge.

Davidson Institute
Contact details
Info@DavidsonGifted.org

Objectives
The Davidson Institute aims to recognise, nurture and support profoundly intelligent young people and to provide opportunities for them to develop their talents to make a positive difference.

Services relevant to parents/carers of children and young people with DME
For families residing outside of the US, the Davidson Gifted Database (www.davidson-gifted.org/search-database) has resources, articles, tips and tools when working with bright youth.

Twice-Exceptionality is an area in which they do provide support, based on need, on an individual level for each family.

Costs
Most programmes and services are free.

Gifted Development Center (GDC)
Contact details
www.gifteddevelopment.org

Email: gifted@gifteddevelopment.com

Objectives
The GDC was established in 1979 and supports giftedness throughout the lifespan. Since it was set up it has helped to change the lives of more than 6400 children and families world-wide, most of whom are 'Twice-Exceptional'. It also builds awareness and understanding of giftedness through research, advocacy and the development of national policy in the US. Their philosophy is child-centred, with a focus on understanding the child's inner world (overexcitabilities, emotions, perceptions, relationships, personality, etc.) rather than on their potential for success.

Services relevant to parents/carers of children and young people with DME
Resources to help parents and carers with their advocacy skills; a shop with a range of books and assessment tools; and a blog called Musings. It also provides a face-to-face assessment service for children with 2e (DME) and has a journal that seeks to address the unique issues of gifted adults (including those with DME).

Costs
There is a charge for assessments, the books and resources, but the blog can be read for free.

Gifted Homeschoolers Forum (GHF)
Contact details
https://ghflearners.org

Twitter: www.twitter.com/ghflearners

Facebook: www.facebook.com/ghflearners (there is also a private group on Facebook)

Instagram: www.instagram.com/ghflearners

Objectives
GHF is a supportive community for gifted learners (including those with 2e/DME) and their parents and carers where they provide connections and information that brings them together and helps to support them to lead happy and healthy lives.

NAGC (National Association for Gifted Children)
Contact details
www.nagc.org; email: nagc@nagc.org

Twitter: @NAGCGIFTED

Facebook: www.facebook.com/nagcgifted

Objectives
NAGC is based in the US. Its mission is to support those who enhance the growth and development of Gifted and Talented children through education, advocacy, community building and research. They help parents and carers, families and others to help Gifted and Talented children as they strive to achieve their personal best and contribute to their communities.

Services relevant to parents/carers of children and young people with DME
Resources; NAGC publications; an online shop; NAGC Networks and Special Interest Groups; NAGC Annual Convention; Parent Tip Sheets; and NAGCEngaged, an online community for professionals and parents to engage with one another.

NAGC is a membership organisation. A parent membership brings the following benefits: a Parenting for High Potential publication; a Teaching for High Potential publication; NAGC Insider monthly e-newsletter; NAGC NewsSource e-newsletter; volunteer opportunities to network; NAGC social media outlets; practical webinars (videos and podcasts); summaries of current research; political, policy and research analyses; advocacy guides; and discounts to the Convention and at the bookshop.

Costs
Lots of resources can be accessed free of charge, but there is a charge for membership, the Convention and some of the publications and resources.

Any other information of relevance to parents and carers
Although it doesn't seem to state it, parents of 2e (DME) children will find articles and support of relevance to them on the site. Also, while NAGC has a lot of information for professionals on its site, there is enough of relevance to parents of pupils with DME to make it worth a look.

NZAGC (New Zealand Association for Gifted Children)
Contact details
https://giftedchildren.org.nz

Email: info@giftedchildren.org.nz

Facebook: www.facebook.com/NZAGC

Objectives
NZAGC is a charitable organisation that supports Gifted children and their families.

Services relevant to parents/carers of children and young people with DME
NZAGC publications, which includes *Tall Poppies* aimed at Gifted children and their families; a list of assessors who deal with giftedness (including DME) and also counselling;

membership – people can either become members nationally or through an affiliated branch; branch membership provides Gifted children, their families and also educators with a range of activities including club days and holidays, courses, regular newsletters and access to a library; national membership is provided at a range of levels from individual to platinum level giving access to different benefits; and an annual Gifted Awareness Week with access to a range of competitions and activities for children and young people.

Costs
There is a cost for membership and some resources, but most online information (such as Gifted Awareness Week) is free.

Any other information of relevance to parents and carers
Most events seem to be face-to-face. There is no specific mention of GLD/2e/DME but the organisation does recognise and support these children.

SENG (Supporting Emotional Needs of the Gifted)
Contact details
www.sengifted.org

Email: office@sengifted.org

Twitter: https://twitter.com/ENG_Gifted

Facebook: https://facebook.com/SENGifted

Instagram: www.instagram.com/sengifted.com

Objectives
SENG is a non-profit organisation based in the US that empowers families and communities to guide Gifted and Talented individuals to reach their goals: intellectually, physically, emotionally, socially and spiritually. It was founded by Dr James Webb in 1981 to offer the gifted community support and guidance through education, research and connection.

SENG believes that with the right intellectual and emotional support, Gifted and Talented and Twice-Exceptional (GT/2e) people can accept themselves and fulfil the potential of their incredible capabilities. Perhaps more importantly, they can learn to work with their high sensitivities to feel balanced, happy and at peace.

Services relevant to parents/carers of children and young people with DME
- SENG Model Parent Group (SMPG) – these run for 8–10 weeks and are structured around *A Guide to Gifted Children* by James Webb and colleagues.
- SENG support groups – designed specifically to address some of the unique issues, needs and challenges faced by varying gifted communities both in the US and beyond. The online platform allows individuals to meet together face-to-face to discuss issues, needs and challenges with the guidance of an expert. SENG's online support groups offer support in a private setting and allow gifted people to connect with each other regardless of their location.
- SENGinars – live, virtual presentations by GT/2e experts on a variety of subjects. Each SENGinar lasts an hour-and-a-half and can be viewed from the comfort of your home. Scheduled on Thursday evenings, usually twice a month, SENG also records each SENGinar and hosts them on their Vimeo channel. All registrants can also view

the SENGinar recording for free, as part of their registration, and they are available for purchase by those who were not registered to attend the training.

- SENG mini conferences – one-day events filled with breakout sessions from GT/2e experts, keynote sessions and more. Typically, SENG also presents a day of continuing education courses and/or SMPG training the day before a mini conference. SENG typically schedules 3–4 mini conferences per year in the US or Canada.

- Annual online conference – this includes lots of webinars and sessions for parents and carers with children who are GT/2e.

- SENG membership – gives parents access to a community of GT/2e people, those who support someone who is GT/2e, professionals and educators through private forums, discounts on programmes and SENGinars, a free Home Edition software from Renzulli Learning…and so much more!

Costs
The majority of SENG's resources and services are free, with additional services to paid members.

TiLT Parenting
Contact details
https://tiltparenting.com

Twitter: https://twitter.comTiltParenting

Facebook: www.facebook.com/tiltparenting

Instagram: www.instagram.com/tiltparenting

Podcast: The TiLT Parenting Podcast (on all major platforms)

Objectives
TiLT Parenting was founded in 2016 as a podcast and community aimed at helping parents and carers raising 'differently wired' children to do so from a place of confidence, connection and joy. It is run by Debbie Reber who is passionate about the idea that being differently wired isn't a deficit; it's a difference. She hopes to change the way difference is perceived and experienced in the world so these exceptional kids, and the parents and carers raising them, can thrive in their schools, in their families and in their lives. Debbie's book, inspired by TiLT Parenting, *Differently Wired: Raising an Exceptional Child in a Conventional World*, was published in June 2018.

Services relevant to parents/carers of children and young people with DME
Regular podcasts; a blog; resources (book lists, suggested podcasts and support organisations on key issues); a back-to-school 3-hour workshop; TiLT Together: Differently Wired Parent Groups (in the US and around the world, including in the UK); Differently Wired 7-day Challenge; and a Differently Wired Membership Club.

Costs
Lots of resources are free of charge, although there is a charge for some of the services, such as the Differently Wired Membership Club.

With Understanding Comes Calm LLC

Contact details

https://withunderstandingcomescalm.com; email: julie@withunderstandingcomescalm.com; Twitter: @julieskolnick; Facebook: www.facebook.com/withunderstandingcomescalm; Instagram: www.instagram.com/letstalk2e; LinkedIn: Julie Rosenbaum Skolnick.

The organisation also provides: Let's Talk 2e parent and educator conferences as well as Parent Empowerment Groups: www.letstalk2e.com; it is also available on YouTube.

Objectives

With Understanding Comes Calm's mission is to empower parents and carers, educators, clinicians and 2e adults to bring out the best and raise self-confidence in their children, students, clients and themselves through education, tailor-made strategies and advocacy training. Julie Skolnick is the Founder.

Services relevant to parents/carers of children and young people with DME

Regular blogs; newsletters; podcasts; other resources (including signposting); webinars; conferences; Virtual Parent Empowerment Groups; one-to-one consulting; hourly consulting for emergencies; and helping prepare partnership plans (including consulting and teaching). 2e Resources Partner Directory, a comprehensive listing of schools and associations in the US organised in five categories: Education, Clinicians, Consultants, Enrichment and Associations: www.2eresources.com

Costs

There are many free resources on the site and also some resources where there is a fee, especially consulting (although there is a free 20-minute consultation call) and conferences.

Any other information of relevance to parents and carers

With Understanding Comes Calm LLC publishes a free monthly newsletter, Gifted & Distractible, and people can subscribe at: www.withunderstandingcomescalm.com/newsletters.

KEY SPECIALISTS IN DME

Dr Devon MacEachron, PHD is a specialist in Twice-Exceptional (2e/DME) and Gifted learners, with a positive psychology focus on strengths and interests. She provides consultation services and also neuropsychological and psychoeducational assessments with actionable game plans to families to enable students to reach their potential. In addition, Dr Devon provides a regular blog.

Contact details: https://drdevon.com; email: dm@drdevon.com; Twitter: @2egifted; Facebook: www.facebook.com/2Egifted

Scott Barry Kaufman is a humanistic psychologist who explores the depths of human potential. He is a specialist on intelligence, creativity and wellbeing and, as well as teaching, produces books, podcasts, a regular blog and articles. He is involved in the Twice-Exceptional world and has done regular online training sessions for parent organisations in the US. He also edits *Beautiful Minds* for *Psychology Today*.

Contact details: https://scottbarrykaufman.com; for some free resources, go to: https://scottbarrykaufman.com/resources; for self-actualisation tests, go to: https://scottbarrykaufman.com/selfactualizationtests; for the latest episodes of *The Psychology Podcast*, go to: https://scottbarrykaufman.com/podcast

Daniel B. Peters, PhD is a psychologist, author and co-founder of Parent Footprint, an interactive parenting education community and website that offers Parent Footprint Awareness Training. He is the host of podcast *The Parent Footprint*, and a regular contributor to *The Huffington Post* and *Psychology Today*.

For over 20 years, Dr Dan has been passionate about helping parents to parent their children with purpose and intention, to guide them in reaching their potential while their children are also reaching their own. Dr Dan is the author of a variety of books, including *Make Your Worrier a Warrior*, a guide to conquering a child's fears. He is also a contributor to *Twice Exceptional: Supporting and Educating Bright and Creative Students with Learning Difficulties* (edited by Scott Barry Kaufman) as well as many articles on topics related to parenting, family, giftedness, Twice-Exceptionality, dyslexia and anxiety. Dr Dan is co-founder/Executive Director of the Summit Center that specialises in the assessment and treatment of children, adolescents and families, with a special emphasis on gifted, talented and creative individuals and families as well as anxiety.

Contact details: www.drdanpeters.com; email via Professional practice: Summit Center: https://summitcenter.us; Facebook: www.facebook.com/drdanpeters; Parent Footprint: https://parentfootprint.com; YouTube: www.youtube.com/user/SummitCenterCA; Twitter: @drdanpeters

MISCELLANEOUS INFORMATION THAT MAY BE OF INTEREST

Big Life Journal creates engaging resources that help children and young people to develop a growth and resilient mindset so they can face life's challenges with confidence: www.biglifejournal-uk.co.uk

Hoagies Gifted provides lots of free information on giftedness and 2e (DME), including a section for parents and carers. It is also on social media, including a closed Gifted Discussion Group on Facebook: www.hoagiesgifted.org; Twitter: @HoagiesGifted; Facebook: www.facebook.com/HoagiesGifted

Laugh Love Learn Blog is about overexcitabilities and living with intensity. The aim is to share positive stories about living with intensity: www.laughlovelearn.co.uk; Facebook: www.facebook.com/laughlovelearn

Glossary of Terms

Acceleration This is a strategy that allows a child to progress through school at a faster than average rate. There are different kinds of acceleration for a child with High Learning Potential (HLP) or Dual or Multiple Exceptionality (DME), including moving up a year (or even missing a year altogether) or learning with older children in one or more subjects.

ADD (Attention Deficit Disorder) This is an outdated term, and is now seen to describe inattentive-type Attention Deficit Hyperactivity Disorder (ADHD) with symptoms such as disorganisation, lack of focus and inattentiveness.

ADHD (Attention Deficit Hyperactivity Disorder) This condition affects people's behaviour. It is a neurodevelopmental disorder characterised by inattention, or excessive activity and impulsivity, which are otherwise not appropriate for a person's age.

Anorexia (or anorexia nervosa) Anorexia is an eating disorder and serious mental health condition where individuals try and keep their weight as low as possible.

AP (alternative provision) This means education organised by local authorities for children who, for a variety of reasons, would not otherwise receive suitable education.

APD (Auditory Processing Disorder, sometimes called Auditory Processing Difficulties) This is not a hearing problem, as individuals with APD usually have normal hearing. APD makes it difficult to understand noisy places, similar sounding words and spoken instructions. It also refers to sensitivities in hearing.

ARFID (Avoidant Restrictive Food Intake Disorder) This is a new diagnosis in the *Diagnostic and Statistical Manual of Mental Disorders*, 5th edn (DSM-5). It was previously referred to as selective eating disorder. It is like anorexia, but does not involve distress about body shape or size.

AS (Asperger's Syndrome) First introduced in 1944, it was removed as a formal diagnosis from the *Diagnostic and Statistical Manual of Mental Disorders* (5th edn) (DSM-5) in 2013. Individuals are diagnosed instead with ASD. Individuals with AS do not have the learning disabilities of those with ASD but may have other challenges. It is often referred to as 'High-Functioning Autism' (HFA) (see below).

ASD (Autism Spectrum Disorder) This is also called Autism Spectrum Condition (ASC), with a variety of characteristics depending on where the individual is on the spectrum.

Asynchronous development A mismatch between the cognitive (thinking), emotional and physical development of individuals with High Learning Potential (HLP) that may lead to uneven development.

BDD (Body Dysmorphic Disorder) A mental health condition where the individual spends a lot of time worrying about perceived flaws in their appearance that are often unnoticeable to others.

Behavioural optometrist A specialist who explores the link between vision, learning and development.

Blended learning An approach in education that combines online learning and interaction with traditional place-based classroom methods.

Bright and quirky Alternative words include 'neurodiverse', 'Twice-Exceptional' (2e) and 'Dual or Multiple Exceptionality' (DME).

BTEC (Business and Technology Education Council) Specialist, practical, work-related qualifications.

CAMHS (Child and Adolescent Mental Health Services or CYPMHS, Children and Young People's Mental Health Services) Services that support children and young people with their mental health.

Chunking This involves breaking down a more difficult process (such as a piece of text or stages in a maths sum) into more manageable sections so individuals can do the piece of work.

Cognition support Support for an individual who has problems with the way they think, such as problems remembering things.

Communication and interaction How an individual exchanges information (using speech, language and other forms of communication) backwards and forwards with someone else.

Coproduction In schools this is about the involvement of pupils and parents or carers in the design and delivery of services. It involves honest and effective dialogue between parents or carers and professionals to improve education for their children.

Depression This is a mental health condition with long-term and ongoing feelings ranging from feelings of unhappiness and hopelessness to anxiety, high emotions and suicidal thoughts as well as physical symptoms.

Differentiation Changes that allow teachers to give pupils of different capabilities the best chance of learning. Classroom methods include allowing pupils to have a flexible pace of learning, collaboration with others, tasks that progress, digital resources, verbal support, outcomes that vary and ongoing assessment. Differentiating like this makes it possible to cater for a wide range of abilities in the classroom.

Differently wired Alternative words include 'neurodiverse', 'Twice-Exceptional' (2e) and 'Dual or Multiple Exceptionality' (DME).

DME (Dual or Multiple Exception/Exceptionality) High ability (High Learning Potential) and a Special Educational Need and Disability (SEND).

Double-jointedness Defined as Joint Hypermobility Syndrome. This is where the individual has very flexible joints that cause them pain.

DSM-5 (*Diagnostic and Statistical Manual of Mental Disorders*, 5th edn) This is the standard classification used by mental health professionals and is mostly used in the US. Clinicians in the UK most often use the ICD-10 (*International Classification of Diseases*, 10th revision) as a diagnostic tool.

Dyscalculia A specific and persistent difficulty in understanding numbers. This can lead to a range of difficulties related to maths.

Dysgraphia A learning disability that relates to writing, where skills in writing are below the individual's age measured through intelligence and education.

Dyslexia A Specific Learning Difficulty that can cause problems with reading, writing and spelling and the skills needed for them (such as planning and organisation).

Dysphagia The medical term for swallowing difficulties.

Dyspraxia Also known as Developmental Coordination Disorder (DCD), it is a condition affecting physical coordination. (It is sometimes informally referred to by parents and carers as the 'clumsy disease'.)

Ed pysch (educational psychologist) Educational psychologists work with children and young people (aged 0–25) who are experiencing problems that hinder their successful learning and participation in school and other activities.

EHCP (Education, Health and Care Plan, sometimes called the EHC Plan) A legal document that describes a child or young person's special educational, health and social care needs and the extra help they will be given to meet those needs to support them to achieve what they want to do in their education.

Executive functioning A set of mental skills that include working memory, processing speed, planning, self-regulation and sorting out tasks.

G&T (Gifted and Talented) One of the terms that may still be used in some schools to refer to pupils and programmes defined as More Able (High Learning Potential, HLP).

GATCo (Gifted and Talented coordinator, also called G&T coordinator) This term is still sometimes used for specialists in school who coordinate support for More Able (High Learning Potential, HLP) pupils.

GLD (Gifted Learning Disabled, Gifted with Learning Disabilities or Gifted with Learning Difficulties) All these phrases are used in some part of the world to refer to children and young people with Special Educational Needs and Disabilities (SEND) and High Learning Potential (HLP) (Dual or Multiple Exceptionality, DME).

Growth mindset A theory of learning where individuals believe that their abilities can be developed through dedication and hard work.

Gustatory Refers to taste. Various processing problems can occur relating to the sense of taste.

HFA (High-Functioning Autism) Autism is a spectrum condition. HFA is an unofficial term used for people who may have been diagnosed with Asperger's Syndrome (AS) in the past. An individual on the high-functioning end of the spectrum may not need the same level of support as people diagnosed with severe autism. However, symptoms may still include sensory difficulties, difficulties with organisation and planning and social awkwardness.

HI (hearing impairment) Hearing impairment or deafness refers to someone who has some level of hearing loss but this level can vary greatly. Hearing loss is usually measured by the quietest sounds someone can hear in decibels.

HLP (High Learning Potential) Another phrase used for Gifted and Talented or More Able children and young people.

Hypermobility Referred to as 'Joint Hypermobility Syndrome' (sometimes informally referred to as double-jointed). This is where the individual has very flexible joints that cause them pain.

Hypersensitivity Extreme sensitivity to one or more senses, such as touch, taste or hearing. It is also called sensory avoiding where individuals avoid sensory input as it is too overwhelming.

Hyposensitivity Under-sensitivity in one or more senses. It is also called sensory seeking where individuals look for more sensory stimulation.

IEP (Individual Education Plan, sometimes called an Individual Learning Plan (ILP)) Used for pupils who are not fulfilling their potential and who have a specific need that can be addressed, for example, by changes in their curriculum, additional resources or a different learning environment from others. It is more informal than an EHCP but is still written down and followed with regular reviews and input from pupils and parents and carers.

Inclusion manager Sometimes its role is as a diversity and inclusion manager. It is the manager in school who is responsible for making sure that all pupils are included in the life of the school and that professionals such as teachers understand inclusion and how it should work so that every child is included in the teaching and learning programme in the school.

Interoception Refers to sensations related to the physical condition of the body. Interoceptors are the internal sensors that provide a sense of what our internal organs are feeling, such as hunger and thirst.

Joint Hypermobility Syndrome (often referred to as double-jointedness) This is where the individual has very flexible joints that cause them pain.

LSA (learning support assistant) Their main role is to provide support for pupils with Special Educational Needs, such as helping to implement their Individual Education Plan (IEP). They usually work on a one-to-one basis with a child, but different schools may have different ways of deploying LSAs.

Mind mapping A mind map is a way of organising tasks, words or concepts to provide an organisational structure to an individual's thoughts. An example would be structuring how to write an essay before writing it.

MLD (moderate learning difficulties, sometimes called global learning difficulties) This applies to children who have difficulty following the curriculum at school, despite having additional help and intervention.

MOOC (Massive Open Online Course) These are distance learning courses run online. They can usually be accessed without paying tuition fees or committing to regular attendance or involvement in learning.

More Able or Most Able There is no national definition of this in England. It has gradually replaced the term 'Gifted and Talented' (G&T) used in schools, but focuses more on achievement.

MSI (multi-sensory impairment) This means the child has impairments with both sight and hearing.

Neurodiverse Refers to the diversity of human brains and minds. It is just a normal part of the infinite ways in which individuals can think or learn differently and not a deficit.

Neurotypical An abbreviation of 'neurologically typical'. It applies to individuals who have typical developmental, intellectual and cognitive abilities.

OCD (Obsessive-Compulsive Disorder) A mental health condition where the individual has obsessive thoughts and compulsive behaviours.

Ocular Motor Dysfunction Also known as Ocular Motility Dysfunction. This occurs when eye movements are poorly controlled or defective and it affects an individual's ability to read, for example.

Olfactory Sense of smell.

Oscillopsia Vision problem in which objects appear to jump, jiggle or vibrate when they are actually stationary.

Pathology A branch of medical science primarily concerning cause, origin and nature of disease.

PDA (Pathological Demand Avoidance) A profile on the autism spectrum. PDA individuals share characteristics of others on the autism spectrum but also have a cluster of additional traits including the need for control and avoidance of everyday demands.

PEP (Personal Education Plan) Looked-after children must have a care plan, of which a PEP is an integral part. It is an evolving record of what needs to happen for looked-after children to enable them to make at least expected progress and to fulfil their potential.

PMLD (profound and multiple learning disability) This is where an individual has a severe learning disability and other disabilities that significantly affect their ability to communicate and be independent.

Processing speed This is the pace at which an individual takes in information, makes sense of it and begins to respond.

Proprioception (also called kinesthesia) This is the body's ability to sense its location, movements and actions. It is the reason an individual can move freely without consciously thinking about their environment.

Reception class Reception class (or Year R), FS2 (foundation second year) is the first year of primary school in England and Wales. The child is usually four or five years old. It comes after nursery and before Year 1 in England and Wales (or before Primary 2 in Northern Ireland).

Rising fives Education offered to all children in the academic year before they start compulsory education.

SEMH (social, emotional and mental health) This term was introduced in the Special Educational Needs and Disabilities (SEND) Code of Practice in 2014. It replaced the terms 'BESD' (behaviour, emotional, social development) and 'EBD' (emotional and behaviour difficulties).

SEN (Special Educational Needs) If a child or young person is struggling at school or college and they need extra support, they're likely to have special educational needs.

SENCo (Special Educational Needs coordinator) A specialist member of staff in school who is responsible for coordinating additional support for pupils with Special Educational Needs and Disabilities (SEND). The SENCo works with parents or carers and other professionals as they are responsible for requesting the involvement of relevant services a pupil might need.

SEND (Special Educational Need(s) and Disability(ies)) A child or young person has special educational needs and disabilities if they are struggling with learning difficulties and/or a disability that means they need special health and education support.

Sensory occupational therapist Occupational therapists work with people of all ages, helping them to carry out the activities that they need or want to do to lead healthy and fulfilling lives. Specialises in supporting individuals with sensory difficulties to help to get these back on track.

SLD (severe learning difficulties) Individuals with SLD are likely to find it difficult to understand, learn and remember new skills, making it more difficult to learn.

Social services They have a legal obligation to safeguard and promote the welfare of vulnerable children and offer a wide range of care services to children and their parents or carers.

SPD (sensory processing difficulties, sometimes referred to as sensory processing disorder) We process information through our senses, and for some children this can be challenging and cause a range of problems including sensory overload.

SpLD (specific learning difficulties) These affect the way information is learned and processed. They are neurological rather than psychological in nature and occur independently of an individual's intelligence. Most common SpLD include dyslexia, dyspraxia, dyscalculia, dysgraphia and Attention Deficit Hyperactivity Disorder (ADHD).

Stealth dyslexia This is a relatively recent term that describes pupils with above-average abilities or gifted reading abilities who use their abilities to hide or mask their dyslexia.

TA (teaching assistant) TAs help to support learning activities in schools and nurseries, particularly educational, emotional and social development. They work with individual children, groups or the whole class depending on the school's strategy.

Tactile Sense of touch.

Transition School transition concerns the move children and young people make between one situation to another. This could be between home and school, from one class to the next at the end of the year or between primary and secondary school or beyond.

Trichotillomania Referred to as trich or hair-pulling disorder. It involves recurrent, irresistible urges to pull hair from all over the body, such as the scalp, eyebrows and eyelids.

Twice-Exceptional (sometimes shortened to 2e) Gifted and Talented children and young people with Special Educational Needs and Disabilities (SEND). Used in countries such as the US (in the UK Dual or Multiple Exceptional, DME, is used).

Verbal comprehension The ability to understand spoken language. Individuals with verbal comprehension difficulties may know the meanings of words but struggle to provide the definitions.

Vertical teaching structures (sometimes called vertical tutoring) Many schools operate horizontal teaching structures where all pupils are the same age. A vertical structure is where groups are equally made up of pupils drawn from all year groups within the school. Some schools put vertical teaching in place for their tutor groups. Some schools go further and do this for their teaching arrangements.

Vestibular Refers to balance and how the body moves against gravity.

VI (visual impairment) Problems related to sight.

Visual perception problems Having the ability to interpret the information that an individual sees.

Working memory The brain system that provides for the temporary storage and manipulation of information to carry out complex tasks such as in language comprehension, learning and reasoning.

References

ADDitude Editors (2013) 'I'm tired of reminding her to do things.' ADDitude, 7 February. Available at: www.additudemag.com/watches-for-adhd

ADHD Foundation (no date) 'Ten point observation list on ADHD behaviour.' Available at: www.adhdfoundation.org.uk/wp-content/uploads/2020/12/10-point-observation-list-on-ADHD-behaviour.pdf

Auticon (no date) 'Another perspective.' Available at: https://auticon.co.uk/our-services

Autistica (no date) 'Signs and symptoms of autism.' Available at: https://www.autistica.org.uk/what-is-autism/what-is-autism

Betts, G. and Neihart, M. (1988) 'Profiles of gifted children.' *Gifted Child Quarterly*. Available at: www.davidsongifted.org/search-database/entry/a10114

Beyond Autism (no date) 'Online courses.' Available at: www.beyondautism.org.uk/professionals/training/online-courses

Boddison, A. (2021) *The Governance Handbook for SEND and Inclusion: Schools that Work for All Learners*. Abingdon: Routledge.

British Dyslexia Association (no date) 'Signs of dyslexia.' Available at: www.bdadyslexia.org.uk/dyslexia/about-dyslexia/signs-of-dyslexia

Brown, D. (2019) *Be Your Best Self: Life Skills for Unstoppable Kids*. London: Button Books.

Cain, S. (2012) 'The power of introverts.' TED Talks on YouTube, 2 March. Available at: www.youtube.com/watch?v=c0KYU2j0TM4

Cullins, A. (2020) 'How to explain growth mindset to kids: Neuroplasticity activities.' *Big Life Journal*, 23 August. Available at: https://biglifejournal.com/blogs/blog/teach-kids-growth-mindset-neuroplasticity-activities

Daniels, S. and Piechowski, M.M. (eds) (2009) *Living with Intensity: Understanding the Sensitivity, Excitability, and the Emotional Development of Gifted Children, Adolescents, and Adults*. Scottsdale, AZ: Great Potential Press, Inc.

DENI (Department of Education) (Northern Ireland) (no date, a) *New SEN Framework*. Available at: www.education-ni.gov.uk/articles/review-special-educational-needs-and-inclusion

DENI (Department of Education) (Northern Ireland) (no date, b) *The Draft Special Education Needs Regulations 202X: A Summary Guide for Parents and Young People*. Available at: www.education-ni.gov.uk/sites/default/files/consultations/education/Summary%20Guide%20-%20SEN%20Regulations%20for%20parents%20and%20young%20people.PDF

DENI (Department of Education) (Northern Ireland) (1998) *Special Educational Needs: A Guide for Parents.* Available at: www.education-ni.gov.uk/sites/default/files/publications/de/special-educational-needs-parents-guide.pdf

DENI (Department of Education) (Northern Ireland) (2021) *New SEN Framework.* Available at: www.education-ni.gov.uk/articles/review-special-educational-needs-and-inclusion

Department for Education (UK) (2008) *Gifted and Talented Education: Helping to Find and Support Children with Dual or Multiple Exceptionalities.* Available at: https://dera.ioe.ac.uk/8314/7/c1bec38baa81045fa9e1f92b98ba6fa6_Redacted.pdf

Department for Education (2011, updated 2013) *Teachers' Standards: Guidance for School Leaders, School Staff and Governing Bodies.* Available at: www.gov.uk/government/publications/teachers-standards

Department for Education (2019) *Elective Home Education: Departmental Guidance for Parents.* Available at: https://assets.publishing.service.gov.uk/government/uploads/system/uploads/attachment_data/file/791528/EHE_guidance_for_parentsafterconsultationv2.2.pdf

Department for Education (2021) *Early Years Foundation Stage Profile: 2021 Handbook.* Available at: https://assets.publishing.service.gov.uk/government/uploads/system/uploads/attachment_data/file/942421/EYFSP_Handbook_2021.pdf

Department for Education and Department of Health (2015) *Special Educational Needs and Disability Code of Practice: 0 to 25 Years. Statutory Guidance for Organisations which Work with and Support Children and Young People Who Have Special Educational Needs or Disabilities,* January. Available at: https://assets.publishing.service.gov.uk/government/uploads/system/uploads/attachment_data/file/398815/SEND_Code_of_Practice_January_2015.pdf

Department of Education, Skills and Employment (Australia) (no date) 'What is the Australian Government doing to support students with disability in schools?' Fact sheet. Available at: www.dese.gov.au/quality-schools-package/fact-sheets/what-australian-government-doing-support-students-disability-schools

Department of Education, Skills and Employment (Australia) (2005) *Disability Standards for Education 2005.* Available at: www.education.gov.au/disability-standards-education-2005

Distin, K. (ed.) (2006) *Gifted Children: A Guide for Parents and Professionals.* London: Jessica Kingsley Publishers.

Distin, S. (2016) 'Why it's a good thing kids ask so many questions.' Tinybop, Inc., Blog, 17 February. Available at: https://tinybop.com/blog/why-its-a-good-thing-kids-ask-so-many-questions

Dweck, C. (2017) *Mindset: Changing the Way You Think to Fulfil Your Potential* (6th edition). London: Robinson.

Dyslexia Scotland (no date) 'What is dyslexia?' Available at: www.dyslexiascotland.org.uk/sites/default/files/library/WhatisDyslexia.pdf

EA (Education Authority) (Northern Ireland) (no date) 'Special Educational Needs.' Available at: www.eani.org.uk/parents/special-educational-needs-sen

Education Otherwise (no date) 'Starting out.' Available at: www.educationotherwise.org/starting-out

Eide, B. and Eide, F. (2005) 'Stealth dyslexia.' *2e Newsletter*, 26 May. Available at: www.davidsongifted.org/search-database/entry/a10435

Eide, B. and Eide, F. (2011) *The Dyslexic Advantage: Unlocking the Hidden Potential of the Dyslexic Brain.* New York: Hudson Street Press.

Evans, C. and Attwood, T. (2018) *Ask Dr Tony: Questions and Answers from the World's Leading Authority on Asperger's Syndrome/High Functioning Autism*. London: Future Horizons.

FutureLearn (no date) 'Frequently asked questions: FutureLearn for schools.' Available at: https://ugc.futurelearn.com/other_assets/FutureLearn+Teacher+FAQs.pdf

Gerhardt, P. and Cohen, M. (2014) *Visual Supports for People with Autism: A Guide for Parents and Professionals*. Bethesda, MD: Woodbine House. Available at: www.autism.org.uk/advice-and-guidance/topics/communication/communication-tools/visual-supports

Gilbert, I. (2019) 'A Tin of Thunks' [tin]. London: Independent Thinking Press.

Goodall, J. and Vorhaus, J., with Carpentieri, J.D., Brooks, G., Akerman, R. and Harris, A. (2011) *Review of Best Practice in Parental Engagement: Practitioners Summary*. Available at: https://assets.publishing.service.gov.uk/government/uploads/system/uploads/attachment_data/file/182507/DFE-RR156_-_Practitioner_Summary.pdf

Griffin Occupational Therapy (no date) 'What is Sensory Processing Disorder (SPD)?' Available at: www.griffinot.com/sensory-processing-disorder

Guare, R., Dawson, P. and Guare, C. (2013) *Smart but Scattered Teens: The 'Executive Skills' Program for Helping Teens Reach Their Potential*. New York: Guilford Press.

HEdNI (Home Education Northern Ireland) (no date) 'Frequently asked questions.' Available at: www.hedni.org/frequently-asked-questions

Herrnstein, R.J. and Murray, C. (1994) *The Bell Curve: Intelligence and Class Structure in American Life*. New York: Free Press.

Hymer, B. and Gershon, M. (2014) *Growth Mindset Pocketbook*. London: Teachers' Pocketbooks.

Iannelli, V. (2020) 'A food diary for tracking your child's nutrition.' *Verywell Family*, 25 March. Available at: https://verywellfamily.com/printable-foor-diary-2633949

Kaufman, S.B. (2018) 'Can introverts be happy in a world that can't stop talking?' *Beautiful Minds*, 5 October. Available at: https://blogs.scientificamerican.com/beautiful-minds/can-introverts-be-happy-in-a-world-that-cant-stop-talking

Lawn, R.B., Slemp, G.R. and Vella-Brodrick, D.A. (2019) 'Quiet flourishing: The authenticity and well-being of trait introverts living in the west depends on extraversion-deficit beliefs.' *Journal of Happiness Studies 20*, 2055–2075. Available at: https://link.springer.com/article/10.1007/s10902-018-0037-5

Lehman, J. (no date) 'Motivating the unmotivated child.' Empowering Parents. Available at: www.empoweringparents.com/article/motivating-the-unmotivated-child

Magee, E. (2020) '63 fun questions to get your kids talking.' Explore Parents, 20 May. Available at: www.parents.com/parenting/better-parenting/advice/questions-every-parent-should-ask-their-kid

The MEHRIT Centre (2016) 'What is Self Reg.' Video on YouTube, 15 June. Available at: www.youtube.com/watch?v=hOlV_kNYAYA

Mental Health Foundation (2018) 'Mental health statistics: Stress.' Results of the Mental Health Foundation's 2018 study. Available at: www.mentalhealth.org.uk/statistics/mental-health-statistics-stress

Merrill, J. (2012) *If This Is a Gift, Can I Send It Back? Surviving in the Land of the Gifted and Twice Exceptional*. Ashland, OR: GHF Press.

Ministry of Education (New Zealand) (2020) *The Education and Disability Legislation Guiding Our Approach to Learning Support*. Available at: https://education.govt.nz/school/student-support/special-education/education-disability-legislation

NAGC (2018) 'Use of WISC-V for Gifted and Talented Children and Twice Exceptional Identification.' August. Available at: www.nagc.org/sites/default/files/Misc_PDFs/WISC-V%20Position%20Statement%20Aug2018.pdf

nasen (no date) 'About whole school SEND.' Available at: https://nasen.org.uk/page/about-whole-school-send-wss

National Improvement Hub (2020) 'A summary of resources relating to highly able learners.' Learning resources, 21 January. Available at: https://education.gov.scot/improvement/learning-resources/a-summary-of-resources-relating-to-highly-able-learners

NHS England (no date) 'Symptoms of Attention Deficit Hyperactivity Disorder.' Available at: www.nhs.uk/conditions/attention-deficit-hyperactivity-disorder-adhd/symptoms

NHS England (2018) 'How many calories does a child of 7–10 need?' Available at: www.nhs.uk/common-health-questions/childrens-health/how-many-calories-does-a-child-of-7-10-need

NHS England (2018) *Ask. Listen. Do. Making Conversations Count in Health, Social Care and Education: Top Tips for Families and Carers.* Available at: www.england.nhs.uk/wp-content/uploads/2018/06/Ask-Listen-Do.pdf

Nisai Group (no date) 'Advice for parents.' Available at: www.nisai.com/our-story/advice-for-parents

Ofsted (2021) *Inspecting Local Authorities Children's Services.* Available at: www.gov.uk/government/publications/inspecting-local-authority-childrens-services-from-2018/inspecting-local-authority-childrens-services

The Open University (no date) 'Admission of applicants under the age of 18.' Available at: https://help.open.ac.uk/documents/policies/admission-of-applicants-under-the-age-18

Potential Plus UK (2017–20) 'High Learning Potential.' Advice Sheet PA101. Available at: https://potentialplusuk.org/wp-content/uploads/2017/02/PA101-High-Learning-Potential-170131a.pdf

Potential Plus UK (2017–20) 'Characteristics of Children with High Learning Potential.' Advice Sheet PA102. Available at: https://potentialplusuk.org/wp-content/uploads/2017/02/PA102-Characteristics-of-Children-with-HLP-170131a.pdf

Potential Plus UK (2017–20) 'Needs of Children with High Learning Potential.' Advice Sheet PA103. Available at: https://potentialplusuk.org/wp-content/uploads/2017/02/PA103-Needs-of-Children-with-High-Learning-Potential-170131a.pdf

Potential Plus UK (2017–20) 'Early Years and High Learning Potential.' Advice Sheet PA104. Available at: https://potentialplusuk.org/wp-content/uploads/2017/02/PA104-Early-Years-and-High-Learning-Potential-170201a.pdf

Potential Plus UK (2018–21) 'Dual or Multiple Exceptionality (DME).' Fact Sheet F01. Available at: https://potentialplusuk.org/wp-content/uploads/2018/09/F01-Dual-or-Multiple-Exceptionality-DME-180913.pdf

Rayner, A. (2021) 'Fun ways for teaching your kids to save money.' RoosterMoney, 29 January. Available at: https://roostermoney.com/gb/fun-ways-teaching-kids-to-save-money

Rooke, M. (2018) *Dyslexia Is My Superpower (Most of the Time).* London: Jessica Kingsley Publishers.

Ropelewski, T. (director) (2015) *2E: Twice Exceptional* [Documentary]. Available at: www.imdb.com/title/tt4841578

Ropelewski, T. (director) (2018) *2e: Teaching the Twice Exceptional* [Documentary]. Available at: www.imdb.com/title/tt7389908

Royal College of Occupational Therapists (no date) 'What is occupational therapy?' Available at: www.rcot.co.uk/about-occupational-therapy/what-is-occupational-therapy

Ryan, A. and Waterman, C. (2018) *Dual and Multiple Exceptionality: The Current State of Play.* London: nasen.

Schoolhouse (no date) 'FAQs – Home education in Scotland.' Available at: www.schoolhouse.org.uk/resources/faqs

Scottish Government (no date) 'Additional support for learning.' Available at: www.gov.scot/policies/schools/additional-support-for-learning

Scottish Government (2004) *A Manual of Good Practice in Special Educational Needs.* Available at: www.gov.scot/publications/manual-good-practice-special-educational-needs/pages/3

Scottish Government (2017) *Supporting Children's Learning: Statutory Guidance on the Education (Additional Support for Learning) Scotland Act 2004 (As Amended): Code of Practice (Third Edition).* Available at: www.gov.scot/binaries/content/documents/govscot/publications/advice-and-guidance/2017/12/supporting-childrens-learning-statutory-guidance-education-additional-support-learning-scotland/documents/00529411-pdf/00529411-pdf/govscot%3Adocument/00529411.pdf?forceDownload=true

Silverman, L.K. (no date) 'Characteristics of Giftedness Scale: Research and review of the literature.' Available at: www.spart5.net/cms/lib07/SC01000802/Centricity/Domain/491/Characteristics_Scale.pdf

Silverman, L.K. (2012) '100 words of wisdom.' *The SENGVine Newsletter*, January. Available at: https://myemail.constantcontact.com/SENGVine-January-2012-Announcements.html?soid=1102289134078&aid=WBJC3ju0ulU

Silverman, L.K., Chitwood, D.G. and Waters, J.L. (1986) 'Young gifted children: Can parents identify giftedness?' *Topics in Early Childhood Special Education* 6, 1, 23–38.

Simister, C.J. (2009) *The Bright Stuff: Playful Ways to Mature Your Child's Extraordinary Mind.* London: Pearson Life.

Simone, R. (2010) *Aspergirls: Empowering Females with Asperger Syndrome.* London: Jessica Kingsley Publishers.

Sloane, P. (2016) *Lateral Thinking Puzzles.* London: Sterling.

SSAT (Schools, Students and Teachers Network) and Dulux (2017) *Exploring Smarter Spaces: How Learning Environment Design Can Help Teachers and Children Thrive in the Learning Environment.* Available at: https://webcontent.ssatuk.co.uk/wp-content/uploads/2018/02/28144939/SSAT-and-Dulux-Smarter-Spaces-Report.pdf

Statista (2020) 'Average value of pocket money per week in the United Kingdom (UK) as of 2020 by age (in GBP).' Available at: www.statista.com/statistics/1006191/average-value-of-pocket-money-in-the-uk-by-age

Trail, B.A. (2011) *Twice-Exceptional Gifted Children: Understanding, Teaching and Counseling Gifted Students.* Waco, TX: Prufrock Press.

UN (United Nations) (1989) *The United Nations Convention on the Rights of the Child.* Available at: www.unicef.org.uk/wp-content/uploads/2010/05/UNCRC_united_nations_convention_on_the_rights_of_the_child.pdf

Wabisabi Learning (no date) '10 essential resources for building your learners' questioning skills: Develop your learners' questioning skills in these fun and challenging ways.' Available at: https://wabisabilearning.com/blogs/inquiry/building-questioning-skills

Wallace, B., Leyden, S., Montgomery, D., Winstanley, C., Pomerantz, M. and Fitton, S. (2010) *Raising the Achievement of All Pupils in an Inclusive Setting: Practical Strategies for Developing Best Practice.* London: Routledge.

Webb, J.T., Amend, E.R., Webb, N.E., Goerss, J., Beljan, P. and Olenchak, F.R. (1st edition 2005, 2nd edition 2016) *Misdiagnosis and Dual Diagnoses of Gifted Children and Adults: ADHD, Bipolar, OCD, Asperger's, Depression, and Other Disorders*. Scottsdale, AZ: Great Potential Press, Inc.

Welsh Assembly Government (2004) *Special Educational Needs: Code of Practice*. Available at: https://gov.wales/special-educational-needs-code-practice

Whitehouse, A. (2021) *Andrew and the Magic Giveash**ometer*. London: Independently published.

Whole School SEND (2021) Ask, Listen, Do: Understanding SEN Support. Available at: www.sendgateway.org.uk/resources/ask-listen-do-understanding-sen-support

Wilson, E. (2013) *Little Tin of Big Worries* [cards]. Preston Deanery: Loggerhead Publishing.

Wiseman, R. (2016) *Queen Bees and Wannabes: Helping Your Daughter Survive Cliques, Gossip, Boyfriends and the Realities of the Girl World*. London: Harmony (3rd edition).

Yates, D. (2021) *2020 Survey of Dual and Multiple Exceptionality*. The Potential Trust.

Yates, D. and Boddison, A. (2020) *The School Handbook for Dual and Multiple Exceptionality: High Learning Potential with Special Educational Needs or Disabilities*. London: Routledge.

Resources Recommended in the Main Text[1]

Comsmart sandtimers in 6 colours and times: www.thewinfordcentre.com/product/comsmart-sand-timer or www.amazon.co.uk

Consortium, calming cat worry toy and coaching cards: www.consortiumworldwide.com/calming-cat-worry-toy-and-coaching-cards-46563

Craftly Ltd, create your own bespoke reward charts, calendars, educational boards and routine charts: www.notonthehighstreet.com/craftly

Duck Duck Moose, award-winning educational apps for children: www.duckduckmoose.com

The Dyslexia Shop, visual timetable boards: https://www.thedyslexiashop.co.uk/visual-timetable-board.html

GoNoodle, YouTube channel for children who can't stop moving: www.youtube.com/channel/UC2YBT7HYqCbbvzu3kKZ3wnw

GoNoodle website channel: www.gonoodle.com

HKD Solutions, UrZone® 6 in 1 safe enclosed space and bed: www.hkdsolutions.com/index.asp

Learning Works for Kids, Dragon dictation app: https://learningworksforkids.com/apps/dragon-dictation

Mantra Lingua, award-winning multilingual education resources: https://uk.mantralingua.com

Mindomo, educate tomorrow's thinkers today: www.mindomo.com/mind-maps-for-education

National Open College Network, products: www.nocn.org.uk/products

Ollie and his Superpowers, a range of resources to help children discover their superpowers and become more resilient: www.ollieandhissuperpowers.com

Open College of the Arts, Our courses: www.oca.ac.uk/our-courses

The Philosophy Man, free P4C resources: www.thephilosophyman.com/free-p4c-resources

Raising Creative Thinkers, a one-place solution for creative education: www.raisingcreativethinkers.com

Seesaw Learning Inc., Shadow Puppet Edu app: https://web.seesaw.me/shadow-puppet-edu

SparkleBox, Homework resources: www.sparklebox.co.uk/misc/homework

---

1   All websites were accessed in March 2021.

'Thunks, Unusual questions to make you think', free slideshare resource based on the work of Ian Gilbert: www.slideshare.net/year5thepines/thunks-9947392

Tink'n'stink, creative resources for extraordinary minds: www.tinknstink.co.uk

TTS, A5 primary homework diary and reading record book: www.tts-group.co.uk/a5-primary-homework-diary-reading-record-book-/1012565.html?cgid=Stationery_--_Office-Planners_Registers_--_Diaries

Yellow Door, a range of early years resources including on emotions and self-regulation: www.yellow-door.net

About Denise Yates

Denise Yates has worked in education and training for over 35 years to enable all individuals to maximise their potential. Over the years, this has included ex-offenders, children with moderate learning difficulties and adults with numeracy and literacy problems and in inner-city areas working with young people at risk of offending.

For 10 years Denise was Chief Executive of the national charity Potential Plus UK (formerly the National Association for Gifted Children). In 2017, Denise left to pursue her passion, which could be summarised as 'hidden potential' – children and young people with Dual or Multiple Exceptionality (DME), those with mental health problems, and those who have been failed by the system, for whatever reason.

A Cambridge economist, Denise is currently, among other things, a trustee of The Potential Trust (a charitable organisation that supports More Able children from low-income backgrounds), a non-executive director of Nisai Education Trust (which is interested in exploring different models of education), and a member of the Above & Beyond Group (which looks to work in partnership with organisations in the UK, in whatever sector, for the benefit of children and young people with gifts and talents, including those with DME).

Denise is a fellow of the RSA and also a trained adviser with Citizens' Advice, and spends one day a week helping individuals and families in her community. In 2020, with Adam Boddison, she wrote *The School Handbook for Dual and Multiple Exceptionality*, and in 2020 she was awarded an MBE in the Queen's Birthday Honours for services to children and young people.

You can contact Denise on Twitter and LinkedIn at @DeniseYates_

About Paul Pickford

Paul Pickford is an award-winning visual artist, based in Salford, specialising in illustration, animation and visual narrative techniques. His skills include a variety of drawing and painting techniques, puppet making, pop-up art and sculpture. He has successfully led workshops in all of these areas working with schools and special needs and community groups. His work has been published as books, comic strips, promotional material, theatre posters and 2-D and 3-D animations. He has experience of working in a range of animation techniques and has designed and made animation sets and characters. He has also worked with clients including the BBC, British Waterways, the NHS and The Groundwork Trust and galleries including The Tate, The Lowry and The Turnpike.

Index